ALSO BY MYRNA BLYTH

For Better and For Worse

Cousin Suzanne

Ladies' Home Journal Vintage Covers

"[S]pills the beans on the way her fellow *Spin Sisters* at the gal mags sell unhappiness with a sugarcoating of liberalism."

—*Vanity Fair*

"When Myrna Blyth left the business of editing women's magazines, she didn't just burn her bridges. She blew them up."

—*Baltimore Sun*

"[A]n industry tell-all with plenty of juicy anecdotes from Blyth's years in the hand-wringing, back-biting world of women's magazines. . . ."

—National Review Online

"[A] devastating teardown of the powerful women who set the tempo in today's media. . . ."

—*Quest*

"After twenty years at the helm of a premier women's magazine, Blyth has written a book that doesn't just bite the hand that fed her, it chomps it off."

—*The Hartford Courant*

"With sharp insights and wicked humor, Myrna Blyth shines an unsparing spotlight on the elite media—and offers a timely, and important, warning to women to not believe the hype."

—Monica Crowley, WABC Radio

"This book is insightful and surprisingly funny—an insider's gutsy take that breaks news and proves at last what many of us have suspected about mainstream media."

—Kellyanne Conway, president and CEO of
The Polling Company/Women Trend

"It is the most sustained attack on women's magazines since Gloria Steinem started *Ms.* in 1972 and suggested that the typical women's magazine was just a "survival kit" for the unliberated, and edited for advertisers, not readers."

—*The New York Times*

"This book has set off a firestorm among Blyth's targets. . . [it] has some of the biggest names in television and publishing in an uproar."

—*Newsweek*

"The hiss of the snaky sisters and their devious deceptions make this book a delicious read."

—*Washington Sunday Times*

"*Spin Sisters* is sure to raise eyebrows and provoke debate both inside the world that helps shapes women's views—and far beyond."

—Julie Eisenhower

"Judging by the insults lobbed at Bernie Goldberg, Ann Coulter, and other media critics, there is one definitive statement that can be made for Myrna Blyth's *Spin Sisters*—every word must be true."

—*Human Events*

"Myrna Blyth's bestseller *Spin Sisters* is a compelling read, replete with interesting ideas and clever turns of phrase."

—*Jerusalem Post*

"[*Spin Sisters*] is a fascinating look at how closed the world of New York media women is and how influential the Spin Sisters can be."

—*Detroit News and Free Press*

THE GLOVES ARE OFF!

"Recovering media-queen Blyth has two main messages. To her former magazine sisters: Get out of your penthouses and live a little, you'll learn a lot about your audience. And to all other women: Sisters, don't let them fool you, they're not Everywoman, whatever they say."

—*New York Post*

"The polite and powerful media women who lunch every day at the same Manhattan restaurants will hate this book. The rest of America . . . will lap it up."

—Jim Brady, *Advertising Age*

"As former CBS News correspondent Bernard Goldberg did with his best-seller *Bias*, longtime *Ladies' Home Journal* editor-in-chief Myrna Blyth is about to blow the political cover of prominent "media queens" like Katie Couric, Barbara Walters, and Diane Sawyer."

—*The Washington Times*

"She is on to something. Forget do-me feminism. A bigger trend today is do-nothing feminism. . . . Ms. Blyth has plenty of personal anecdotes about the self-satisfied world she knows so well. . . . She's got a point, and one worth making. But she may never eat lunch at Michael's again."

—*The Wall Street Journal*

"I can't think of too many mainstream journalists who are willing to take you behind the scenes for an up-close and personal look at how some of the best-known journalists in America slant the news to fit their own biases. But that's exactly what Myrna Blyth does in *Spin Sisters*, an exposé that will almost certainly wipe those big smiles off the faces of Katie, Diane, Barbara, and a few other important divas in the world of big-time journalism."

—Bernard Goldberg, author of *Bias*

"If you're a man wondering why women seem out of it, or a woman wondering why you feel guilty or scared, read *Spin Sisters* by Myrna Blyth. Blyth . . . explains in a fascinating three hundred pages that women's media, particularly television and magazines, are dedicated to selling products by selling the idea that all women are stressed-out, under- (or over-) sexed victims with bodies that can be saved by a few nips and tucks, a few creams and lotions, and a few trips to the hottest designers—not to mention shoe stores or psychiatrists."

—*Richmond Times Dispatch*

SPIN SISTERS

How the Women of the

Media Sell Unhappiness—

and Liberalism—

to the Women of America

MYRNA BLYTH

ST. MARTIN'S GRIFFIN ❦ NEW YORK

www.stmartins.com

Library of Congress Cataloging-in-Publication Data

Blyth, Myrna.
    Spin sisters : how the women of the media sell unhappiness—
and liberalism—to the women of America / Myrna Blyth.—1st St.
Martin's Griffin ed.
    p. cm.
Includes bibliographical references (p. 311) and index (p. 329).

ISBN 0-312-33607-1 (pbk)
ISBN 978-0312-33607-3
    1. Women's periodicals, American. 2. Women—Press cover-
age—United States. 3. Journalism—Objectivity—United States.
4. Women on television. I. Title.

PN4879.B58   2005
051'.082.082—dc22

                                             2004051441

P1

CONTENTS

Spin Sisters: \\'spin\\'sis-ters\\n. (2003) Members of the female media elite, a Girls' Club of editors, producers, print and television journalists with similar attitudes and opinions who influence the way millions of American women think and feel about their lives, their world, and themselves.

INTRODUCTION

Newsweek called it "one of the glitzier Manhattan media events in ages." Was it a book party? A fund-raiser? A fashion show or a film opening?

Not exactly.

It was, believe it or not, a baby shower on a sunny May afternoon. It was unlike any baby shower you've ever attended.

The hostess was Senator Hillary Rodham Clinton and the pregnant guest of honor, her former press secretary, Lisa Caputo. It was just weeks before the Hillabaloo of the launch of the senator's book, which she called *Living History* and most critics called Whitewash. The guests at the shower, held at an elegant Fifth Avenue apartment with a spectacular $5 million view of Central Park, were the Spin Sisters of media elites—a sorority of journalists, television, publishing, and public relations executives all dressed in seasonally appropriate pastel pantsuits. Barbara Walters in lavender, Diane Sawyer in cream, colum-

1

nist Liz Smith in yellow. A bevy of Democratic activists and big-time party contributors were there as well, nibbling on smoked salmon finger sandwiches and sipping lemonade. Lisa was not only the sole pregnant woman in the room, she was one of the few women there young enough to actually get pregnant.

Several hundred miles away in South Carolina, writer Meryl Gordon, who was covering the debate of lackluster Democratic presidential hopefuls for *New York* magazine, fretted because she knew she was missing what she considered a far more interesting occasion. Political consultant Mandy Grunwald, who was advising one of the potential candidates, sympathized. "It's the mother of all baby showers."[1]

Except nobody opened any of the prettily packaged presents and cooed over little bibs and booties. No one sat around eating slabs of cake decorated with blue ("It's a Boy!") whipped-cream flowers. Not one woman even got a chance to tell the story of her own dramatic twenty-seven-hour labor.

What was the hot topic du jour? The whispered conversations were about which Media Queen would score the big "get," the first prime-time interview Hillary would give to promote her $8 million autobiography. Sorry, Diane in cream, advantage to Barbara in lavender. As it turned out, Hillary, who was able to forgive Bill for Monica, was also able to forgive Barbara for her sympathetic Monica interview.

One surprised guest, a PR woman new to this circle, said to me as we nibbled our chocolate chip cookies and eyed Barbara and Diane eyeing each other, "But aren't we supposed to be talking about *the baby!?!?!*"

You would have thought. Anywhere else in America, with any other group of women, the impending arrival—and I don't mean of Hillary's book—would have been the center of attention. But not with this crowd.

So why was I there? I have to admit it: I could be considered a Spin Sister, too. For more than twenty years, I was the editor-in-chief of

Ladies' Home Journal and founding editor of *MORE* magazine. As the *Journal* editor, I had interviewed Hillary several times. I knew Lisa Caputo from her frantic White House days, but we are hardly close friends. I had been invited to what is usually a personal kind of party because there was nothing very personal about it. This was business, the serious business of networking, and the guest list was nothing more than a reflection of how women in Manhattan media circles often meld their professional and personal lives. And even their political lives.

To be honest, attending that shower made me very uncomfortable for a couple of reasons. Partly because I don't agree with the very liberal political opinions shared by almost all my fellow guests. I also know many American women don't agree with them either, a fact the Spin Sisters find hard to believe or accept. While over the years my politics had changed even more dramatically than my hair color, the views of the other women in the room had stayed the same. The second most popular topic of conversation that afternoon was what dreadful, stupid, moronic thing George W. Bush would do next.

I also felt awkward because, by that time, I had spent months thinking about some of the women in the room and their enormous influence on the women of America, an influence I had come to believe was manipulative and often damaging.

Walking home after the party, I also realized that I had to acknowledge from the start that I was part of the Girls' Club whose members are expert at telling and selling stories to American women. Stories that, nowadays, are usually about your difficult stress-filled life and your treacherous stress-filled world. I knew I had to let you know that along with my "sisters" I am partly to blame for creating the negative messages of victimization and unhappiness that bombard women today. Messages that women can't avoid daily, weekly, and monthly.

What do I mean? Check out a newsstand and read the cover lines on the dozens and dozens of magazines published for women every month. Those brightly colored blurbs in seventy-two-point type, like so many I have written, blare out a stream of warnings about the dangers women face along with lists of cures for those many, many problems women are now assumed to have.

Too much weight, too little time.

Too many kids, too few eggs.

The right man at the wrong time.

The wrong man at the right time.

And enough diseases to satisfy the worst hypochondriac among us.

Professor Robert Kubey of Rutgers University, a leader in media research, told me that when he read just one copy of *Self* magazine he was amazed by the tone of the features and the advertisements. "I didn't realize," he said, with a laugh, "that a woman could have so many things wrong with her."[2]

Welcome, Professor, to the world of women's magazines, a nearly $7 billion-a-year business, which nowadays is primarily based on telling women that their lives, the lives of contemporary American women, are often too tough for them to handle and that they should feel very sorry for themselves.

The story told on television—which, if you are like most women you probably watch almost five hours a day—is just as downbeat, if not even bleaker.[3] On cable, you can find frantic heroine-in-jeopardy movies playing almost any hour of the day or night. The networks' nightly newsmagazines are just as bad with hyped-up stories of murder and mayhem, usually at the hands of abusive husbands or boyfriends, evil corporations, or incompetent doctors. Even on morning television, we constantly view tales of miserable, victimized women. And always underlying this nonstop gloom-and-doom media barrage is one simple message: It could be you!

This distorted vision of your life is absolutely crazy, since you also happen to be the best-educated, healthiest, wealthiest, longest-lived women with more opportunities for personal fulfillment than any other generation in history. What has always characterized American women has been our strength, energy, and competence, our desire to be actively and positively involved in improving our lives and the lives of our families. Over the past fifty years, the creativity and productivity of women in this country, unleashed and utilized as never before, has been one of the most important reasons that America is now the strongest, richest, and most diverse country on earth.

So what is going on here? How did this happen? And how does the constant negative image of women's lives in magazines and on television, the frequent portrayal of women as victims, affect the way you think about yourself and the world?

I decided to write this book to try to answer these questions. In the process, it also became both a personal and professional self-examination that was very difficult at times. Nobody likes to look back and admit, hey, I wish I hadn't done that. But here goes.

I confess, I confess that as an editor I promoted the Female Fear Factor for all it was worth and just like my colleagues used scary headlines, month after month, to attract readers.

Over the years, it became easy for us all to tell women they had so many reasons to complain, to encourage their constant whining and moaning and kvetching. And to always treat them, the most fortunate women in the world, with pity rather than with respect.

At the same time all of us in the media played endlessly on women's insecurities, especially about their bodies. Such messages can be so undermining that 52 percent of women declared in a recent survey that they would give up a year of their lives in order to stay at an ideal weight.[4] A whole year of life!

That declaration really stunned me, even though I know that, most months, the largest-circulation magazines for women never publish an issue without a diet story. Yet, at about the same time women were telling researchers they'd be willing to trade longer life for fewer pounds, another study found that the gaunt, hollow-eyed models on the pages of magazines are often so thin that their bodies could be medically classified as "emaciated."[5] The result? Not very surprising. Even women who are not overweight feel fat and depressed enough to volunteer to give up some of their precious time on earth.

The magazines you read, and the morning television shows you watch often claim to be revealing secrets: "The 7 Secrets of How to Fight Stress," "The Secret of Staying Thin Forever," "The Secret Sex Move No Man Can Resist." Yeah, sure.

Well, now I'll let you in on the *real* secret: The way media for women tries to attract and keep your attention is by selling the notion that you are perpetually frazzled, frumpy, fearful, or failing. Even if you are not—and most of you aren't.

That's why I ought to do a little penance. I can do this, I think, by helping you understand how an army of editors, journalists, TV executives, producers, and publicists, who I know so well, create, pass along, and profit from those constant undermining messages.

I also want to help you learn more about the women who really succeed big in media and how they operate—the divas like Katie, and Barbara and Diane, my fellow partygoers, who are among the most influential women in our country.

Isn't it interesting that although Dan Rather and Tom Brokaw and Peter Jennings are widely recognized they would never be even close to the top on a list of the most important men in America? But a Most Important Women list never appears without these Media Queens right up there in the very top spots.

Even though you may disagree with some of what I have to say, please hear me out. For I am also certain that there is a liberal tilt in media aimed especially at women—and so much of media is aimed right at you. That's because advertisers and marketers are constantly seeking women, who hold the purse strings in our economy. Women make or influence 85 percent of all spending decisions, representing an enormous $6 trillion worth of annual purchasing power.[6]

It's well known that the overwhelming majority of media professionals vote Democratic.[7] In fact, most Spin Sisters are even more likely than men to identify themselves as liberal Democrats, especially in the Manhattan media circles in which I've traveled. Quite honestly, it is kind of lonely when absolutely nobody ever agrees with you. At one point during the Lisa Caputo baby shower, I said to another guest, "I think I am the only woman in the room who has ever even voted for a Republican. I suppose you had to have one." She replied, "You were invited despite that fact." Now, wasn't that special?

I've found myself smiling a lot lately listening to Democrat leaders and others on the left whining that the media has been "taken over" by conservatives. Well, that hasn't happened in the Girls' Club and certainly not in media aimed at women. Let's face it. Finding conservatives or even moderate Republicans like me in the Spin Sister media elite is as likely as finding a size 16 model on the cover of *Vogue*.

But don't think the Girls' Club's liberal bent is being driven by a "vast feminist conspiracy." That just isn't so. Nowadays the influence of hard-line feminists, outside of women's studies departments, is practically zilch. Nor do female editors and producers sit around and plot insidious ways to get a loaded political message across to female readers and viewers. Believe me, even at the shower Hillary hosted, the group was more excited about a Prada jacket that one of the guests had bought at a sample sale than a piece of legislation that the junior senator had proposed.

But that doesn't mean that the liberal content these Spin Sisters write or produce doesn't have both a cultural and political influence. Whether it's on the Lifetime channel or in the pages of *Glamour,* there is an assumption on the part of those who produce or appear on television or who edit magazines or handle public relations that all women think the same way about important issues. And must think the same way as the overwhelming majority of the Girls' Club who share the same left-of-center opinions when they are lunching together at the same restaurants in Manhattan, weekending together in the Hamptons, or spending a spring afternoon at an extremely awkward baby shower in a lavish Fifth Avenue co-op.

I know from long experience that media for women tells you endlessly about the stress in your life, about the way you should look, about what should make you feel sorry for yourself, or very, very fearful about your health and the environment. In much the same way you are given a one-sided message about politics, too, by always being told more government is the best solution to fix many of the problems in your life. That's a philosophically loaded message that is the culmination of all the other stories you are told about how tough life is for women, even middle-class women.

Here's another secret, but not one that would ever be part of a cover line or a coming-up-next blurb on *Today*: The Spin Sisters are a lot more liberal than most women in America. Yet they have no doubt that their beliefs are the ones all women should hold, and that they know the only "right" way for women—just because they are women—to think. They are convinced that when it comes to politics they know what's good for you even better than you may know yourself.

Liberal bias in media may infuriate some men but doesn't necessarily change their thinking. They may bark a few choice words at Dan or Peter and then change the channel until they find Bill O'Reilly. But when focused on women, the media's liberal bias is more pervasive, more insidious, and more effective. Especially when it's coupled with negative messages about victimization and unhappiness aimed at you over and over by the same liberal media.

Over the years I've observed dozens of focus groups and initiated countless surveys to learn more about women's attitudes. Each time I found out what I already knew—that women are basically smart and practical. Yet you must contend on a daily basis with a media onslaught that tells you how tough life is for you and how hard it is for you to cope.

I'm not saying our lives are perfect or easy. Any woman in the throes of toilet training, teen driving, or a temperamental boss knows better than that. But don't most of us just handle it as women have always done? Not according to most media aimed at women who tell you you're overwhelmed and near helpless in the face of the obstacles of life.

You deserve better than that. I believe what I say will help you disregard such myths no matter how slickly they are packaged or who is selling them to you. I also hope I can get you to think more positively about yourself and your ability to manage your own life. I know most women are realistic and sensible. Much too smart, I trust, to continue to be conned or snowed or spun, especially once they have some inside information. And that's where I come in. After a lot of soul-searching, I wrote this book to tell the truth about the business I know so well—about its power and influence, its manipulations, and its sometimes misguided politics. I didn't write it for Republicans or Democrats, liberals or conservatives. I wrote it for every woman who is overdue for some truth-telling when it comes to what the media has been selling them for too long. On the following pages, I am certain I will give you—and, perhaps, even the Spin Sisters themselves—something new to think and talk about.

CHAPTER 1

Spin, Sisters, Spin

Remember way back when Rosie O'Donnell was the "Queen of Nice," when her syndicated talk show was almost as popular as Oprah's? For an hour every weekday, she seemed like such a cheery girlfriend, always so good-humored and smiling. Why, we were even supposed to believe that Rosie—such a cut-up—really, really, *really* had a crush on Tom Cruise.

That was all before a German publishing conglomerate turned *McCall's*, America's oldest women's magazine, into *Rosie*, a publication that was supposed to appeal to millions of readers who were allegedly just like Rosie, described by the magazine as a young working mother interested in kids, cooking, and crafts. Were they kidding? How many lesbian moms with multimillion-dollar bank balances, bodyguards for their kids, and a political point of view to the left of

Madonna's live on your block? Calling Rosie typical is like saying Princess Di was just a single mom trying to juggle two kids, keep a wardrobe up-to-date, and still find time for volunteer work.

Now, anyone who actually knew Rosie and admired her gift for comedy might have called her talented and very funny but, quite frankly, never nice. I suppose it's possible to find something phonier than Rosie's relentlessly upbeat on-camera persona—Pamela Anderson's chest comes to mind—but it's not easy. Still, that didn't stop the media from gushing over Rosie's daily doses of hearty good nature. And pretending that she, in her uniform of dark man-tailored suits, was maybe just a wee bit tomboyish. In cover stories in a battery of women's magazines including *Redbook, Marie Claire, Good Housekeeping* and, I admit it, *Ladies' Home Journal,* her "niceness" was hailed, and Rosie was extolled as a talented comedienne, a good mother, and a generous philanthropist, some of which may be true.

But nobody ever mentioned she was also hell on wheels.

I was part of the spin. As the *Journal* editor, I had the job of organizing several cover stories on Rosie, including photo shoots. It was never pleasant. Rosie did not like to have her picture taken. Rosie did not like to tell anyone her correct clothing size. So when she arrived at the studio where the magazine's cover was to be shot, the dozens of outfits hanging on the rack waiting there for her didn't fit. Already angry when she walked in, that made Rosie even madder. Rosie also didn't like the photographer who was taking her picture. And she didn't like the makeup artist or the hair stylist or the fashion consultant, all of whom had been hired at great expense to make her look as attractive as possible. Rosie didn't even like to smile.

But you'd never know it to see the final cover with Rosie beaming from the newsstands like your new best friend with a bright and peppy cover blurb to cap off the charade. That was part of the spin, too.

Once I gave a luncheon for Rosie. It seemed like a good idea at the time. To get her to be the guest of honor, the magazine contributed a large sum in her name to one of her favorite charities. This, by the way, happens all the time. It's the way celebrities hit up publications to give to the star's pet philanthropic projects. Our luncheon for a couple of hundred guests at the Rainbow Room, on the top of Rockefeller Center, was held during the first year of Rosie's talk show, when she was very popular. Many of the guests were fans and were eager to get close to her. They assumed Rosie in person was like the Rosie she played on TV. But Rosie, looking bored and sulky, was having none of it.

She sat glumly on a raised dais with Libby Pataki, the pleasant, down-to-earth wife of the governor of New York, and me. When a perfectly polite woman came up and asked for an autograph, the Queen of Nice harrumphed that she didn't give them. Libby Pataki murmured something noncommittal like "Oh, that's interesting." Rosie looked annoyed. When she finally got up to speak, she turned and snidely said, "Listen, Lib, you don't like that I don't give autographs? Well, I only give them to kids. To anyone older than that, I say, you want my autograph? Get a fuggin' life."

Rude and crude. But Rosie was the star of the moment. Everyone laughed and applauded, thrilled that Rosie had shared with us the nasty way she brushed off her fans. This wasn't a crowd who would ever challenge a celebrity's inappropriate behavior, much less take on the hottest ticket in town. "That Rosie, she's so outrageous. Isn't she great?" they chattered, reaffirming each other's instinct to never, never, never criticize a star.

A Coming-Out Party

While she hosted her daily talk show, Rosie employed a contingent of very experienced publicists from PMK/HBH, the most powerful celebrity public relations firm in the country, who accompanied her virtually everywhere. In fact, one publicist insisted that when the *Journal* did a cover shoot in Miami with Rosie, she, too, had to be flown there, at the magazine's expense, just to make sure her client was "comfortable." Highly paid hand-holders go with the territory when it comes to celebrity day care.

When Rosie decided to end her daily television talk show, she was also about to publish a book about her life called *Find Me*. In a hit-and-run maneuver, Rosie wanted finally to tell the truth about her homosexuality to the American public. Although leaving television, she expected to continue to oversee her magazine.

Her "coming out" was a carefully orchestrated two-month-long media campaign, overseen by Cindi Berger, a top PMK publicist, described by the *New York Post* as one of "The 50 Most Powerful Women in New York." Cindi is one of the Precinct Commanders of the Access Police, the handlers who control press entrée to movie, music, and television stars with an iron fist. She oversees a whole stable of "problem kid" clients including Sharon Stone and Mariah Carey and those insightful foreign policy analysts, the Dixie Chicks, whose headline-making behavior makes them all media favorites. Cindi is in charge of deciding which of her stars will be made available to appear on which magazine cover, which network television newsmagazine show will get the exclusive interview and which will be shut out. You thought editors and producers picked who would appear on their covers and shows? Not exactly. But more about that later.

Cindi, who says she shares Rosie's political philosophy as most in the media do, was in favor of her client's new honesty but wanted to package the disclosure very carefully. She arranged for a highly pro-moted two-hour prime-time interview special on ABC with Diane Sawyer.

The Sawyer interview would focus not on the talk show host's own personal story but rather on a related issue that was important to Rosie, her outrage that in the state of Florida where she lived, homosexual couples were not allowed to adopt children. Cindi had carefully researched opinions about the issue and believed women in general would be interested in Rosie's point of view.

Then, to further take the edge off Rosie's admission, Barbara Walters, another of Cindi's clients, pitched in. Weeks before the Sawyer interview, Barbara casually mentioned on her show, *The View,* that Rosie was gay, as if it were no big deal. But what *was* made a big deal was Rosie's determination to assist the ACLU in overturning the Florida adoption law. That aspect of the prime-time special was promoted twice on *Good Morning America* and on ABC affiliates' local news programs. *World News Tonight* anchor Peter Jennings carried an excerpt from the special as if it were major news. Even the show's title, "Rosie's Story: For the Sake of the Children," fit right in to the carefully created ACLU propaganda campaign.

Finally, the big night of the Sawyer special arrived. Political correctness reigned, and everything was done, as it usually is, to make sure that celebrity equaled credibility. If a star says it, hey, it must be so. No Media Queen would be so churlish as to contradict or even ask one tough question during a highly promoted prime-time interview that was sure to garner really big ratings.

During the program a gay couple who had tried to adopt several hard-to-place foster kids were featured and portrayed very sympathetically. On camera, a sociologist, Dr. Judith Stacey, ripped to shreds the notion that it was damaging or inappropriate for gays to adopt. Dr. Stacey is the Streisand Professor of Contemporary Gender Studies at the University of Southern California. Yes, *that* Streisand. The only person willing to express and to explain his support for the Florida law was a mild-mannered young then-state senator named Randy Ball. Savvier Florida politicians may have realized that their television skills would be no match for Rosie and a sleekly produced major network special in the debating department.

When Ball said he opposed Rosie's position because he adhered to the Bible and its views on homosexuality, Diane Sawyer looked pained and practically sniffed at such intolerance. But when Rosie explained her religious philosophy with a rhyming lyric from the long-running musical *Les Mis*—"My soul belongs to God, I know. I made that bargain long ago"—Diane seemed to brim over with respect.[1]

Now, I happen to know the author of the English lyrics of *Les Miserables*. He is a British journalist named Herbie Kretzmer, known as the Kosher Butcher of Fleet Street when he was a theater critic because of his particularly acerbic reviews. I imagine he thanks God every morning for the royalties he gets from the world's most successful musical, but I don't think he considers himself either divinely inspired or on par with the authors of the Old Testament.

To no one's surprise, least of all mine, Diane's *Primetime* interview got high ratings—and Rosie's book hit *The New York Times* best-seller list. According to a satisfied Cindi Berger, everyone out there really knew all along that Rosie's flirting with "her Tommy" Cruise was just shtick and that her carefully stage-managed revelation was no big deal. And Rosie herself, gleeful that all constraints were off after the finale of her talk show, told a nightclub audience a few weeks later with relish, "The bitch ain't so nice anymore."

The War of the Rosies

And so another successful episode in audience manipulation seemed to end as planned for everyone involved in this clever little marketing scheme. Rosie and her publisher had a best-seller, Diane and ABC had a ratings hit, Cindi and PMK had scored for their client, and the National Gay and Lesbian Task Force found themselves and their issues discussed round the clock on network and cable television.

But then a funny thing happened. The newsstand sales of *Rosie* magazine plummeted from a high of over 700,000 copies a month at the magazine's launch to a low of around 200,000.[2] Despite one of the most carefully constructed coming outs since New Coke, half a million women just stopped buying.

Were those young mothers out there who cared about "kids, cooking, and crafts" shocked that Rosie was gay? Maybe some were. Did they disagree with her far left political views? Again, some probably did. But I don't think either her sexual proclivities or her politics were the reason for such a steep decline in sales. I think that the readers of *Rosie*, whether they cared about Rosie's disclosure or not, just couldn't help but realize they had been had. Rosie wasn't who she had pretended to be. And those readers decided they were just not going to be scammed at $3.50 a copy anymore. Because of the dramatic sales decline it wasn't long before the publishers of *Rosie* magazine, Gruner + Jahr, began an ugly fight with the star about the direction of the magazine. Both sides aired their differences in public and then sued each other for millions. It wasn't pretty.

The drama of the rise and fall of *Rosie* made headlines all over the country, but the selling and telling of Rosie wasn't that extraordinary, at least not to me. Seeing a celebrity image created out of whole cloth was nothing new. Believe me, it happens all the time. But what doesn't happen very often is the chance to see a media rollout as tightly controlled as Britney Spears's virginity watch go south.

Why am I telling you this story?

Because it's a perfect example of calculated Girls' Club spin. Obviously Cindi's goal was to make the women watching the *Primetime* special unquestioningly (and unthinkingly) sympathetic to Rosie by framing her coming out as part of a one-woman crusade to change what she argued was an antiquated, bigoted Florida law. To accomplish this she was assisted by Diane and, to some degree, by Barbara, and the rest of the gang at ABC. After watching the special, if you weren't sympathetic to Rosie "for the sake of the children," you felt there was something very wrong with you. If you didn't agree with

Rosie, well, then you didn't really care about needy kids. And who wants to feel she doesn't care about kids?

Gotcha!

Of course, Rosie messed it up when she declared so gleefully that the bitch was back. (Her publisher's counterclaim was that the bitch had been there all along, having temper tantrums in her corner office.) But then who could blame daytime viewers and magazine readers for thinking for so long Rosie *was* the Queen of Nice? She had been packaged and sold to you as exactly that by the best in the business. Only when Rosie let down her hair (metaphorically speaking) and then chopped it off (not so metaphorically), did women realize that Rosie just wasn't such a cheery, smiling Cutie Patootie after all.

Still, if false notions about celebrity were all women's media was selling, it probably wouldn't matter much. But that isn't the case. What you are also told and sold are some very negative messages about your own lives, and that's a lot more important. Women's media often wants you to buy notions of unhappiness and victimization and all the political baggage that goes with it in just the same way Cindi and Diane and Peter and Barbara wanted you to buy Rosie's "selfless" coming out and her political agenda. Behind that spectacular snow job was the power of the evening news, an evening newsmagazine, and a morning talk show complemented by celebrity news shows and lots of coverage in newspapers and weekly magazines hyping the story.

Read All About It

Messages about your own lives are often sold to you in print, as well, without as much fanfare as on TV but with every bit as much effect. Remember that Rosie wanted to dump her daily talk show but keep control of her magazine. She desperately wanted to continue to share her views about depression, decoupage, and Tom DeLay with her readers every month. Oprah, the most influential female performer ever on television, is also a proponent of the power of print. Even with an hour of airtime each weekday and millions of viewers, she still felt she needed a magazine to promote her vision and her views to her fans.

Of course I understand the appeal and importance of women's magazines, even though most male editors and writers remain journalistic chauvinists. They just don't get it. Guys think of women's magazines as beneath them, as not important enough—pulp nonfiction created for a strange netherworld of Pampers, pasta recipes, and menopause in which men suspect women exist. Wrong. Women's magazines are powerful. Of the ten largest and most profitable magazines in the country, five are edited specifically for women and the other five have large female audiences. And sure, these magazines may occasionally talk about diapers and the difference between rigatoni and fusilli, but they also mold the way women think and feel about their lives and their world.

Female social commentators all across the spectrum definitely know this, and use it. Betty Friedan, Susan Faludi, and Naomi Wolf on the left and Danielle Crittenden, Christina Hoff Sommers, and Michelle Malkin on the right don't agree on much, but they have all written about the effect women's magazines have on shaping the views of their millions of devoted readers.[3]

Women's studies professors have published long research papers analyzing the influence of these magazines. Professor Sherrie A. Inness, who writes frequently about women and media, declares women's magazines "convince millions that the views expressed by [such] magazines are just, fair and truthful," even when their views are limited to one "monolithic" perspective.[4] British social commentator Valerie Bryson writes, "Many women who are uninterested in politics as defined by men gain political information and values not from serious newspapers and broadcasts but from women's magazines and daytime television."[5]

That's important because nowadays the "political information" you get, girlfriend to girlfriend, often has a definite "one-perspective" liberal tilt. Believe me, I know the formula: diseases and diets, sob stories and social issues, and stress, stress, stress. And I know the impact such a formula can have on one's ideas and emotions.

So forget the laundry piling up faster than the national debt, grab a glass of wine, and let me give you the chance to hear from a few writers and editors who feel it is their duty to tell you about how tough your life is because they claim their life is so tough, too. And, just like Rosie, they don't mind bitching. They are the media's Nay Nay Sisterhood who feel sorry for you because they feel so darn sorry for themselves.

CHAPTER 2

How We Got from There to Here

In a dust jacket trimmed with Pepto-Bismol pink, Allison Pearson's novel *I Don't Know How She Does It: The Life of Kate Reddy, Working Mother* climbed up the best-seller list in stiletto heels. Ms. Pearson, an award-winning columnist for the *London Evening Standard,* had written a book that reviewers just couldn't help but love because it was about someone who was "witty," "brainy," and "a babe" whose life was a lot like theirs.

The novel's heroine, Kate Reddy—"blondish hair," "decent legs"—is a British hedge fund manager and working mom who absolutely, definitely Has It All. High-salaried career; two adorable, healthy children; a competent nanny; and a husband so helpful and good-humored he not only changes "nappies" but has a cute classification system for the baby's bowel movements.

For my husband, also English, changing diapers was something akin to sumo wrestling—not very high on his to-do list. But Kate's willing pooper-scooper of a husband isn't the only thing that sets Kate Reddy apart. Unlike most of us, this young mother also has 1) a London town house, 2) several good girlfriends with whom she exchanges witty but warmhearted e-mails, 3) a daily cleaning woman in addition to the nanny, 4) a taxi driver who is always on call to act as her personal chauffeur, and 5) a potential lover, a dishy American multimillionaire George Clooney look-alike, so gentlemanly that he undresses Kate when she's drunk, even removes her contact lenses (God knows how, it is never explained), but respects her too damn much to take advantage of her.

But is our Kate happy? Not a bit of it.

According to her own self-analysis and to the reviewers who *soooo* empathized, Kate's "highly stressed" working mother's life is filled with anxiety, guilt, and "deep sea diver tiredness." Harry Potter lookalike Margaret Carlson, best known for her liberal girl gig on CNN's *The Capital Gang,* understood completely how tough and demanding it was for poor downtrodden Kate. "Nearly every female [with] both a child and a byline," she confided to the readers of *Time,* "has stripmined Pearson's theme: how to squeeze babies, marriage, and a highpowered job into a day that cannot be stretched beyond 24 hours."[1] Call me crazy, but a nanny, cleaning lady, chauffeur, and supportive husband should make life a little easier, shouldn't it?

How About a Little Brie with the Whine, Girls?

There are practically herds of Kates-in-the-flesh roaming the glitzy media world of editors, writers, producers, and stylists. But Pearson was too shrewd to make her heroine a journalist, because, she says, it is not quite "ball breaking enough." Pearson's own life sounds like the

London version of media elite comfy: She works from her flat, has a full-time nanny for her kids, and only has to leave the house to appear on television, or fly to L.A. to interview a celebrity for her column, or discuss the $2 million movie deal she made for the film rights to her book. Not exactly heavy lifting. When we once asked ordinary women in a *Ladies' Home Journal* poll what they thought would be the absolutely ideal job, they all wanted to be "a best-selling novelist." No fools, they know that it is highly paid part-time work that you can do at home.

I met a Manhattan version of Kate recently, a young editor who wanted to see me because she was interested in working on a magazine that I was developing. She was the daughter of a former neighbor, and I hadn't seen her since she was very young. Back in the early 1970s, her mother and I were a distinct minority—women with young children in an Upper West Side apartment building. That was then. Nobody wanted to have children. This is now. The place is overrun with strollers, often double or even triple strollers for after-fertility-treatment twins and triplets.

This young woman's mother had once been something of a local celebrity. When she was pregnant with her second child, she didn't make it to the hospital and had the baby on her kitchen floor. When we heard the big news, we all prayed that she had a regular cleaning lady. I don't think our building's superintendent, first on the scene, ever quite recovered from the ordeal. Mind you, this was long before video-taped midwife-assisted home deliveries became the rage. Now when you tell your children how they made you suffer, you have the proof.

Although I didn't really have a job for this young woman, I was curious to see how the little girl who lived downstairs had turned out. Not surprisingly, she looked like her mother at her age, thin, dark, and very pretty. She told me, over our breakfast fruit plates and English muffins, that she was married and had two children, and was doing very well as an editor at a well-known magazine.

As we drank our lattes, she filled in more details about her life. She had a large apartment, a weekend home, and the prerequisite nanny who took care of the kids. Her husband, whom she met right after college, was very supportive of her career. She had wanted to start a magazine rather like the one my company was developing. He had tried to copyright what she thought would be the perfect title as a special birthday gift for her. A good job, two kids, a very thoughtful guy. My real-life Kate, not cracking wise on the pages of a slick novel, surely would be content. Right?

Wrong. With the kind of instant intimacy women can achieve before their second cup of coffee grows cold, my young friend lowered her head and told me she was overwhelmed and stressed. In less than a minute, she morphed from perky on-the-make, looking-for-her-next-job, editor-in-chief-wannabe to Sad Sack in DKNY. Her shoulders drooped; her voice became teary. She said with a sigh for full effect that she "just can't cope."

Oh, dear. But what exactly was her problem? Frankly, her life sounded pretty damn good to me.

Now it was her turn to be a little surprised. Surely I understood?

When she's at work, she feels like she should be at home. When she's at home, her children are difficult and annoying. She worries about being a good mother. She worries about getting ahead. And she doesn't have Any Time for Herself, as if the woman at work and the mother at home were somehow unrelated to her. As if she only truly existed when she could be totally focused on her own interests or needs.

Well, okay, I agreed with her, it has always been tough to work and have small children. I knew that. Her mother knew that. I remember how irritating my kids could be. Small kids *are* annoying, but what did she expect? Bridge partners? And you do worry about them nonstop. But as I looked across the breakfast table, I wondered why this extremely fortunate young woman found life so difficult that it brought tears to her lovely, perfectly made-up eyes? Surely she was smart enough to know her life would be the envy of many women? And why was she so totally comfortable complaining to a near stranger who she expected to automatically sympathize with her? Much as the heroine of *I Don't Know How She Does It* expects everyone to ignore her breathtaking brain power, her Armani wardrobe, her six-figure salary, and just do the decent thing—pity her.

Kristin Van Ogtrop is another very unhappy and, in her case, ticked-off member of the Spin Sisters, that exclusive sorority of women whose lives and careers revolve around the media, especially women's media, and who often are describing themselves when they believe they are describing you. Kristin is "the executive editor of an enormously popular women's magazine" as she identifies herself in *The Bitch in the House,* a collection of personal essays by women writers and editors who share an amazing ability to whine endlessly about the state of their generally upscale, interesting lives.

She is one of the collection's twenty-six-women-behaving-badly authors who expect your understanding, your sympathy, and, of course, that you feel their pain. She calls her brightly written essay "Attila the Honey I'm Home"—and tells us about her days editing a long manuscript, going to meetings, checking with the nanny, as if the poor girl had been sentenced to life at hard labor in Attica. Her diary of whining tells us she was "Driven to the TV studio for hair and makeup . . . to go on live at 7:40 [A.M.] . . . appearing as an 'expert' on a local morning show. I have a hair stylist I've never met before and he makes the back of my head look ridiculous, like a ski jump."[2] Well, now, this *is* traumatic—doing television appearances without your own personal stylist in tow. To coin a phrase, I don't know how she does it.

Cathi Hanauer, the collection's editor, who claims "this book was born out of anger," is also full of complaints. Among them: The cat wakes her up! *The cat wakes her up!* Oh, and the FedEx man arrives unexpectedly. Hitler invading Poland, now, that was an unexpected visitor to get stressed about, not Hanauer's version of *Girl Interrupted*.

Unlike Kristin, a New York suburbanite, Cathi lives in a small town in Massachusetts with her husband and her two children. She works at home on her writing and for several years had a steady income writing the book review column for *Mademoiselle*. Still she groans, "Cartons of books I was supposed to be reading . . . arrived by the week."[3] Well, yes. Funny how there's this pesky little connection between getting paid and doing work.

These are just two of twenty-six "bitches in the house," and I could go on, but you get the idea. Just call it the "Luckiest Women in the World Blues." Kristin, Cathi, novelist Allison Pearson, and my young editor friend are part of the swelling chorus of Media Princesses who believe that it is simply impossible to be a woman today. Even if you are an enormously fortunate upper-middle-class woman, as most of them are, it doesn't change a thing. For these talented and privileged women, with little understanding of the lives most non-Club women lead, just getting through the day is a drama of heroic proportions. Cathi Hanauer writes in her Introduction to *The Bitch in the House*, "Two healthy children, a nice home, an interesting job . . . what could I possibly be mad at? Yet I was mad." As were her friends, "ambitious women (often writers) juggling jobs and marriages and, sometimes, small children—[who] were also resentful, guilty, stressed out."[4]

Well, I have three words for these women—get a grip! I don't mean to seem unsympathetic. Wait a minute, yes, I do. These are educated, talented, clever women with so many wonderful opportunities before them—careers, children, husbands, personal growth—and yet to hear them complain, you'd think them totally incapable of handling even the smallest irritants of life. I don't put answering the door or the phone in the same category as facing a life-threatening illness or dealing with what we all faced on September 11. Those are real tragedies—life doesn't get any more real than that.

So how, I ask you, did we get Here from There? How did we go from the days when a woman had only one option in life—to marry (young), have kids (fast), and fill in the rest of our leisure time cooking, cleaning, chauffeuring, and worrying about the ring around his collar—to today when so many Kates can Have It All, with a nanny to help, and are miserable? How did we go from having no choices about our lives to having so many choices that it has made some of us a little crazy—and so very self-involved? When did independence turn into narcissism and self-indulgence? Why did we stop being concerned about the real problems women face? And what part did media and those involved in media play in this perception switch that happened so quickly that a generation or two of women now suffer from permanent emotional whiplash?

I can give you a short guide to these thirty long years of change in women's roles, lives, and attitudes because I not only lived it, I edited it. When I told a friend, ten years my junior, who had quit her high-powered White House job to stay home with her son, about some of the advice that had been dished out in *Ladies' Homes Journal* and other magazines I had worked for over the years, she laughed, and said, "You've got to be like McNamara and confess your crimes."

Okay, I will. But I have to admit that for years I thought I was a head cheerleader, encouraging, applauding, even shouting at women when necessary to make the most of the opportunities we now have. I have spent my entire adult life in the magazine business, almost always editing magazines for women, and I considered myself lucky, very lucky. Not everyone gets to interview both Princess Diana *and* the winner of an Oprah look-alike contest who turned out to be a female impersonator. Who knew?

I loved working on women's magazines because I thought I was fortunate to be both living and telling the best and most interesting story of our time—the improvement in the lives of women—to those who were benefiting from these enormous gains. As the years went by, I saw women's magazines change to reflect the changing roles of women in society. Nothing wrong with that, but the story that began as an exciting movement for equal rights and morphed into a wonderful celebration of opportunity today has become a depressing, discouraging gain-means-pain tale of woe sold to women readers as the grim new reality of their lives. It wasn't always that way.

Yeah! Yeah! Yeah!

My first job was at a magazine for teenage girls, when I was practically a teenager myself. It was called *Ingenue*, and it was the early 1960s when the first wave of baby boomers made teenagers and their fads suddenly important. Though we may try, some of us will never forget ironing our hair or sleeping on rollers the size of beer cans, wearing miniskirts we wouldn't be caught dead in today, and buying albums by shaggy-haired crooners who shocked our parents but drove us mad.

With a press pass proudly hung around my neck, I attended the Beatles' first American press conference, the hottest media event of the year. Because I represented a teenage magazine, I got to sit in the first row and ask the Fab Four what our readers wanted to know, wonderfully innocent questions like, "Beatle Paul, who cuts your hair?" and "Beatle John, what do you really, *really* think of American girls?" Okay, so I wasn't exactly Woodward and Bernstein, but I was having the time of my life.

I even followed the Beatles to Miami Beach on assignment, where they took some needed R&R after wowing our readers and every other little girl over eleven with their hair-shaking performance on the *Ed Sullivan Show*. Life would never be the same again for millions of fathers who sat stunned as their heretofore normal, well-adjusted daughters, glued to the family television, turned into hysterical, weeping lunatics before their very eyes. I was just old enough to avoid throwing myself into the frenzy that accompanied the biggest British invasion since the War of 1812, but I headed south to Florida thrilled to be in the position that millions of girls would have killed for—to actually meet the Beatles. This was big, really big.

When I arrived the Fontainebleau Hotel was so jammed with fans and beer-swilling British journalists that they stuck me in a poolside cabana without a door and comped me for a dinner and performance by a disgruntled Frank Sinatra. Ol' Blue Eyes was sullen that the new guys in town weren't even interested in paying their respects. Watching Sinatra's angry performance, it was the first time I observed generations clash. Out with the old, in with the new. I would see this happen over and over again in the years ahead and most often in relation to women and how we were told to live our lives.

Celebrity journalism in those days was so genteel that no one, not even the tough Fleet Street reporters who knew the Beatles' every move, reported that John, Paul, George, and Ringo spent most of their time in their rooms with a coterie of eager-to-please groupies. I didn't let my *Ingenue* readers in on that little piece of gossip, believing that perhaps the nearly demented teenage girls of America weren't ready to hear that their conquering heroes wanted more than to "Hold Your Hand." They were having such a good time, the Beatles even refused to leave their Florida fun to return to Britain to receive an award from the prime minister at a long-planned luncheon. No problem. The Conservative prime minister Harold Macmillan changed the date to accommodate the fun-loving Lads from Liverpool. The power of celebrity to reshape events had truly begun.

Yes, it was swell at *Ingenue* while it lasted, but I also learned my first tough-minded lesson in magazine publishing there. Never try to sell a magazine to readers who can't pronounce its name.

After *Ingenue* folded, I began to freelance for *Redbook,* which called itself "the magazine for young mamas." I pounded out short stories about being a young wife and mother when women's magazines had at least three or four stories in each issue about being a young wife and mother.

The themes of my little stories in that long-ago time were always the same: small children can be a pain (surprise, surprise), but they are worth it. Husbands can be even a bigger pain, but they are worth it, too. These tidbits of prose were easy for me to write because I honestly believed the message. I still do.

But that was the way we all were in those days, when Betty Friedan was just beginning to shake the foundations of the neat little world of women's magazines and television sitcoms. When I was growing up, a nice middle-class girl was supposed to get married and produce children—definitely in that order. That was it. Your mother and everyone else told you so. And media reinforced the message with all the finesse of a sledgehammer. *Leave It to Beaver* or *Father Knows Best* had about as much subtlety as Roseanne on a good day.

Women's magazines did much the same and with much the same reach. In the great heyday of women's service magazines—*Ladies' Home Journal, Redbook, Good Housekeeping, McCall's, Family Circle, Woman's Day,* and *Better Homes & Gardens,* known as the Seven Sisters—they had a combined circulation of 40 million at a time when there were 76 million women in our country. Men, back from the war, were climbing the corporate ladder while both family size and home ownership was burgeoning. It was a time when Conformity Was All, and these magazines assumed that their readers were mothers at home, devoted to their children, dutifully taking care of hardworking husbands.

The Happy Housewife

I grew up in a new ranch house in a new community in a suburb on Long Island with an older brother and the requisite hardworking dad and homemaker mom who kept her magazines—she subscribed to five of the Seven Sisters—on the coffee table and followed their recipes for Lady Baltimore Cake and Fruit Salad Surprise in Jellied Aspic. I remember, and not fondly, marshmallows and maraschino cherries suspended in lime green Jell-O, a dish only a hungry toddler could love.

The magazines also assumed their readers, no matter what their social class, wanted to be treated like "ladies." Senator Barbara Mikulski once explained, "When World War II was over my aunts and other relatives wanted to get out" and stop working in the factories where they had been employed. "They wanted to be 'ladies' and they wanted their daughters to be 'ladies.'"[5] Hard as it is now to believe in this age of pregnant actresses prancing naked across the covers of national magazines, this great concern with prissy respectability even influenced the celebrity reporting of the day. Marilyn Monroe, the most sensational star of the time, was never featured in the traditional women's magazines. She wistfully told Edward R. Murrow on a *Person to Person* broadcast that, although she had appeared on the cover of many magazines, she longed to be in *Ladies' Home Journal*. It didn't happen until years after she was dead. Today, most editors or producers or Media Queens, for that matter, would do practically anything, no matter how undignified, for the rights to "I Was the President's Mistress" and would never think twice about running it. To get her Monica Lewinsky interview, Barbara Walters courted Monica's lawyer, William Ginsburg, in dozens of demeaning ways, including hopping on the D.C. shuttle to hand deliver a box of bran flakes, his favorite lunch, that wasn't served after noon at his Washington hotel.

In the '50s and early 1960s, women's magazines occasionally wrote about women with problems but were edited as if the magazine's readers' lives were virtually problem free. The editors knew the readers might be interested in a tale of a woman with an alcoholic sister or a *Ladies' Home Journal* "Can This Marriage be Saved?" story entitled

"I Live with a Tyrannical Husband," and who didn't? But these pieces were not coupled with "news to use" advice for readers as potential victims as they always are today, like "Could Acupuncture Prick Up Your Sex Drive?" or "Are You Going to Hell?"—terribly useful features that appeared not so long ago in *Glamour.*[6] Back then, magazines' implicit stance was that their readers might be interested and sympathetic to other women's difficulties, but they were really too nice to have such problems themselves.

Television sent the same message. The shows on the new TV sets families gathered round to watch every night—programs like *Father Knows Best* and *The Adventures of Ozzie and Harriet* and the advertisements that were part of the shows—confirmed that there was simply no other life possible for a woman. And why should there be?

Even if you were born long after *Leave It to Beaver* debuted in 1957—hey, even if your *mother* was born after that—you have seen June Cleaver in her starched shirtdress and heels with a feather duster in hand. And you know what a compelling image the calm, unharried, always ladylike Happy Homemaker can be. No wonder this decades-old icon of a more placid time still plays in reruns in the back of so many women's heads.

But there was a dark side to being June, too. In my demanding suburban high school, I took three years of Latin and chemistry and physics, but I also had to take a course in homemaking. Elizabeth Dole once told me that she had been afraid she wasn't going to graduate from high school because she couldn't sew a zipper in a skirt: No Duke or Harvard Law if she couldn't get that damn thing in straight.

That's because you were graded in home ec just like any other course, and if you didn't do well—if you sewed your A-line skirt inside out or spilled raw tapioca in the teacher's perfectly ratted bouffant hair as a friend of mine did—you could kiss the honor roll goodbye. You didn't want *that* to happen. You were supposed to do well in school and go on to college. But getting a guy, *the* guy, was always a girl's primary goal.

On the last night of school my senior year in college, I remember vividly my beautiful best friend weeping into her vodka-and-grape juice Purple Cow because she had always expected to get married the Saturday after graduation, and it wasn't going to happen. And we were at *Bennington,* the most progressive, free-spirited women's college in the country.

I wasn't that nuts about getting married. Nah, I'd given myself till at least age twenty-three. I made it just under the wire, tying the traditional knot though with a decidedly untraditional guy—a British journalist. But let's fast forward a little, a mere five or six years. While I was pounding out those stories about the joys of being a young wife and mother, the times were definitely changing.

Betty Crocker Out, Betty Friedan In

By 1970, what was called the women's liberation movement was bursting into bloom, the subject of excited, enthusiastic cover stories in *Time, Newsweek,* and *The New York Times Magazine,* and analyzed sympathetically in documentaries on ABC, NBC, and CBS. Even Walter Cronkite was curious to find out about "what women now want." And if "Uncle" Walter wanted to know, everyone wanted to know. I, safely married as I was supposed to be with a couple of babies under my belt, watched and listened and realized that somewhere between meeting the Beatles and boiling baby bottles, I had gotten seriously out of step. How could this be, I wondered? I'd done everything the magazines and television had told me to do, hadn't I? Where did I go wrong?

It was Betty Friedan who answered the question for me and millions like me and kick-started the women's movement in the process with her book *The Feminine Mystique*. Betty was a brainy, cranky, suburban wife and mother who wrote articles for all the major women's magazines. For years, she interviewed suburban housewives like herself, like the magazines' readers, for her pieces in *McCall's* and *Redbook* and *Ladies' Home Journal*. She had grown to believe that these Happy Homemakers, real-life versions of June Cleaver, weren't happy at all. Betty found them to be bored, frustrated, and suffering from what she called "the problem that has no name."[7]

These trapped, middle-class housewives cooked and gardened and crafted and were bored stiff, Betty maintained, by the repetitive and often pointless tasks of housework. Of course, sitting here all these years later, this all seems just a little ironic. Didn't the women Betty saw as trapped in empty lives fill their days with exactly the same kind of domestic chores—napkin folding, pumpkin carving, cookie baking—that Martha Stewart so cleverly gussied up, repackaged, and shrewdly marketed to women of exactly the same economic circumstances thirty years later?

Women also thought they had plenty of time for themselves, the free time that women today say they now so desperately crave. So much damn time that, according to Betty, those long quiet hours left these women depressed, sexually frustrated, and popping Miltown, the "in" tranquilizer of the day, like Altoids.

Betty even compared women's lives of "nothingness [and] emptiness" to those of concentration camp inmates.[8] Remember, this was less than two decades after the liberation of Auschwitz when the horrors of the camps were still fresh. To compare the lives of American women with victims of the Holocaust I thought, then and now, was way over the top. I have always admired Betty, but, in this instance, she was indulging in a women's magazine technique that is still used today whenever possible: grossly exaggerate the challenges facing ordinary women as far more difficult and even tragic than they really are to make a political point.

Okay, I was in tune with some aspects of the women's liberation movement, which was developing all around me, but it wasn't always an easy transition for me and thousands of other women trying to grasp what was happening. Betty Crocker was out; Betty Friedan was in.

Betty's message was fairly limited. She thought middle-class women should stop wasting their college educations and just go to work. Some "sisters" took up the cause, however, in a more aggressive way. In March of 1970, two hundred giggling, shouting feminists, a few worried about whether they were going to be finished in time for their weekly hair appointment, occupied the offices of the editor of *Ladies' Home Journal* for eleven hours. They were there—after alerting *The New York Times* about their daring raid—to express their dissatisfaction with the contents of the magazine (and all women's magazines) and demand changes in what women's media was serving up. John Mack Carter, the *Journal's* dapper and talented editor at the time, listened to what he later called their "shrill accusations and the radical dialectic." But I can tell you, he was more worried that they would not let him out of his office for bathroom breaks than anything else. Finally he agreed to let the editors and writers in the group produce a special section for the magazine that, he promised, would be published. It appeared in the *Journal* the following August. Most of the readers were underwhelmed by their radicalized sisters' content, but John had deftly avoided a trip to the urologist.

The lead article echoed Betty's cure-all exhorting women to get off their duffs and get a job: "Just what is it that men have that we envy? The freedom, the right, the encouragement, the responsibility to go outside the home and work for a living. We want that responsibility because we believe that the social rewards for holding down a job are critical to one's sense of dignity and self worth."[9]

I bought it. I did. Because I liked to work. Because I was ambitious. Because I felt lucky to be working. As I told my mother, somewhat smugly, I was able to "fulfill myself" in this way. My mother, who had worked as a secretary before she was married, just didn't get it. Why work if you can get your husband to do it for you?

Of course, I was kidding myself, like a lot of middle-class women at the beginning of the women's movement. I believed work was more about self-development than a paycheck. Right. And rhinoplasty is about better breathing. At the time, my husband had just left a big job as a foreign correspondent for a major newspaper and was starting his own news service. I wrote fiction, worked part-time as an editor, helped him in his office while raising our two boys. I could not yet admit to myself, and it would take me years to do so, that I had to work because we needed the money, and we kept needing the money.

A lot of women, especially those entering college at that time, romanticized work in exactly the same way I did. We all thought a happy ending would be the big corporate job and the big corporate title with the prestige and fat paycheck that went with them. "Congratulations, Miss Jones, you are our first female vice president . . ." and the music swells. They were primed to believe total emotional satisfaction would come from the work and success. Lime Jell-O would never clutter their fridge.

But as women's magazines embraced this new feminism and smart, self-confident women declared their independence from home and housework in talk shows and sitcoms, the new working woman never noticed that most men didn't end up with the big corporate job and the big corporate title, either. Twenty years later, many of these same women would discover that, truth be told, most work is deeply ordinary, but for now, their briefcases were a badge of honor. The days when a woman's worth was measured by the early potty-training habits of her children or the ease of her meat loaf recipe were definitely over.

It wasn't long before younger feminists took over the movement and quickly shouldered a middle-aged, argumentative Friedan out of the way. Trashing traditional women's roles was a large part of their message. The most militant "women's libbers" of the time declared that marriage was a patriarchal system devised merely to keep women in their place. Getting pregnant and having children was "barbaric."[10] (Well, maybe they had a point there.) So working like hell was the best option left.

Great. My two children, my greatest achievements to date other than my close encounter with the Beatles, were as passé and out of style as the Happy Homemaker's shirtwaist. In today's child-centered, baby-loving world, it is hard to imagine that by the early '70s, being pregnant was considered not so much a happy event but, frankly, a little gross. Even obstetricians were faintly sadistic about pregnancy. I had a friend who always referred to hers as Dr. Mengele.

I had my son on the exact day the doctor forecast when we first found out I was pregnant. When I arrived at the hospital on what I thought was our mutually agreed-upon date, I discovered my obstetrician was out of town, and a perfect stranger of a doctor delivered my first child. My own doctor waltzed in a couple of days later, made a perfunctory apology, and explained that he had been "called away" to a medical convention. An emergency medical convention!! Medical chutzpah, circa 1970. File this nutty excuse, worthy of Monty Python, in the same category as flying pigs and friendly mothers-in-law.

You also looked like hell when you were pregnant. It was the age of the miniskirt, and my four maternity outfits, red, pale blue, dark blue, and buttercup yellow, all looked like pillow cases with sleeves. I can remember watching Johnny Carson on TV one night while I was nursing my son. Gloria Steinem, television's favorite feminist, was the guest. She looked gorgeous, as usual, with her short skirt and great legs, long fall of shining hair and thick false eyelashes. She was telling Johnny that women had to focus on themselves and that sisterhood was powerful. I remember thinking that if Gloria really were my sister, I wished there was more of a family resemblance.

Real Women Carry Briefcases

You've probably heard some feminist authors like Susan Faludi claim that the messages of feminism had a hard time being heard in mass media; it just wasn't so. By the end of the 1970s, the image of the new, independent Career Woman, single and dressed for success in a gray flannel pinstriped suit and polka-dot bow-tied blouse, was constantly endorsed as desirable and appealing. Rise up and lose that shirtwaist! Now women were being sold a career in exactly the same drumbanging way that the Happy Homemaker had been marketed and sold to their mothers.

The new message was that women—or, at least, the women who mattered—were changing their lives and doing it in new and exciting ways. You, too, could and should. *Prime Time,* a book based on a long-term study of thousands of television programs from the late 1950s through the mid-1990s, found that the theme of women's rights became "prominent" during the decade of the '70s and that "characters who deride women's abilities in any way were invariably shot down."[11]

Not only were television sitcoms like *That Girl* and later *The Mary Tyler Moore Show* very popular, Phil Donahue's talk show, the predecessor to Mighty Oprah's, was extraordinarily influential. Donahue, as liberal then as he is today, preached feminist ideas from 1967 onward to the millions of housewives who loyally watched him every afternoon. Donahue and actor Alan Alda, the wisecracking lead surgeon on television's M*A*S*H, became the sexy symbols of "New Men," sympathetic and supportive of the women's movement. They were always being quoted and cooed over in women's magazines as examples of men who changed, understood, got it. Men unafraid to show just how in touch they were with their feminine side. Not like the lunk who shared your bed.

If you followed the network news closely, you also saw that from the start, television news was sympathetic to feminist goals of equal pay for equal work, increased availability of child care, and reproductive rights. During the '70s, many more female reporters appeared on camera—including Lesley Stahl on CBS and Ann Compton on ABC— who added more emotion (and an array of changing hairstyles) to the news they reported. This more personal style of journalism, turned into an art form by Barbara Walters, who became the co-anchor on the *ABC Evening News* in 1976, would eventually feminize, to a major degree, both the content and the style of much of television news coverage.

Women's magazines, including *Ladies' Home Journal,* which had been most invested in selling women's traditional roles, changed so dramatically they often left their readers behind, reeling. In the mid-1970s, thirty-nine editors of women's magazines wrote editorials urging the ratification of the Equal Rights Amendment. Because the leaders of the women's movement had declared that the personal was political, the editors assumed all readers would be open to the same political message. All women should agree just because, well, because we were women. So began in earnest the unwavering belief that continues today among the editors of women's magazines that women— or rather the women who matter—think alike.

Big mistake. The ERA campaign totally backfired. Those sophisticated New York editors were outmaneuvered by Phyllis Schlafly, a brilliant operative in the guise of a midwestern housewife. Schlafly, with great skill and by marshaling enormous grassroots support, managed to derail the Equal Rights Amendment just three states short of ratification.[12]

Schlafly and Friedan, now both in their eighties, are lionesses in winter, somewhat removed from the battle but still involved in the issues facing women today. I spoke with them both while working on this book. Betty, who always knew in her heart that women would want to marry and have children, even if they worked, told me that she felt women were now "equal enough." But she was disappointed that too many women have lost the spirit and enthusiasm to make the most of the opportunities available to them. "Remember that song, 'I Am Woman, I Can Do Anything, I Am Invincible?' Why don't women feel like that anymore?" she lamented rather plaintively.[13]

Schlafly, the daughter of a hardworking mother, and mother herself to two career-women daughters, still runs her political organization, the Eagle Forum, and writes a twice-weekly newspaper column. "I never said women shouldn't work," she insists. "I just said I didn't want to pay for their child care."[14]

In women's media circles, Schlafly has always been decried as a right-wing extremist, a nut, someone who makes the Wicked Witch of the West look like Mary Poppins.[15] Nice. Her own life story reads like a Barbara Taylor Bradford novel—a woman who worked hard and achieved much against great odds. But no self-respecting Spin Sister would be caught dead doing a piece on this woman who, by any objective measure, has led an extraordinary life. Invite her to lunch? Only when hell freezes over or liposuction is a covered benefit, whichever comes first. I love to describe her life and career to friends and colleagues: working her way through university in a munitions factory, winning a fellowship to Radcliffe for graduate work, attending law school in her fifties, an expert on arms control, the author of a major work of political philosophy. Oh, and a wife and mother of six children. My media buddies are wildly impressed by her achievements. Until I mention her name.

Carol Story, longtime CBS' *The Early Show* producer, remembers working on an afternoon talk show in Cleveland in the 1970s that competed with Donahue. "Schlafly was the guest. I guess it was around the time of the ERA debate. I remember she said women would rather hug a baby than a typewriter. Behind the camera, we were all feminists, and we laughed at her. Hey, she turned out to be right!"[16]

Victims of Our Own Success

During the late 1970s, I was working at *Family Circle*, which was then the biggest-selling women's magazine in the world. I started out as fiction editor, which I used to say was about as important as being food editor at *Playboy*. While other women's magazines were fiercely debating the right life for women and losing their readers, *Family Circle*, along with its arch-rival, *Woman's Day*, was "sticking to its knitting" and crocheting, of Granny Squares that is. Telling women, during those Jimmy Carter years of skyrocketing inflation, how to throw together a tasty dinner for four with half a pound of hamburger and how to make monkey dolls out of socks to put under the Christmas tree.

I became editor-in-chief of *Ladies' Home Journal* in 1981, as women were beginning to move into jobs with the kind of power and responsibility our mothers never dreamed of. The *Journal* is over 120 years old. Recently I saw myself described as "founding editor." Not exactly. When I arrived, the magazine was in such lousy shape that one friend congratulated me on being appointed captain of the *Titanic*. The debate about the right place for a woman had worn away the readership and confused the advertisers. The magazine was near collapse.

No problem. I was full of energy and enthusiasm because I thought women had finally found the right answer to that question. I believed women could, at last, just do what they wanted and feel good about it. And do it without a catfight, without putting down the choice any other woman made.

My first readers' survey seemed to confirm my optimism. Eighty-six thousand women told me they liked the "opportunities they now had." Good. They didn't want to live the way their mothers had lived. Good. But they also said the "happiest day of their life" was the day they married or had a child.[17] It made perfect sense to me because it was exactly how I felt, too. What bothered them the most was "not being treated with respect." But they weren't complaining. Eighty-seven percent said they were glad they were women because "women can do anything."

In my first years at the *Journal,* I was the cheerleader-in-chief, complete with pom-poms and a megaphone, running many articles about the opportunities women now had, saluting achieving women, describing how well we were doing. Occasionally, I admit, a questioning note would appear. "Do I have it all but no time to enjoy it?" a working woman lamented in one piece.[18] There was a lead story, "The New One-Paycheck Family,"[19] about women who had quit work to stay home with their young children. In the piece, the mothers made it clear they were doing so because they wanted to be with their children, not because their children really needed them. While in another piece, "Work Plus Baby—The New Reality," Dr. Ivan Jacobson of Columbia University advised women to get right back to work and fast. "I do think the convalescence period after childbirth was exaggerated . . ." he declared, no doubt from his extensive personal experience. "Look, a woman having a second or third baby has always had to get back to tending to a household and toddlers and a husband. Maybe going to an office is easier than that. In any case, I'd definitely say six weeks is the maximum time off needed for just about any woman."[20] Really.

In that same article, a significant new trend was revealed. Mothers acknowledge how hard it is to leave their babies and "seem to compensate by being particularly intense about mothering." Shades of things to come.

Okay, so the pressures of the next decade were already beginning to emerge. Still, it was a good and exciting time for women, trying to combine the old and new, building on the values that had always been important to us, making use of new strengths. Women did not have to conform to only one role. Having choices was better than not having them. Wasn't it?

As I sat in my editor's chair, I really believed that media would never again sell a simplistic, one-sided image of women to women. Hell, I would never do that now that I was in charge, would I? Besides, women wouldn't stand for it. We liked having choices. Didn't we?

But then we all discovered something unexpected. Having choices is complicated. Not impossible, not horrible, but complicated. We found out that there is a downside to almost every choice you make and that can be very, very scary. Most of us learned to cope just as our mothers and grandmothers had done before us. We sucked it up, traded panty hose for pant suits, and thanked God every day for the invention of the microwave. But not everyone handled this revelation with equal grace or grit.

And so media has spent the last ten years creating an all-encompassing *new* image for women, an exaggeration of our reality, much as the Happy Homemaker was an exaggeration—in truth, more women were in the workforce in the 1950s than in the 1940s[21]—just as Connie Career Woman in her bow-tie blouse and three-button suit was another exaggerated stereotype.

Today, like stars of an awful horror movie, we've all become victims—dare I say it?—of our own success. Now the message is: If you are a woman, just *because* you are a woman, you inevitably have problems. That your very life—even if you live a perfectly ordinary one—is the source of serious difficulties.

Instead of celebrating our opportunities, the media portrays smart, educated, talented, resourceful women as harried, hurried, incompetent losers, always, but always, getting it wrong.

If you are single, they say you still need to get a man and get him as aggressively as possible by using wiles that would make the "working girl" on the corner hang up her thong in exhaustion.

If you are single and don't have a man or a child, the media tells you that you will end up, as Sylvia Ann Hewlett dolefully predicts in *Creating a Life*, with ravenous unsatisfied baby hunger having made a "creeping nonchoice," squandering your fertility. How many bags of lowfat popcorn have you put away watching this theme played over and over again in sappy Lifetime movies?

Hewlett's much-publicized book sold poorly, but got a total media blitz, including a cover story in *Time* and a frightening segment on *60 Minutes* that was rerun within a couple of months just in case you didn't get the message the first time.

Of course, if you do have a baby or two and stay home with them, you are sentenced to life without the possibility of parole on the Mommy Track, where, according to the media, you can kiss your economic independence, self-respect, and even your sanity good-bye.

If you do have a child, you will also have to give up your sex life as one *New York* magazine writer reported, describing "The Curse of the Breast-feeding Mother": Bug-eyed with horror and disdain, she explains how your whole life changes. Nursing mothers stop wanting sex. "I stared down, imagining my entire sensual future resting on my rack. I was a fox; I didn't want to be a cow."[22]

And if you do it all—work, marriage, kids, and occasionally even perform the sex act—you can still complain, like Kate Reddy of *I Don't Know How She Does It*: "Mum thinks I have it all . . . I can't tell her, can I? It would be like finding out that after Cinderella got to live in the palace, the Prince put her back on hearth-cleaning duty."

Well, Mum knows English Princesses have had a tough go of it lately.

So we end up with today's baffled woman who is told no matter what she does—or how she does it—she can't win.

That's Why They Call It the Blues

Thirty-five years ago, the women's movement began as a struggle for equal opportunity. Over the next two decades, "You go, grrrls!" was

the message sent by most women's magazines and beamed from our
TV screens as Mary Richards summoned the courage to take on Mr.
Grant, and Murphy Brown got in somebody's face nearly every week.
And when it came to "bitches in the house," Krystle and Alexis were
the real deal. But in recent years, we've swerved from empowerment
to victimhood. Why? Why would a media that is so dependent on
women audiences lead you down such a gloomy path?

And is it even true? Are you *really* that stressed or always half-sick
with killer cramps, killer bloat, killer PMS, or the recently discovered
"perimenopause," an all-purpose condition that can go on for years
and may possibly afflict you almost as soon as you use up your first
box or two of superabsorbent minipads.

Do women truly think, as *Good Housekeeping* recently declared in
a throwaway line, that some days "just making it to midnight without
a major catastrophe is an accomplishment,"[23] as if most days for most
readers were as fraught with terror and trauma as September 11? Do
we routinely wake up from nightmares about "deadly molds" or
"killer hot dogs"? Do we spend our days worrying whether antiper-
spirants cause breast cancer or wondering if a long airline ride will
cause a fatal blood clot? Or are we just observing today's favorite
media technique to paint women's lives to women audiences as a picture of accumulated woes, a picture that, by the way, belies the true
circumstances of how most women live.

Or can there be another reason?

Back in the '70s, the stories I wrote were always didactic and gave
readers, in the guise of fiction, a clear lesson about how to live their
lives. In some ways, it's not very different today. Articles that are
supposed to be fair-minded are often slanted, albeit naively, to give
women ideologically tinted messages about how to view themselves
and understand their world.

A mid-1990s Media Research Center study of thirteen women's
magazines pointed out that in a six-month period there were over a

hundred features that touched in some way on social issues, including health care and the environment. In almost all of the stories, the message was the same: We have a big problem. It's scary and could affect any woman or her children. It could affect You. To fix this problem, we need government action, and we need it now! Other solutions were rarely offered. In fact, twenty-three articles actually told readers to get out there and make government get involved.[24] This attitude continues today. In researching this book I read every issue, between January 2000 and December 2002, of nine women's magazines including *Cosmopolitan, Family Circle, Good Housekeeping, Glamour, Marie Claire, Redbook, Vogue, Woman's Day* and, of course, *LHJ*. In the articles that touched on political issues there were seventy-one calls for action, either requiring government involvement or endorsing organizations that advocate greater government action. The underpinning of all of this, the story behind all these stories, is the assumption that, being a woman, you will understand and agree. You will share a uniform "woman's point-of-view," the belief that women today are constantly victimized and that such victimization is beyond our control and more pervasive than even the good life most of us enjoy.

I also took a look at the cover lines on a sampling of major women's magazines—*Good Housekeeping, Redbook, Cosmopolitan,* and *Glamour* along with *Ladies' Home Journal*, of course, for an even longer period, from 1990 through 2002. These large and successful magazines have a joint readership of over 60 million women, many in their twenties, thirties, and forties. By almost any measure, happy days were here again in the '90s. Most American families were better off financially than ever. Life expectancy had increased. Infant mortality and breast cancer mortality rates had declined. Teenage pregnancy had decreased. More students than ever before, especially women, had graduated from high school and were off to college. All these factors affected the lives of women who read magazines.

Yet the covers told a different story, one of women growing more and more beleaguered, endangered, and unhappy during these thirteen years.

Take just one year: 1992. During that entire year, there was not one cover line about stress or being exhausted or just plain unhappy with your life on the cover of *Redbook* magazine, whose readership is primarily women in their thirties. By 2001, there were ten cover lines about beating stress, three about having no energy, two about how to become happier, and one about finding time for yourself. And it wasn't the attack on the World Trade Center that made women so stressed—that would be understandable. Every issue of the magazine, except December's, was planned, edited, printed, and out the door before September 11.

On *Good Housekeeping*'s 1992 covers, I couldn't find one line about dieting, and I believe American women did eat that year. Eight years later in 2000, there were eleven cover lines about dieting, two about exercising for a better body, and one about looking younger. All women's magazines increased their cover lines and their features about health as well during this decade, based on the belief that a month without a potential new disease to worry about was like a day without sunshine. In the *Journal* I followed the fashion and began to use two or three health lines almost every issue as if every woman had some type of incipient medical problem, major or minor, whether it was "killer cramps," "bloat," an eating disorder, or sun spots, spider veins, or "acne at *your* age."

Throughout the decade, all the magazines, the *Journal* included, also published and promoted many stories about crimes against women and children, even though crime statistics were plummeting across the country.

Glamour for one, all through the '90s, became focused less on fashion and more on features about violence against women, running many articles on the subject: "Stalked! Why No Woman Is Safe!" (August 1992), "He's Going to Kill Me! Is Anybody Listening?" (September

1994), "Could He Be a Stalker? Danger Signals You Might Miss" (June 1997). In 2000, while *Good Housekeeping*'s diet-conscious readers seemed menaced by the proliferation of Krispy Kreme franchises, *Glamour*'s readers were in the crosshairs of an AK-47. "*Glamour* Investigates the Gunning Down of American Women" (January 2000), with the blurb on the story declaring that although women are killed by guns "lawmakers seem to do little about it." In this same issue was a story about a woman harassed by a police officer, the implication of the two stories taken together is that if the robbers don't get you, the cops probably will.

But women's magazines weren't the only culprits. Year by year, television newsmagazines and talk shows, video copycats of women's magazines, focused more and more on frightening crime and health stories, sometimes battling with the magazines for exclusive rights to precisely the same stories. Watched primarily by women, these programs, which proliferated in the '90s, were in the Fear Factor business long before the real *Fear Factor* hit ratings gold for NBC.

I know as an editor it became the style to tell women over and over they had lots of reasons to worry and complain. So much so that talking about personal responsibility or making tough choices and living with them seemed downright harsh. Av Westin, the television executive who created the newsmagazine *20/20*, which became the template for so many of the magazine shows that followed, told me, "We started every story with a victim. That's what we said. 'We need a victim. Find me the victim.'"[25] In magazines, we also got into the destructive, demeaning habit of looking at the world of women victim-first. Of course, this made us—the editors, producers, and newsmagazine anchors, Spin Sisters all—seem *so* understanding and caring about women. As if the only thing women deserved was sympathy. Our formula became a combination of self-indulgence, self-pity, and celebrity, not a menu to be proud of but one that seemed to fit the "I feel your pain" 1990s and the beginning of this decade especially well.

Contrary to what we've spun, we *have* come a long way, baby, over the past thirty years. This is the best of times for American women. Every statistic proves it. Yet you are being sold, day after day and month after month in soppy TV movies and scary TV news-magazines and on the slick pages of colorful magazines, the most negative interpretation of your lives.

Let me show you exactly what I mean. And there is no better way to do that than to tackle the myth of stress and to try to beat it—for all our sakes!

CHAPTER 3

Got Stress?

Ho, ho, ho. 'Tis the season to be jolly. Or is it? Once upon a time, the holidays were something we looked forward to celebrating. Decorating the tree was fun even with more dead lights dangling from its branches than you find in most Third World countries after dark. Tramping from store to store for the perfect gift was worth it even if you spent the day after Christmas desperately seeking the sales receipts somewhere in the pile of crumpled shopping bags waiting in the closet for the round-trip back to Bloomingdale's or FAO Schwarz. And even though every year I would swear off the annual pilgrimage to Macy's for a photo and a heart-to-heart with old St. Nick, the picture of my kids was always sooo cute; and twelve months later, there I'd be, back for more. I still treasure one portrait that makes it clear that all my older son really needed from Santa, just as in the song, was his two front teeth.

Sure, a two-hour wait with a couple of cranky toddlers for thirty seconds with Father Christmas has its drawbacks, I'd be the first to admit. So would the two hundred other slightly crazed moms trapped in a line that moved at the speed of a bad French movie. But depression inducing? I really don't think so. Yet if you pick up almost any women's magazine from the moment there's a chill in the air or switch on a morning show or Oprah when the mistletoe is gaily hanging, and, fa-la-la, you'd think we were preparing for Armageddon, not eggnog and tobogganing. *Stress! Stress! Stress!* scream the cover lines. Holidays, we are told, are nothing but the Twelve Days of Stress-mas. Nowadays you might not believe that once upon a time Christmas was, like, the happiest time of the year.

Coming Up on *Today*: Dr. Grinch

I nearly choked on my bagel laughing one morning in 2001 as I watched Ann Curry, the *Today* show's chic, sophisticated counterweight to Her Cuteness, Katie Couric, furrow her perfect brows in deep consternation and concern. It was two days after Christmas, just a few months after 9/11, and Dr. Judith Reichman, *Today*'s doctor on call, had arrived like the cavalry, as Ann put it, to rescue women viewers from the threat of what she delicately called "gender-special emotional and physical problems" that can come from "dangerous holiday stress." As if buying and receiving presents were somehow life threatening.[1]

Now, I agree that the holiday season can be a little trying. Aunt Mary's uncanny ability to belch through every carefully prepared course of Christmas dinner with the regularity of a German train schedule comes to mind as a possible irritant. So does the "diamonds are forever" anniversary ring you oohed over with hubby on more than one occasion and which morphs into a lovely sweater set under the tree exactly like the one he gave you last year in exactly the same cornflower blue. But is this the stuff of serious stress?

Girls, aren't we really tough enough to stuff a turkey and open a can or two of yams without a near mental or physical breakdown? Well, according to Dr. Reichman, we are not.

To listen to Reichman, holiday stress can lead to, well, a veritable cornucopia of personal disasters. With Ann dutifully egging her on, the good doctor spent what seemed like twenty minutes ticking off the devastating tragedies that this demanding, downright dangerous season can trigger. There's depression, insomnia, lack of concentration, and general "sad feelings." Early periods, late periods, more PMS, bloating, and breast tenderness. Weight gain—Dr. Reichman claimed each of us, over Christmas, will put on anywhere from three to five pounds which, by the way, has been found to be untrue. Worst of all, said Dr. Grinch ominously, "That's weight we never lose."

And what about the hot toddies or that Christmas cocktail you're likely to indulge in? Well, if you're a woman and you drink, says Dr. Reichman, you're "far more likely not to be able to drive right." Gee, what if a male doctor had said that? Wouldn't such flagrant chauvinism make you a little annoyed? Demon alcohol can also lead to Bad Judgment, which leads to Sexually Transmitted Diseases and Unwanted Pregnancies. And speaking of STDs, did you know that the 22 percent of women who have been infected with genital herpes are more likely to suffer a recurrence during the holidays because they are more stressed and their natural killer cells don't work properly?

Ann didn't know that either but looked properly pained when she found out.

There are also more cold sores to look forward to, and as Ann puts it in the fine tradition of TV medical journalism, "lest anybody think that stress is not dangerous, I mean, it can also cause people with high blood pressure to have more pressure in their—their blood vessels . . . it's very dangerous." Thanks for the clinical explanation, Ann.

But in case the doctor's Christmas list of looming stress-related health disasters gets you (dare I say it) stressed, Dr. Reichman is filled to the brim like a good cup of Christmas cheer with helpful suggestions. Take hot baths, meditate, do yoga, or consider medication, she advocates. If you get an infection, take care of it. Now, why didn't I think of that? Chew gum while you're cooking so you don't nibble. And Dr. Reichman's pièce de résistance? If you are going to someone else's house for dinner or a party, and they will be serving fattening food (do you know anyone who doesn't at a Christmas party?) "bring healthy alternatives." I'm sure your host and hostess, who just plunked down the equivalent of a mortgage payment for a festive catered buffet, won't mind a bit when you show up with a terrine of tofu pâté and a thermos of soy punch in your rhinestone-studded evening bag.

I know Dr. Reichman and her trusty interviewer were serious and meant well. Holidays can be times when our energy and spirits don't match the season. But are they really so much more stressful than those our mothers and grandmothers organized? After all, we've got frozen hors d'oeuvres we can pass off as our own (I always do), Internet shopping, tape dispensers, and cell phones. But, bah humbug, we've not only stopped counting our blessings, we don't even acknowledge them. Instead, we've got stress. We've got it all year long.

Just watch women's television programming or pick up a copy of almost any magazine, and you'll see that stress has become the cellulite of today. It is the constant, unquestioned problem stalking every woman from morning till night.

Twenty years ago "cellulite" was a peculiarly female malady that every woman over the age of sixteen was alleged to have residing somewhere south of her hipbone. It was pervasive and unavoidable, just another fun feature of being a woman. Promoted by the beauty industry in France, cellulite was that disfiguring, water-filled "orange-peel skin" that popped up on your thighs and bottom when given a good squeeze, sort of like your own personal bubble wrap. So, like post-maternity hemorrhoids and menopausal moods, you were supposed to try very hard to make it go away. In those *Dallas* and *Dynasty* days, it was presumed women still had enough time to focus on the finer details of their anatomy, to ruthlessly examine their thighs, shriek with horror, and rush out to buy overpriced creams and potions with names like Lift Extreme-Nutri-Collagene Concentre as a cure for lumpy, bumpy rumps.

I don't believe any man ever said to his wife or girlfriend, "Oooh, baby, you've got cellulite. I'm outta here." If asked, most of them would probably tell you cellulite is some kind of new battery. But cellulite was supposed to make you crazy and was sold to you that way, too.

Archfeminist Susan J. Douglas, in her rollicking book *Where the Girls Are*, does a great riff on how women were made to feel inadequate if they couldn't turn their bottoms into the then much-desired "buns of steel" and how the great international beauty-industrial complex realized there was "gold in them thar thighs." And sought to extract it.

Still, Douglas does stretch it when she affirms, "The flawless rump became the most important female body part of the 1980s because its cultivation and display fit in so well with the great myth of Reaganism: that superficial appearances really can be equated with a person's deepest character strengths and weaknesses."[2] Huh?

Following that free-floating logic, dare one say that the all-purpose, overwhelming Soccer Mom Stress, pushed by women's media for the past decade, fits in so well with the great myth of Clintonism: that we all deserve an "I feel your pain" kind of sympathy for practically anything and everything that might be the least bit difficult. Do we really need hand-holding just to get through a hectic day or to make that most challenging of suppertime decisions: Hamburger Helper or Domino's? Not exactly Sophie's Choice. But if we all are made to feel like victims of stress it follows that we ought to feel sorry for *all* other victims, whether or not they truly deserve our concern. After all, misery loves company.

Of course, women, like men, have—and have always had—genuine stress and the problems that produce it. Our immigrant and pioneering foremothers, our grandmothers who scraped and scrimped their way through the Depression, our moms who sent their husbands off to Omaha Beach, the centuries of mothers who watched the baby's temperature spike without the Children's Tylenol that would get it down in half an hour, all had stress. They worried and prayed and wept. Just think back to the women in your own family and what they coped with through the generations.

My Hungarian grandmother came to America, where she could not speak the language, with a husband who barely made a living as a pants presser in a sweatshop. Yet she raised five children in a tenement, four sons and a daughter, who all grew up to be hardworking and successful. And she was not very different from hundreds of thousands of other Eastern European, Irish, and Italian mothers, all raising children at that time on New York's Lower East Side. Frankly, I don't know how they did it without aromatherapy or Zoloft.

In recent years, stress has been defined downward, so far downward that we believe almost any minor annoyance can give us serious stress. Lately, we're supposed to lose it over every load of laundry that doesn't get done, every extra cookie that we eat, every time our teenager changes his moods. But how, in the best time for women in the history of the world, did we come to accept that such trivialities stretch our limits?

I can sum it up fast—money, honey. Stress sells. It sells self-indulgence, which in turn sells everything from Botox injections to body creams, spa visits to yoga mats. If the selling of cellulite was the prototype, spawning millions of dollars in sales for the cosmetics industry in the '80s, stress is today's ready-for-market, all-purpose affliction from which no woman is immune.

Does women's media focus on stress, its causes, and cures, because women have more of it today? Or do we feel more stressed because the Spin Sisters keep *telling* us that we are so overwhelmingly stressed? That's the classic chicken-or-egg which-came-first dilemma women find themselves in today. With thirty years of experience, my gut says that stress is real but oversold, wildly oversold. The media have become addicted to stress because it is such a marketable staple for women's magazines, morning talk shows, and evening news segments.

Month after month in the pages of the top women's magazines, millions of women—the single *Cosmo* girl out to get her man, the *Family Circle* SUV-driving Soccer Mom, and every female in between—are told over and over: "Poor girl, you are trying to cope with a tsunami of stress in your daily life, and it's simply impossible." Real issues that cause gut-clenching anxiety—like most women's number-one problem, not having enough money to pay the bills—are never mentioned. Why? Because that's a problem that cannot be solved by taking a hot bath. Especially when both the ad pages and the magazine copy tell you just how desperately you need that twenty-five-dollar bottle of L'Occitane lavender bubble bath, imported from Provence, to pour in the tub to de-stress yourself.

Where did stress come from, anyway? Would you believe Canada?

The Original Rat Race

The word *stress,* at least in its current meaning, was coined in the mid-1950s by a Canadian medical researcher, Hans Selye, who was the author of two extremely popular books, *The Stress of Life,* published in 1956, and *Stress without Distress* in 1974. Selye was born in Hungary and came to the United States after medical school to study at Johns

Hopkins. He found Hopkins's "informal academic attitude" just too darn stressful, as we would say now, and transferred to Montreal's McGill Medical School where he conducted the research that was the basis for his now almost universally accepted theories on stress.

Selye's original research was so downright weird it deserves recounting. After injecting rats with everything from liquefied cow ovaries to toxic formaldehyde, Dr. Selye noticed that the rats experienced physiological changes. Very Interesting.

Next he exposed the rats "to the frigid Canadian winter by leaving them on the windswept roof of the McGill Medical building." Then he put them in a real rat race "in revolving barrel-like treadmills driven by electric motors, so that they had to constantly run to stay upright." Others were dumped into a water barrel so they had to keep swimming to keep from drowning. Hans would have been a great personal trainer. Finally, in a move that should have earned him a spot in the PETA Hall of Shame, he sewed open the eyelids of the poor rats, forcing them to constantly stare into a very bright light.[3]

From these experiments he concluded there was "biological stress" that created damaging bodily changes. Call me crazy, but somehow, I think if I were left on a freezing roof, trapped on a revolving treadmill or in a barrel of water, and injected with large doses of embalming chemicals, my body might have had just the teeny, tiniest negative reaction, too. But Selye's experiments were accepted and thus stress was born—at least in North America.

Dr. Anne Becker, an assistant professor of medical anthropology at Harvard Medical School, puts our focus on stress in perspective: "No matter where you live, there are going to be stresses. . . . Americans are very concerned about stress, but other cultures accept that it's part of the landscape. The question is how . . . much you pay attention to it and how much you name it." I think the answer is we're now in the habit of doing that way too much.

To counteract stress, one women's magazine recommends drinking a tea, popular in Fiji, made with kava, which it describes as "a natural anxiety remedy." (In my world, I call that Chardonnay.) The magazine does go on to caution its readers: "The FDA has advised consumers that [kava] might be associated with liver injury. It may also cause a scaly skin rash called kava dermopathy."[4] But other than that, go for it!

The magazine's enthusiasm for this beverage is based partly on the fact that it works so well for those relaxed Fijians "that they have no word for stress" in Fiji. But there was no word for stress in France or Germany until Selye lectured there in the mid-'50s about his studies on "le stress" and "der stress."

These days, what is often missed in the media's discussion of the biological impact of stress on women is the fact that even Selye believed only major life events could create in humans similar forms of "biological stress" that he had observed in his rats. And by major life events, he did not mean such things as forgetting the half-time snacks for the peewee soccer game or the morning crawl to the office, or your husband's ability to find every sports channel on the remote and his total inability to locate the laundry hamper.

By Selye's definition, major stress creators were the death of a spouse, the loss of a job, a move to a strange, new place—experiences on a scale comparable to a rat having its eyelids sewn open—not the small inconveniences of daily life. He also believed there was good and necessary stress that he called eustress—forces that push us to be energetic, ambitious, even heroic.

Time on Our Hands

Nowadays, whether it's *Redbook* or a sappy or scary segment on *Today* or *Good Morning America*, we are told over and over again that the rapid pace of our lives and our lack of free time explains the increased levels of stress we all are assumed to feel. But, hard as this news flash may be to accept, it is not true that we are busier than we used to be or that we have less leisure time than our mothers had. We believe only what we have been taught to believe.

Robert D. Putnam, who wrote the foreword to *Time for Life,* the book based on the University of Maryland's well-known Americans' Use of Time Project, said this about the disconnect between the perception and reality of our lives: "Subjectively, Americans today undeniably 'feel' more rushed now than a generation ago. By the clock, however, and by their own minute-by-minute chronologies, Americans since 1965 appear to have gained nearly an hour more free time per day. We seriously overestimate how much time we spend at work and we dramatically underestimate how much free time we have at our disposal."[5]

Time for Life also notes that in the 1960s, the average amount of free time women had—time not spent working, sleeping, eating, or taking care of the children—was 33.9 hours a week. Today we have 38.7 hours, nearly five additional hours. That's primarily because, with the help of labor-saving devices, moms spend a lot less time doing chores. Even working mothers, always worried about not spending enough "quantity" or "quality" time with their children, average as much time with the kids as their nonworking mothers did a generation ago.

So why don't we believe we have more free time than women of our mothers' generation? Maybe we don't feel that we have that extra time because of what we do with it. Research shows almost all the "added leisure" gained over the last thirty years is being spent—where else?—on the couch, in front of the tube. The increase in TV watching has, in fact, cut into the time we allocate to almost everything else in our lives. And remember that women, on average, watch television nearly five hours a day.

Rutgers professor Robert Kubey has spent years studying the effect television has on·our emotions. In *Scientific American,* Kubey and his collaborator Mihaly Csikszentmihalyi wrote: "The amount of time people spend watching television is astonishing. . . . Fully half of their leisure time, and more than on any single activity, save work and sleep. . . . To some commentators this devotion means simply that people enjoy TV and make a conscious effort to watch it. But if that is the whole story why do so many people experience misgiving about how much they view?"[6]

Could the problem also be what we are watching? Programs that reinforce misconceptions about women's lives and help increase feelings of stress? Check out some highlights of just one anxiety-producing weekend of movies from Lifetime, which calls itself Television for Women. Lifetime's own Web site hyped the movies this way to lure viewers and not, as you might think, to turn them off.[7] That weekend, women could watch:

EMPTY CRADLE: Determined to keep her boyfriend from leaving, an unbalanced nurse fakes a pregnancy, then kidnaps a baby and claims it as her own. Told her baby was born dead, the birth mother of the missing baby refuses to accept the facts surrounding her infant's alleged death, and fights her family, the hospital, and the police in order to uncover the real truth of her baby's disappearance.

Just your average maternity ward experience.

Followed by:

AWAKE TO DANGER: A teenage girl recovering from a coma tries to remember the events of the night her mother died, but as she gets closer to remembering, her mother's killer closes in on her.

Whatever happened to teenage problems like zits and Spanish finals?

Followed by:

LOVE, LIES AND MURDER, A MINISERIES: The true story of the bizarre murder plot of a father, who enlists the help of his teenage daughter and seventeen-year-old sister-in-law to brutally murder his wife.

The family that slays together, etc. . . .

Followed by:

WHEN NO ONE WOULD LISTEN: A battered wife attempts to escape from her irrational and violent husband, but he finally resorts to holding her hostage.

I give up.

And all these films were programmed on just one weekend.

Like so many women's magazines, Lifetime claims that its central mission is to be supportive of women. So is a Wonderbra, but some things are better left unseen—and that includes most Lifetime movies dressed up as "reality" television. Maybe there are things more out of touch with reality than Lifetime—the Victoria's Secret catalogue and Michael Jackson leap to mind. Still, if you watched nothing but the sappy programs and movies on Lifetime, you might be tempted to believe all men are 1) unfaithful rats, 2) abusive monsters, 3) dishonest scumbags, or 4) all of the above. Women, on the other hand, spend their lives on Lifetime either as übervictims facing such typical tragedies as an astronaut's bout with breast cancer in outer space or as supermom crusaders risking it all to fight for the latest liberal cause célèbre.

The Wall Street Journal's media critic, Tunku Varadarajan, and I think a lot alike when it comes to such programming. He writes:

"Dipping into the Lifetime channel may leave viewers so rattled by the fear of violence, wrongful incarceration, sexual discrimination, or death by disease that they become convinced that they've got one of the many disorders that the network is dedicated to combating." He continues, "The preponderance of its female characters seem to fit roughly into two categories—victims, of whom there are many, and flinty achievers who triumph despite the cavemen who eat testosterone for brunch and want to keep them in their place."

Then he asked the question I found myself asking after watching what seemed like a lifetime of Lifetime: "Is the sapping depression I feel a symptom of prolonged exposure to appalling TV?"[8] After weeks of sitting through one ridiculous movie after another, as I did researching this book, I came to the conclusion that this was self-induced torture only Hans Selye might respect. There is only so much Patty Duke, Meredith Baxter, and Melissa Gilbert I can take, even in the name of research.

It's not just what we watch but the mere act of watching itself that can be a downer. Back to Professor Kubey's study, which found that when people watched TV, they felt "relaxed and passive." Okay so far. When the TV was turned off, feelings of "passivity and lowered alertness continued," but according to Kubey, "the sense of relaxation ends." In its place, participants in his study complained that television viewing had "sucked out their energy, leaving them depleted." We all know that bleary, zonked-out, I-wish-I-hadn't-wasted-so-much-time-watching *Loves, Lies and Murder* feeling.

Apparently the only thing that makes many viewers feel better is turning the TV back on in time for *When No One Would Listen,* even though it may mean watching a woman being molested for the third time that day. Kubey compares television to habit-forming drugs: "A tranquilizer that leaves the body rapidly is much more likely to cause dependence than one that leaves the body slowly, precisely because the user is more aware that the drug's effects are wearing off. . . . [Viewers'] sense that they will feel less relaxed if they stop viewing may be a significant factor in not turning the set off. Viewing begets more viewing."[9] So, watching television can be depressing, but turning it off can make you feel even more depressed—so depressed that, in fact, you turn the television back on.

Maybe you should have gone to chill out at a spa, which of course is exactly the point.

Please Don't Disturb!

Another reason women tend to feel hurried and harried and discount our extra hours of free time is because, in the past decade, we have redefined for ourselves what leisure time is. Or maybe it's been redefined for us. Once leisure simply meant time spent not doing what we *had* to do, like work or chores. No longer. Now, for women, it means "private time," the name of a column *Glamour* introduced in the mid-1980s, or time for yourself, spent alone, or perhaps with one's girlfriends but definitely without the spouse and kids. Going to the beach with the family, having a barbecue: work. Having a pedicure the day before: leisure. And not having time for the pedicure, that's stress.

In one episode of *Sex and the City*, Charlotte, newly separated from her husband, describes how relieved she feels because now that he is gone she finally has the time to spend hours examining her pores in the bathroom mirror. Carrie, Miranda, and Samantha all are totally supportive and sympathetic to her plight. Who needs a husband if he is so demanding you can't spend an hour or two checking out the pores on your nose?

In *I Don't Know How She Does It*, Kate Reddy both beats stress and celebrates success by shopping with her assistant who has become a girlfriend. "Faced with the choice between the tan kitten heels and the navy slingbacks, we chose both. And then we took the black stilettos because they were too beautiful not to own and the toffee boots because they were a total bargain."

During the last decade, especially in media for younger women, liberation and narcissism have merged thanks in large part to magazines like *Cosmopolitan* and *Glamour,* which promote a self-centered lifestyle as the key to becoming a fulfilled and happy woman. But the "me, me, me" focus isn't just for singles anymore. Even magazines aimed at married women and mothers tend to portray narcissism as the natural extension of both feminism and femininity. So, as women achieve more, they are told by media and marketers that they naturally deserve more—from new Tampax pearl plastic tampons ("As Extraordinary as You Are") to $400 Jimmy Choo shoes, $300 Kate Spade bags, $450 TSE cashmere T shirts. When it comes to pampering, we've gone from being worth it to being owed it.

Self-nurturing has become a cottage industry created by endless articles that preach a new feminist gospel—that indulging yourself is an important part of being a healthy, well-adjusted woman. And that if you are not buying what you deserve or pampering yourself, you are endangering your well-being in a significant way.

Oprah's magazine, *O,* ran the mother of all stress articles entitled, "Stress Relief: 105 Ways to Get Calm." The twenty-page opus starts like every article about stress relief. It tells you—quelle surprise!—to take a bath—a nice warm bubble bath. It takes the writer exactly seven sentences to begin complaining about her inability to relax as she agonizes over her life: "How did my medicine cabinet get chipped? . . . How does a woman live more than forty years without having one idea for tomorrow's ideas meeting? . . . I need a new bath mat. . . . I hate my clothes. I hate my hair. I hate my towels. . . . What if I never come up with another idea and I lose my job and I'm forced to live on the street without a place to recharge my electric toothbrush?"[10] Enough already!

Redbook's May 2002 issue blared: "This Little Word Stops Stress!"[11] The "little word" is "No!" *Redbook*'s readers are advised to say it frequently to those who are nearest and dearest to them. Here's how the piece starts out:

> The leader of the junior high youth group came toward me with the kind of huge smile that could only mean one thing: She had a scary question to ask. Could I, she wondered, chaperone the Junior High Holiday Sleepover?

Ohmigod! What a dreadful, intrusive thing to ask. Needless to say, the writer, with much fear and loathing, reacts as if she'd been ordered to lead a squadron into Iraq without flight training. After whining some excuses, she confesses, "I was so worried she'd call me back I couldn't sleep for two nights." Fortunately, someone else was found to do the dirty deed, but it got the writer thinking about how really terrific it was to say no—and who else could she advise readers to blow off?

Her suggestions? Just say no to that unhappy friend who wants you to listen, to your boss who needs you to work late, to "your wonderful extended family . . . especially . . . your mother" who wants to spend some extra time with you. Tell her it's your "policy" to "only attend birthdays, weddings, and major holidays." When "your harried neighbor" is begging for your baby-sitter's number, go for humor. Say 'Oh, no, That's the one number I'll never divulge' . . . think you're being selfish? We repeat: You're not required to give up anything . . . if you need it for yourself. Got it?"

"Remember," advises Harvard's Dr. Alice Domar, who has made a career of giving advice about stress to writers for women's magazines when she isn't writing about the subject herself, "your plan for yourself—even if it's just to eat popcorn with the kids in front of a *Shrek* video—is just as important as any other." So tell your boss who wants you to stay late no, you can't, and leave the office. Easy to say if you're a professor at Harvard and a best-selling author.

No, this is not a satire, though, God knows, I wish it were. It is just another feature about stress, suggesting that focusing on your needs, turning away from others, and being "selfish" is the way a contemporary woman should behave because her life is so "difficult."

Personally, I hate it. Looking back, I regret the many "coping with stress" pieces I am sure I commissioned, though none, I think, was quite as silly or self-centered as this one. I hate the knee-jerk reaction that I, along with most other women's magazine editors, have to slap on a "stress" cover line whenever we can. But most of all I hate selling women this notion that somehow ordinary life—having kids, working, popping the popcorn and watching a video of *Shrek,* and even chaperoning the Junior High Sleepover—is so damn difficult. It isn't. We all know it isn't, and it is insulting to tell women it is and wrong to encourage them to think if they are not actively "nurturing themselves," they are somehow failing.

In *O*'s "105 Ways to Beat Stress," readers, most of whom clip coupons and would find chasing the dog in Jimmy Choo's something akin to an Olympic event, are told to "let your guard down, put your feet up, and give your spirit a breather." Where? At an O-recommended "stress-free zone" like the palatial Grand Hotel at Villa Feltrinelli on Italy's Lake Garda, starting at $550 a night. Or you can track rhinos and giraffes at South Africa's Sabi Sabi Private Game Reserve and end the day with a swim in a private pool and dinner served by your own butler for only $500 a night. Or learn French cooking at a fifteenth-century manor house in the Oxfordshire countryside at the low, low price of $690 a night.[12]

Out of its eleven recommendations, *O* does suggest one low-cost "zone"—the New Camaldoli Hermitage, a Benedictine monastery in Big Sur where, for the bargain basement rate of only $60 a night, you can meditate in spartan quarters, join in choral singing, and sit down to a simple dinner in the monk's communal kitchen. Can you think of a more fun getaway? I can just hear myself pitching my husband, "Jeffrey, how does this sound for a quick escape? A week of plain food with a group of perfectly nice Benedictine monks?"

Or you can simply fall back on that old workhorse, the spa. You won't be alone. The spa industry is booming. In 2001, women (and a few men) made more than 155 million visits to the country's 9,600 spas, which include day spas, resort spas, and medical spas, spending $11 billion in the process as they pampered themselves head to toe—literally.[13]

Even in far tougher economic times, day spas grew by 20 percent per year.[14] No wonder, since we had hammered into us so relentlessly that the treatments at these spas—the seaweed wraps, the aromatherapy, the body scrub with salts from the Dead Sea, and the shiatsu foot massage—are necessities for well-being rather than indulgences. Spending $2,500 for a five-day package of hikes, yoga, and hot-stone massages at the Canyon Ranch or Miraval, two spas in Tucson, has become a moral imperative, not an occasional extravagance.

Let's just look at magazines and TV shows that are full of great ideas to help you fight stress. There's yoga—one of the newest weapons in the battle against stress and one that has spawned a whole new industry of products, from clothing, instruction, and equipment to workshops, books, CDs, and videos. Almost 10 million Americans practiced yoga in 2001, spending more than a billion dollars on paraphernalia. In fact, *Yoga Journal* estimates that the average practitioner puts out $1,500 a year getting in touch with her inner self.

After a tough day on the mats, we can go home, lock our bathroom door, and sink into a hot tub and into one of the hottest antistress tickets of all—aromatherapy. One estimate puts the U.S. market at $470 million.[15] That's a lot of candle wax and scented oil.

And lest we forget our good friends in the pharmaceutical industry, some of women's magazines and TV's biggest advertisers, antidepressants have become among the most dispensed drugs—at 130 million prescriptions, or close to $10 billion in total sales.[16] Some put the figures even higher.

Whether it's yoga, spas, support groups, or "mother's little helpers," the underlying message to women is as clear as your skin after a seaweed scrub: You *deserve* to be self-indulgent. You have earned it; and, besides, you need the shopping and/or the spa to keep you sane and healthy because you are working so hard and are so stressed. The fact that the media promotes ideas that support the products of their advertisers is merely coincidence. Yeah. Right.

The Most Stressed-Out People in the World

But who exactly is so incapable of handling all this stress? Why, the very people behind the stress pieces on *Good Morning America* and *Today* and the evening news. The writers and editors who are churning out all those articles like "This Little Word Stops Stress." Those whom Professor Todd Gitlin of Columbia University, an astute, often-quoted critic of the media, says are the most stressed-out people in the world, the ones who feel most overwhelmed today. He calls them "speed freaks . . . journalists who rush the news . . . and marketers who wrap goods in it. Almost all of whom live in the fast lane themselves, socialize with others who live (or wish to live) in the fast lane . . . and nudge still others into that same fast lane."[17] Women in media who work as editors and producers may actually be the most stressed of all working women. The members of the Spin Sorority have become, as Professor Gitlin notes, a multitasking, ad-scanning, channel-grazing, Web-surfing, call-waiting, cell-phoning, chat-grouping, desktop-organizing, remote-controlling, IPod-wearing, BlackBerry-using, computer-editing, readership-counting, ratings-watching work crazies. Usually in fiercely competitive jobs, sometimes treated cavalierly by their employers, overloaded with information and demands, they often work long hours and are always on deadline. And to add to the strain, those in media love to dish about others in media—especially about their failures.

In the cat-eat-cat world of fashion magazines, Grace Mirabella found out she had lost her job at *Vogue,* where she had been editor-in-chief for seventeen years, when a friend told her that on a TV show gossip columnist Liz Smith reported that Grace was fired. Grace's diminutive boss, Si Newhouse, chairman of Condé Nast, publishers of a string of glossies including *Glamour, Architectural Digest,* and *Vanity Fair* and known in the trade as Condé Nasty, called only afterward to tell Grace that yes, sorry, she was toast. Newhouse, who is one of America's richest men, often fires editors by phone. And usually when they are on long, much-needed vacations. Nice.

Tina Brown, probably the most written-about editor of this generation, has talked about how relaxed and happy she was for the first time in years after the failure of *Talk* magazine because she is off the carousel for a while. Being Tina Brown, she, of course, recuperated from her stress on media mogul Barry Diller's yacht in the Mediterranean.

Employed or unemployed, the whole media world is gossipy, self-conscious, and tense. Media princesses are always rushing off to the Canyon Ranch in Tucson or the Berkshires, The Ashram, or Rancho La Puerta in Baja California, mostly free of charge, of course, because members of the press are often comped to work off their anxieties with hikes and herbal wraps. Media Princesses also get the stress-reducing pampering in New York that they recommend to their readers—like massages at Bliss and facials at Skinklinic—again, often for free.

Producer Carol Story at *The Early Show* says, "Nobody has as much stress as a young television producer trying to succeed in such a difficult business. It makes many of these women very negative and very self-critical." Lisa Zeff, Executive Producer at ABC's news production unit, agrees, "There is sometimes a lot of travel to dangerous places and that is always exhausting and difficult. And when a woman gets older in this business and tries to have a child, she can feel overwhelmed." Being overwhelmed is the story she wants to share, and it's your lucky day because she wants to share it with you.

Although we all like to claim our lives have speeded up, Professor Gitlin points out this is simply not true. Cars, trains, and planes are no faster than they were ten years ago. What *has* increased is the amount of information available to the average person and the speed with which that information is dispensed. In the last ten years, we have become a four-hundred-channel universe that can take my husband nearly a half an hour to zap through on his quick-draw remote.

The MTV innovation of fast-cut video images has invaded the rest of the networks. When it comes to print, hundreds of new magazines have been launched each year during the past decade. Even in 2002, a year characterized by a reeling advertising downturn, there were *seven hundred* magazine start-ups. And seven hundred more in the first nine months of 2003, when the climate improved. You've probably gotten the junk mail to prove it. As for the Internet, there are hundreds of thousands of Web sites to surf. My husband, a world-class news junkie, can also go on-line and get lost for three or four hours reading dozens of newspapers in the English-speaking world. One of Cathi Hanauer's *Bitch in the House* complaints is that her husband has time to check out *Salon* on-line, and she doesn't.

Media people are most affected by this explosion of information. As Professor Todd Gitlin declares, "They are the ones who feel there is always something more to read, to see, to hear, to surf. They more than anyone feel everything has speeded up, that they are busier than ever before, and they are constantly stressed because there is always something left undone." And they assume all women are as stressed and unhappy as they are. Sometimes I think critic Neal Gabler had it right when he said, "Life has become a show staged for the media."

But are ordinary women really comfortable with this frenzied assessment of their presumably frenzied lives? I've sat through plenty of focus groups where women were asked what more they wanted in their lives. Like the young editor with whom I had breakfast, they always say that they want more time for themselves whether they are working mothers of young children or women who neither work nor have children living at home. They all have the same wish—more time.

But when you ask women what they would do with that time they insist they crave, they are often stumped. They look around at each other uncomfortably and shrug until someone finally says, "I'd sleep more or have a manicure, or just maybe exercise because I really know I should." During these same focus groups, when we'd ask women who they admire they didn't mention celebrities or politicians, or rarely even Oprah or Hillary. Instead, they usually talk about their own mothers—women who had large families, worked in traditional "pink ghetto" jobs as teachers or nurses, didn't enjoy conveniences like dishwashers or microwaves, had absolutely no time for themselves (and didn't expect any). These women see their own mothers as uncomplaining, strong, and heroic, and wish they could be more like them.

But then their mothers did not have every megaphone of their culture telling them how they couldn't possibly do it all, even when they dealt with problems far more serious than many we face today and often with far fewer resources.

Real Women Can Cope

How do most women handle genuine stress? Better than men. That's what new research is beginning to show. Women live longer than men and part of the explanation used to be that we just had less stress in our lives. That was never true. But back then doctors believed stress had a direct causative link to ulcers and heart attacks thanks to Hans Selye and others. In the mid-'80s, J. Robbin Warren and Barry Marshall, doctors from Western Australia, proved that peptic ulcers were caused by the *H. pylori* bacteria and not the rat race of life. It was so hard for these young, unknown doctors to convince the medical establishment that ulcers were not stress-related that one of them resorted to drinking a bacteria-laced solution to prove his case. Only when he immediately came down with symptoms was their research taken seriously. Recent reports in the *British Medical Journal* have even discounted the long-assumed link between stress and heart disease. One twenty-year-long study of middle-aged men, conducted by Bristol, Glasgow, and Birmingham universities, found that signs of heart disease and deaths due to it were lower among men reporting high stress in their lives than those who maintained they were virtually stress free.[18]

I'm no doctor, but I believe that real stress, the kind stemming from a major life event Selye talked about, *can* lead to emotional and physical problems. But ordinary life doesn't, and that's a distinction rarely made when the media talks about women's so-called stressful lives today.

So who does the public think has more stress—men or women? A Yankelovich study found that 71 percent of both men and women believe "with all the demands made on women most of them are having a tough time." Yet at the same time, only slightly more than 50 percent of women in the same study, when asked about their own personal situations, said they were "stressed." And of that group, over 60 percent said they actually preferred being stressed to being bored.[19] Melinda Marshall, a Westchester author and mother of three who writes about women, says, "We need to say we are stressed nowadays. We just have to. If you don't have stress in your life, it isn't interesting, it isn't important."

Whether stress junkies or not, women may all have a built-in hormonal advantage to help us cope. Dr. Shelley E. Taylor, a professor of psychology at the University of California in Los Angeles and author of *The Tending Instinct,* bases her theory of our natural advantage on more than two hundred research studies. She believes that women have a powerful system for fighting stress based on the female hormone oxytocin, which operates in concert with estrogen. Oxytocin, a mood regulator, which decreases anxiety and depression, is associated with typical female behavior such as childbirth and nurturing the young. When we are stressed, Dr. Taylor believes, females naturally "tend and befriend, turning to friends and family to nurture us much as we nurture those who we know need emotional support."[20]

Maybe this is the reason women complain to each other, and are, ultimately, cheered up by the mere act of complaining. It is the age-old biological way we deal with our own upsets and bond with each other. It's our natural stress-reduction mechanism, more effective than a visit to a day spa or a shopping spree for yet another pair of toffee-colored boots, no matter how delectable they may be.

But when faced with real problems, with real crises, women rarely talk about the stress they are under. Instead, we focus on being strong and coping. Many of the widows of the victims of 9/11 have demonstrated that valiantly. As Lisa Beamer wrote so movingly in her book *Let's Roll,* "Even now, in the midst of great sorrow, there is much to be thankful for—a great family, wonderful friends, and a strong community of faith. I try to appreciate my blessings every day."

We all have friends who have coped with breast cancer, or the serious illness of a child, or the loss of a beloved mate, with practicality as well as strength and grace. I've always noticed that during tough times women don't dwell on the stress of the situation, don't even talk about it, but concentrate on how best to handle the problem they are facing. A single mother with a couple of kids, struggling to earn a living, or a woman whose husband has colon cancer seem to me always to focus on who needs her rather than on her own understandably high level of stress.

When I first came to the *Journal* as the editor I reread the issues of the magazines I had read in my mother's kitchen growing up. Recently I looked at them again and was amazed at the emphasis they put on the moral dimension of being a woman. In the 1950s and in the 1960s, the presumption that all women were like June Cleaver went in tandem with the belief that women were good and strong. Women were viewed as the moral center of the family and of the community. For example, many articles in the mid-1960s *Journal* were about the civil rights movement and made it clear that this was a moral issue in which women had to take a clear stand. In 1965, a housewife and mother of five named Viola Liuzzo left her home in the Midwest to take part in a civil rights march in Alabama. She was murdered for her beliefs. In letters to the editors afterward readers debated whether she was right to leave her family even to take part in the movement that was so important to her.

Though less educated than we are today, and less self-sufficient financially, women were seen as able to cope with whatever hardship they had to face. Maybe because the readers of those magazines had grown up during a depression and lived through a war, they were seen as tough and resilient. Or maybe that's just what was expected of women, and what we expected of ourselves. Somewhere along the way, we seem to have discarded both our sense of competency about handling the smaller problems in our lives and the selflessness and good cheer that puts such problems in perspective.

I hate to put the rap on feminism for doing this. Feminism told us to want more for ourselves, and I agree with that. But has a distortion of feminism morphed into a fragile self-centeredness that we are told, over and over again, should make us feel unable to handle the complex and interesting life that wanting more has given us? In media, at least, this seems to be the case.

Stress. We all have it. We all want to get rid of it. There's not much we can do about it. So we deal with it. Frankly, I think this stress-justified "making time for yourself" chore is a bit of a crock. It's also an extra burden that we don't need. There, I've said it. It's fine if you want to meditate or do yoga or have a massage if you find the time and really think it's worth it. But let's admit it: these activities, even if they relax you, are not as important as spending an extra hour at work if necessary or with your kids—or, remember him? your husband, who these days usually comes far down on the list somewhere after tai chi or spinning class.

At certain times in your life, doing for those for whom you are responsible is a lot more important than spending a half an hour breathing deeply and clenching and unclenching all your muscles from your forehead to your tailbone to your toes as described in *Family Circle*'s adaptation of Alice Domar's book *Self Nurture*. There's more to life than talking over your problems with your golden retriever, "creating mental rest stops," sipping chamomile tea, or the old standby, taking a bath.[21]

I Love My Job!

Maybe somebody should clue in the parents who gathered together in September 2001 for a *20/20* segment called "There's No Place Like the Office."[22] Reporter Lynn Sherr sat down to talk to these typical working parents to hype what turned out to be another newsmagazine story on the latest "my life is sooo stressed" whine-o-gram. For these folks, who appeared to be middle-class professionals, the gripe wasn't rush-hour traffic or a boss with the sensitivity of Homer Simpson. The attractive, articulate women weren't complaining about the glass ceiling, and the smiling, seemingly well-adjusted men didn't bitch about their pay package.

So what was their problem?

They just couldn't stand being around their kids. They weren't even embarrassed to admit it. Why? Because, according to these working moms and dads, their kids were annoying. No, for this group of stressed-out workers, their problem wasn't balancing work and home, it was just home—where the kids are.

And when Sherr asked the group point-blank, "Which is more stressful?" Answer: "The home." "Where would you rather be?" Without hesitation, the group agreed immediately—"At the office."

To drive home the point, Sherr introduced a particularly child-stressed parent, Barbara Lewis, a thirty-something widow from Houston who opined "work is my refuge." According to Sherr, when Barbara heads to the office, she's going to a place "where she's relaxed, appreciated, fulfilled, and happy. And more and more parents are choosing work over home." What exactly is the dastardly threat keeping Barbara at the office as long as she can manage it? Well, her three-year-old daughter, of course, who, it seems, is a bit of a Chatty Cathy. Do you know many three-year-old girls who aren't?

Perhaps our entire society has parental amnesia and now forgets that small children, by their very nature, are annoying. Or is it because we have become so desirous of having children and made our society so totally child focused that we no longer admit that kids aren't born toilet trained, have temper tantrums rather than anger issues, and most come from the "factory" with a black belt in projectile vomiting.

On 20/20, those stress-inducing kids wanted to do such outrageous things as wake their parents up in the morning, curl up in bed and cuddle, and even talk to mom once in a while and expect a reply. One mother complained that her little girl asked if Mommy also liked the television program she was watching. Can you imagine? I mean, these kids sounded tough.

Barbara Lewis explained how she simply couldn't wait to drop her child off and get to work because it was so orderly, so neat, so pleasant there. At the office, there were other interesting adults to talk to, and where she worked, she also had many extra-special perks. Not a bit like home. An upscale cappuccino bar, rather than an overused and underwashed Mr. Coffee in the kitchen. A concierge who helped employees take care of birthday and baby gifts by ordering the presents for them. A doctor on site for office visits, a post office, a bank, an exercise gym, and even free over-the-counter cough medicine.

Barbara confided that her little daughter was, of course, important to her, but she just couldn't resist the lure of her calm, controlled office life and found herself working longer and longer hours.

But then, once in a while, something happens, and fate comes along to pour a glass of ice water over our heads and show us that what we were kvetching about is, in reality, no problem at all.

Because where did Barbara work?

Enron.

Now, that, I concede, is *stress*.

Go with the Flow

I remember my mother telling me when my kids were small and I was working hard that it was the best time of my life. I'm not sure it was, but now I know it was a busy, happy time that does not come again. And it should be enjoyed and appreciated far more than complained about. Once the kids are older you do have time for yourself because they need you less, and that is the way it is supposed to be. I'm sure my mother, when she commented on my busy pace, was at a time in her life when she had too much time for herself. Having too little to do may not be as stressful as having too much to do, but I wager having too much time for yourself can be a lot more depressing.

University of Illinois professor Ed Diener, nicknamed Dr. Happiness for his pioneering research into who's happy and why, says Americans are actually some of the happiest people on earth. From 80 to 85 percent of us feel positive more than half the time.[23] What makes us happy? Not a new Prada bag or a trip to the Canyon Ranch but being around family and friends, measuring ourselves and our success by our own yardstick, and, believe it or not, being busy. Really busy. Mihaly Csikszentmihalyi, a Claremont Graduate University psychologist, says people are happiest when they are involved in "absorbing activities that cause them to forget themselves, lose track of time and stop worrying." He even has a name for all the appointments, the chores, the challenging responsibilities, big and small, that we are told should overwhelm us. He calls it flow, and says it helps us feel our best.[24]

So let's just forget about the trip to the cleaners that didn't get done, the bed that didn't get made, or the homemade muffins that never got baked. Got stress? Sure, but we can handle it—if we stop listening to the constant "your life is hell" message spun by a stressed-out media that tries to make us feel like victims of our often good, opportunity-filled lives. Sure, some days we may feel like rats in a revolving barrel, but we're just as tough as our mothers and grandmothers, and we usually have a lot more advantages. Maybe we should just go with the flow—and enjoy.

Now that we've debunked some of the myth of nonstop stress, let's get physical.

CHAPTER 4

The Feminine Physique

In September 2002, a true media miracle happened. A famous actress took off her clothes for a photo shoot. That, in itself, of course, is not a miracle. It happens every day of the week. Just check out any available picture of skanky Christina Aguilera. But when this celeb doffed *her* clothes for a magazine feature, when she let it all hang out, and I do mean *all*, we discovered that this now forty-ish actress with a reputation for one of the best bods in Hollywood wasn't, in fact, perfect. Actually, she looked a lot worse than everyone imagined she would.

The reaction? Just the opposite of what you might think. The readers loved it. And loved Jamie Lee Curtis in her none-too-flattering black sports bra and spandex briefs. They loved her for revealing her "soft fatty little tummy," her "back fat," and her "Grandma Helen hips."

"It's about time!" women across America cried. "Somebody who looks like us featured on the pages of a women's magazine. Now, that *is* a miracle."

The Scream Queen of the *Halloween* movies, who bared her breasts in *Trading Places,* did a striptease in *True Lies,* and did look quite perfect in *Perfect,* wanted finally, at age forty-three, to get real. The story and the revealing, unretouched photos were all her idea. She wanted one picture of herself, the Real Jamie, without makeup and in her plain, utilitarian undies—you know, the kind we wear to the doctor's and to bed alone. She wanted another of the Glam Jamie after thirteen beauty and fashion experts had spent three hours painting, primping, tweezing, and squeezing her into the kind of sexy little dress that matched her sexy screen image. But the picture of Real Jamie, she insisted, had to be just as prominent as the standard movie-star shot. I know this because the magazine in which Jamie Lee was gutsy enough to reveal all was *MORE,* a magazine I created and edited.

"There's a reality to the way I look without my clothes on," Jamie Lee said when she came to us with the idea, and it was *her* idea. It had to be. Believe me, you have about as much chance getting a movie star to do a reality shot as winning the Powerball lottery. "People assume that I'm walking around in a little spaghetti-strap dress. The Perfect Jamie, the great figure. I don't want the unsuspecting forty-year-old women of the world to think that I've got it going on. It's such a fraud."

She also admitted in the article, "I've done it all . . . I've had a little plastic surgery. I've had a little lipo. I've had a little Botox. And you know what? None of it works. None of it!" Jamie Lee, who now writes children's books about learning to like yourself, even came up with the title for her story. She insisted on calling it "True Thighs." You gotta love this girl, don't you?

The Jamie Lee interview and photo were covered everywhere, in newspapers and on TV in America and around the world. All in all, the story about Jamie Lee garnered over 200 million "impressions" which means 200 million people heard or read about Jamie Lee's amazing act of defiance, her decision to just look like her own true self. Real Jamie loved the attention. "I knew it would be that big a deal," she told me happily. Even though she said her movie days were over, all the publicity helped land her a role in *Freaky Friday* playing the mom. In Hollywood, being honest is rare enough to be a real attention grabber.

How did Jamie Lee really look without a body stocking? Not bad. Not great, but okay; and that's how the hundreds and hundreds of surprised but grateful readers felt who e-mailed to thank us for pulling back the "glamour curtain." She looked like a woman who tries to keep fit but doesn't say no to a dish of Häagen-Dazs one or maybe three nights a week. Comfortingly familiar. She looked like us, and, well, we liked it. We really, really liked it.

The next month's cover story was more typical, about Cybill Shepherd, who had just lost twenty-five pounds and looked terrific in and out of a series of outfits from a sparkly minidress to her bare bottom. But here's the dirty little secret. Cybill also needed at least a baker's dozen of fawning beauty and fashion experts to prep her for the camera. And thanks to computer technology that can make imperfections disappear faster than billing records in Hillary Clinton's boudoir, she could pose in an even more revealing getup than Glam Jamie.

Now I've told you how much women loved the Real Jamie in her black sports bra and briefs. How did they react to Cybill? In a word or two, they hated her. And were disappointed with the magazine for switching gears and gals. Cybill's penchant for raunchy locker room sex talk didn't help, either. Neither did her trashy tale of a long-ago fling with Elvis or her decision to share with the readers a question she poses to all potential dates: "I ask if they've ever masturbated in front of someone."

One reader's response was fairly typical: "I'd like to ask what were you thinking, but I think someone else has coined that phrase but *what were you thinking?* From the sublime to the ridiculous, Jamie being a real woman to Cybill being her own fantasy."

The Beauty Part

Now, I would probably call myself a feminist—though some women's studies professors might not agree after reading this book—but I am not anti-femininity. Believe me, peaceful coexistence is possible. Personally, I like makeup, perfume, and all that stuff, and I don't think there is anything demeaning about trying to look your best. When I went to Russia in 1990 at the time the Soviet Union was dissolving to interview Raisa Gorbachev and to put out a Russian edition of *LHJ*, I brought makeup and nail polish with me and gave little gift bags to the women I met, including top editors and members of the Politburo. Back then, they weren't insulted; they were delighted. In those days, they were starved for these products. Wanting to look good seems to be a positive for women akin to healthy animals grooming themselves.

Strident feminists used to say that it was men, those pigs, who demanded that we go to extremes to make ourselves look good. Men who made women obsessive about their looks, because we were competing with each other to attract them. They blamed our patriarchal society for keeping us buying M.A.C, using Mr. Tweezerman, and suffering through drippy Clairol color treatments every six weeks. And yet a lot of what beauty and fashion magazines sell us nowadays is a level of primping and purchasing that is far too subtle for most men—at least straight men—to notice, care about, or even appreciate.

I don't think men are as demanding about our looks as we have become ourselves. A man wants a woman who is sexually attractive. That's enough for him. He doesn't care if she has had an expensive facial or is carrying that Kate Spade bag. Few guys notice whether you have had a pedicure before you break out your flip-flops for the summer season. Even fewer, outside of the fashion business, can tell whether you're wearing $400 Manolo Blahnik mules or Payless knockoffs. I am not saying guys don't watch the Victoria's Secret TV specials. They do, and not because they are planning what to buy you for Christmas. But in spite of Victoria, her secrets, or even the *Sports Illustrated* swimsuit edition, men, it seems to me, are a lot less demanding of the women in their own lives than we are of ourselves.

In fact, most of our pampering and shopping seems unrelated to men at all these days. Media directed at women have made überthinness, übergrooming, and übershopping self-indulgent values that have gone far beyond the means of attracting men. They've become an end in themselves. Nowadays when we shop, we sometimes buy because we have been told or told ourselves we deserve it. Especially when something is expensive, and probably unnecessary, you dig out the plastic because, well, you're worth it. Today, *all* women deserve more, right? So go out and buy all that you deserve. Certainly beauty and fashion magazines and their advertisers love selling that good-for-them, not-so-good-for-you equation. Thanks to the Spin Sisters, hitting the mall has become retail therapy, especially if we are also bonding with our girlfriends. Carrie and Miranda in *Sex and the City* prowl stores or treat themselves to another facial when they have been dumped by a guy, not when they are trying to look good for him.

But not all women are alike when it comes to the importance of their appearance. Some are much more fashion sensitive than others. The truth, I believe, is that most women are self-improvers and want to look good at least some of the time. And that's healthy, I think. But in a world where we are bombarded by so much airbrushed perfection, a lot of women also want to hear that they are all right when they just look all right. At least once in a while. And media for women practically never gives them this message.

How can they? Many editors and art directors themselves are often personally obsessed with beauty and fashion, invested in looking good no matter what. They know and frequent the best hair dressers, makeup artists, dermatologists, facialists, cosmetic dentists, cosmetic surgeons, and often get their services for free in exchange for a mention or two. They are also hooked on luxuries like $1,200 Prada bags and Crème de la Mer's $165-a-jar lotion, which they also get free or at exclusive sample sales to give them status in their fashionista world. In their interests, their tastes, and their lifestyle, they have almost nothing in common with any woman living beyond a three-mile radius of Bergdorf Goodman's. They want to put out glamorous, aspirational magazines that appeal to them personally and to the equally chic and trendy women—and, let's be honest, gay guys—who dominate the world of beauty and fashion. These are the people—not readers—with whom they work, gossip, party, and whose attention and approval they desperately want.

Hey, I have spent years listening to stylists in $200 Seven jeans and editors, who should know better, tell me the sheer puce-colored skirt cut on the bias with the ragged hemline they want in a photo spread is "soooo in and soooo adorable." They gush like fourteen-year-old pop tarts, who probably would agree with them. But when I protest that it looks like a well-worn relic from Madonna's "Papa, Don't Preach" period, I've been told, "You just don't get it." And they were right. I didn't. Most of the time I fought the but-nobody-can-wear-any-of-this-stuff" fight and won—but I sometimes gave in and published pictures of clothes that were too expensive for our readers and unwearable by them as well. Readers always, always write to complain that clothes in magazines are too expensive. Although *Vogue* publishes photos of see-through blouses that can cost up to $3,000, the average reader of *Vogue* has a household income of around $55,000 a year.[1] And a $3,000 blouse is not on her shopping list.

But most women's magazines would never consider featuring a slightly out-of-shape, fashionless, post-forty actress like Jamie Lee in a cover story. Only the youngest, thinnest models and hippest celebs will do, thank you very much. And why? For much the same reason that stress has become an editorial regular in most women's mags— money, money, and more money. Almost all women's magazines depend on beauty and fashion advertising to a very large degree to keep them afloat. And it is very hard to get advertising without running beauty and fashion editorial pages dotted with beauty and fashion credits for advertisers. Beauty and fashion advertisers, without even a flick of conscience, are committed to telling you that what was "in" is now "out" so that you feel you must buy something new this very minute, and are so invested in image themselves that they are excited only by the young, thin, and the hip. Even though only some of us are young, few of us are thin, and almost none of us are hip.

Or would even want to be because what beauty and fashion advertisers think is hip is often weird, tasteless, and sometimes even depraved. To introduce its spring 2003 collection, Gucci, the luxury goods maker, created a "G-spot ad" photographed by Mario Testino, one of Princess Diana's favorite lensmen, which caused enormous outrage even in anything-goes Europe. It showed a young model pushed against a wall as she pulled down her knickers, revealing pubic hair shaved into the *G* logo of Gucci. The ad appeared in British *Vogue*, whose editor pooh-poohed the many complaints it elicited, calling it cutting edge, as if that were sufficient defense for what was obviously gross, exploitative, and cynical.[2]

But an editor defending a big advertiser, even willing to stoop to pornography to sell a handbag, isn't surprising because it is that dependence on advertising dollars that drives much of the content you read and the photos you see in women's magazines. Today, beauty and fashion magazines go far beyond showing us pretty girls in pretty dresses and inspiring us to look our best. When a young Cybill Shepherd was a blond and beautiful model in the 1970s, she could be twenty pounds heavier than she claimed, have the seams cut open so she could stuff herself into the sample sizes she had to model, and still be on the cover of *Glamour* four times a year because she was such an All-American Girl, in looks, anyway. Not anymore. Nowadays, magazine standards of beauty and physical size have been taken to such extremes that readers have been left far behind.

But the mags tell us we must keep trying, and a lot of us do, at least, for a while. They make us feel that we are fat, frumpy, and fading fast, but not to worry, our Spin Sisters are there to help. Salvation by subscription. Like your best girlfriend, they tell you how to lose weight—as if you didn't know—and how to look younger, today's two basic beauty imperatives. And if you want to cure the frumpies, they tell you to go out and buy the products they promote in their editorial copy, fashion spreads, and celebrity coverage, which are—I bet you've noticed—interchangeable with the products featured in their advertisements. Television and movies reinforce the images and attitudes that fill the pages of many women's magazines that very, very thin is in and that there is something wrong if you are over twenty-five and not trying to look younger than your age. "We hold up the ideal to women," one top beauty advertiser told me, "an ideal she can never achieve—but we want her to keep trying."

It's a little like the poor greyhounds who chase the always elusive rabbit around and around the track—the prize is always in sight but no matter how hard they run, catching the rabbit is pure fantasy. It will never happen, can't happen. How does this make many women feel? Either turned off about herself or about beauty and fashion. Sometimes both. A magazine study found that 62 percent of women say shopping for a bathing suit is more painful than giving birth, and half of us would rather clean the kitty litter box than go through the agony![3] The average American woman is five foot four and probably wears a size 12.[4] She's a lot more curvy than svelte but that's not exactly a sin anywhere besides the cafeteria at Condé Nast. But after looking through a copy of *Vogue* or *Harper's Bazaar* or *Elle* filled with an array of very young women who are seven inches taller and fifty pounds thinner than the rest of us, it's no wonder we feel like stand-ins for the Pillsbury Doughboy. We feel guilty when we eat anything we really want to eat. And we're suckers for any magazine with a wonder-diet cover line.

How to Stay Thin Forever!

So let's dish diets. The way magazines do all the time. Not by saying that the food industry has taught Americans to eat the largest portions served on earth and ask for more. (Food companies are important advertisers, too.) Not by saying that losing pounds can be extremely difficult and complex for many people and that trying to ascertain why has stumped research scientists for decades. Not even by saying accept yourself as long as your weight is at a healthy level. But rather by promising that, in a thousand words or less, they will tell you once and for all how to lose it, keep it off, and stay thin forever. And you are supposed to buy it. A lot of us do.

Every day of the week in this country, 52 million people are on a diet.[5] Nearly half of all women (45 percent) are trying to lose weight.[6] Dieting has become a $40-billion-a-year business as we spend and spend on everything from Weight Watchers to Suzanne Sommers's Thighmaster.[7]

On average each month, there are at least twenty-six cover lines on magazines promising you the one and only way to stop pushing those "glutton buttons." I have heard editors snicker with delighted glee when they have thought up cover lines as snappy—and demeaning— as that one. That's because, month after month, on many magazines for women, the weight-loss cover line is usually their most prominent blurb, as if there were actually something new to say about the subject. No issue of *Good Housekeeping* these days, it seems, can get the seal of approval without an article that tells you what you already know—that you should maybe eat less and exercise more if you want to lose the extra pounds.

Most magazine diets are based on eating about twelve hundred calories a day and offer fairly complicated recipes that produce tiny, often unappetizing, tastings of food more appropriately served in a cute paper bag with a toy inside. Recipes that tell you to whip up a delicious omelet with two egg whites, two ounces of nonfat cheese, three slices of red pepper on a nonstick pan. But who, especially if she has a weight problem, can spend that much time in the kitchen fixing something to eat and end up eating so little? In a way, the magazines count on that. Because if you were, by some miracle, successful on one of their diets, who would buy another magazine with a diet cover line just a couple of weeks later? Would you?

Very rarely are the diets tested in real-life situations before they are published. But then nobody ever complains because most women only stay on them for a couple of days. The helpful tips that accompany the diets can be even less practical. *Redbook* once told its readers, "Drink ten glasses of ice water a day to burn two hundred calories."[8] Ten glasses of ice water to rid yourself of the caloric equivalent of a couple of Chips Ahoys? As Grandmother would say, "Oy, my kidneys."

In my study of women's magazines, my researcher and I found that during the three-year period we tracked, there were 425 articles about weight loss and body problems—most of them in diet stories, fitness advice, and fashion tricks for camouflaging your flaws. Not surprisingly, 97 percent of the issues we looked at featured a diet or body-improvement article on their covers. The idea that a woman could actually be happy with her body and its supposed imperfections was only mentioned twelve times in the three-year period. But we shouldn't just blame magazines. All media aimed at women has gotten into the weight-loss game, as if they were sharing big, important news. Over the past decade, all health news has increased dramatically on television, especially stories about diets. We have heard about the cabbage soup diet, used by Elizabeth Hurley to get back into shape after her baby. (The side effects from that one are, as Elizabeth admitted, "very unpleasant.") Then there's the Macrobiotic Diet championed by gal pals Madonna and Gwyneth Paltrow, who bonded in London over "bancha twig" tea, the diet drink of preference for these two superstars, and, I would guess, a bevy of other small furry creatures with big teeth. Cindy Crawford, Kristin Davis, Courtney Love, and Jennifer Aniston got thin, in Jennifer's case *very* thin, on the very expensive Zone Diet with its prepackaged, delivered-straight-to-your-doorstep meals.[9]

Even Cathy in the comic strip has a favorite eating plan. She was noticeably thinner—at least she was drawn that way—after she went on the Kick-Start Bran Flake cereal diet. Celebrity diets have become such fodder for the media that in England there was a quarterly called *Celebrity Bodies*. It detailed the who, what, and how much of every weight-reduction scheme tried by everyone from Fergie (Weight Watchers) to Kate Winslet, who director James Cameron, during the filming of *Titanic,* used to call Kate Weighs-a-lot. It was probably water weight, anyway.

And you always know it's sweeps month when morning television debuts another diet challenge to help build ratings. We have watched the ever-serene Diane Sawyer lose twenty-five pounds and get trim and toned. We have watched Katie Couric get blonder and buffer. And we have watched Oprah, whose personal diet chef was Rosie Daley, author of two best-sellers, and whose personal trainer is Bob Greene, author of three best-sellers, get thin and fat and thin again so many times that she has become the national poster child for yo-yo dieting.

Thanks in great part to the media, American women have grown so obsessed about their weight that some studies show 74 percent of women in their thirties and forties think about their weight at least once a day.[10] Even African American women who, in the past, were more accepting of their weight and more positive about their body image, have become diet conscious. In a survey of two thousand women conducted by *Essence* magazine, over 71 percent said they were on a diet.[11] Some of us start thinking about what we are going to eat or not going to eat from the moment we wake up in the morning. Yet as a nation we have grown fatter these past ten years, and obesity is an increasing health problem. We can't, excuse the pun, make light of that. But most women think we are overweight whether we are or not, especially after looking at the buffed and beautified models who grace the pages of women's magazines cover to cover.

The *Marketing to Women* study of the types of models used in women's magazine ads confirmed something most of us probably knew. It's not just that we're all too fat, it's that all models are way too thin. There is now a total and complete Tyranny of the Skinny. It wasn't always that way. Today, the models in seven out of ten magazine fashion layouts and ads border on the skeletal. Thirty years ago, in 1972, that number was only three in ten.[12] In Great Britain a while back, some advertisers threatened to pull their ads from *Vogue*, in protest, to encourage fashion magazines to use models with healthier body types. But the campaign quickly petered out. In fact, up-market advertisers, the ones who are more likely to appear in *Vogue* or *Elle* or *InStyle* like Prada or Gucci or Versace, tend to use the thinnest and youngest models available.

If superthin models weren't enough, the celebs that decorate the pages of magazines like *US* and *InStyle* and headline much of the television and movies we watch make most of us feel even if we are not seriously overweight that there is something wrong with our bodies. That's because of the rise of the Incredible Shrinking Actress, women like Calista Flockhart and Courteney Cox who so dominate our media. With all those friends, wouldn't you think one of them would buy Courteney dinner?

A recent survey by the National Organization of Women, which I agree with for once, called this phenomenon of superstars coming in smaller and smaller packages, the Jennifer Aniston Rule. In a fairly informal count of network shows, NOW found 140 women who were model thin while only 31 appeared to wear a size ten or larger.[13] Even more annoying, all those dorky male leads on sitcoms, who are supposed to look funny and do, have attractive, thin wives and girlfriends. Think about it. Cheryl and Jim on *According to Jim*, Kate and Drew on *The Drew Carey Show*, Carrie and Doug on *The King of Queens*. Even Marge and Homer Simpson. While this male fantasy—average working stiff with beer belly gets really gorgeous girl—does happen in real life (oh, at least once every millennium) it is standard fare on TV. But we never see the mirror opposite. We don't see Roseanne settled in marital bliss with, say, Brad Pitt or Ben Affleck. When it comes to women, thin is "in" whether it's the lowly sitcom, high drama, or even Lifetime, the network for women, and it impacts all of us.

Teenage girls are especially influenced by media images of superthinness. There have been many studies of the effect teenage magazines, especially, have on girls' developing self-image. A researcher at Brigham and Women's Hospital in Boston found that the more frequently girls read magazines, the more likely they were to diet. Even though over 70 percent of them were not overweight.[14]

Older women share many of these same reactions, beating them-selves up constantly for not being thin enough or toned enough or young-looking enough. (Thank you, again, Jamie Lee, for trying.) Believe me, when you see a female celebrity in person she is always far thinner than you imagine she would be. Even the more mature, womanly types like Sela Ward or Susan Sarandon don't seem to have a spare inch in the flesh. In person, they seem skinny rather than sexy. And if you have lunch with them, they don't eat. They don't just play with their food; they simply don't order. Or if they do, it's a salad with everything, except the lettuce, on the side. That's because being thin is their job.

Looking young is their job, too. For years, celebs said they looked young because they never ate meat, exercised, had good genes, and drank water. Yeah, sure. Now a few of them, like Jamie Lee and *Every-body Loves Raymond*'s Patricia Heaton, who is the mother of four lit-tle boys, are honest about their nips and tucks. Patricia Heaton is a rarity in Hollywood in several ways. She is unabashedly pro-life. When asked how other Hollywood types reacted to her unusual-for-Tinseltown views, she sweetly says, "On a personal level, as a Christ-ian, it will not be Barbra Streisand I'm standing in front of when I have to make an accounting of my life."[15]

Let's be honest. Celebs and models work at looking good six or seven hours a day and have professionals working with them. When supermodel Cheryl Tiegs, at fifty-one, was one of the first cover models on *MORE*, someone complained that she didn't look like an average fifty-year-old woman. I said, "No, she looked better than you when she was twenty-one, and she still looks better than you." She's a model, after all. I trusted that *MORE*'s readers were mature enough to understand that.

I once asked Steve Florio, the president of Condé Nast, and then the father of a teenage daughter, what he thought of the superthin models that were used in *Vogue*. He told me that Anna Wintour, the magazine's sleek, bony editor, had assured him that the models are naturally slender and are all hearty, healthy eaters. Sure they are, and Bill Clinton never had sexual relations with that woman. Wintour herself is so admired for her sleekness that she couldn't resist commenting on the "plumpness" of Liz Tilberis, a onetime rival, in the obituary she wrote after Tilberis died of ovarian cancer.[16]

The fashion world is rife with stories of models who are always starving themselves and suffer from anorexia and bulimia. Kate Dillon, Carre Otis, and Emme, who are now all plus-size models, have spoken openly about their long, painful battle to stay thin before giving in to a more comfortable size. Though larger models are now occasionally used in fashion magazines with great fanfare, Anna Wintour makes it clear: "I don't think you're going to see this trend on the runway."[17] The only fuller-figured model that designers really like is Sophie Dahl, a gorgeous, milky-skinned, upper-class Englishwoman and granddaughter of the children's book writer Roald Dahl. And when her career needed a boost, she lost thirty-five pounds.

A few years ago, Karen Elson, a British model credited with launching "freak chic," was booted from a Dolce & Gabbana show in Milan for the capital crime of being too fat. Elson, a nineteen-year-old redhead known for her healthy good looks, is five feet nine with a 32-24-34 figure and wears a British size 8 which is an American size 6. But that wasn't thin enough for the always trendy D & G. Elson took the snub graciously. "Milan is like New York. It's serious business and money, money, money. If you don't fit the clothes, you don't do the shows."[18]

Nobody but nobody escapes the Tyranny of the Skinny if they want to appear in magazines. Wintour, who was the model for the demon editor in last year's best-seller *The Devil Wears Prada,* once ordered Oprah to lose twenty pounds before she would agree to photograph the most famous and successful woman in America for *Vogue.* Oprah obeyed.

Obsessed with Being Thin

In truth, the prejudice against the obese is one of the few vestiges of bias that is still permissible in our society today. Along with a lack of tolerance for the devoutly religious, it may be the only bigotry that has actually increased in our supposedly tolerant times. Although I have never worried much about my weight, I have always been interested in weight loss because some members of my family have had very serious weight problems, and I know how terribly painful that can be. On my mother's side, I think there has always been a fat gene dogpaddling from generation to generation in the family gene pool. One of my sons could have a weight problem if he let himself go. One time, when we got together, I told him how great I thought he looked. Translation: He looked *really* thin! But being a mother, I had to add, "Your suit looks a little big, dear." He asked me if I realized that for years, every time I saw him the first thing out of my mouth was almost always something about his weight. And now that he had slimmed down, I was complaining about the fit of his clothes. I hadn't understood, until that moment, how much my one-note focus had bothered him, a guy. How would I have made a daughter feel if I were always going on about her weight? I also realized that playing on people's sensitivity about their weight and offering little help to really solve this complicated problem is one of the shabbiest of all media scams.

I once asked a writer named Leslie Lampert to wear a fat suit for a week. The article she wrote, called "Fat Like Me," was done long before Gwyneth Paltrow donned a similar fat suit for *Shallow Hal*. Leslie, who claimed she was always obsessing about food, found during that week when she looked like she weighed over 250 pounds, that people detest the obese. Snooty saleswomen ignored her in shops. Perfect strangers mocked her on the street. Her own children were embarrassed when she picked them up after school. When she went out to a trendy Manhattan bistro with a male friend, the maître d' seated them at a remote table, near the kitchen, although there were lots of better ones available. When she went to the bathroom, two women sitting nearby asked Leslie's "date" what a cute guy like him was doing with someone who looked as if gravy were her favorite beverage.

The fashion and beauty editors, these stylish Spin Sisters, are as consumed with being thin as the models they work with even if it is almost impossible for them to whittle themselves down to a size 2 or 0. (Only in the fashion world is being a zero a positive.) Kate Betts, the former editor of *Harper's Bazaar* who dumped Renée Zellweger from the cover for being too fat, recalls, "When the look of the moment was more anorexic than usual, there was supposedly a sign in the bathroom of one of the major American fashion magazines that said, 'Don't vomit in here.'"[19] Nasty little stories like this are shared all the time. Once a young assistant who worked around the clock to organize a fashion magazine party was told the following day she should not attend. She was too "big" for the uniform the staff would be wearing. An editor at a beauty and fashion magazine admits, "The big competition is who is skinnier. I remember one girl saying that her boss hated her. I asked why. And she said, 'Because I am skinny and pretty.' And you know what? I think it was true. Her boss really did hate her because she was skinny and pretty."[20]

During the time she was editor-in-chief of *Bazaar*, Betts struggled with her own weight. At the same time Betts was dissing Zellweger, who was starring as the chubby but lovable Bridget Jones, she was trying to lose the weight she had gained while pregnant. "You're not fat," friends would say consolingly. "You've just given birth to a ten-pound baby." She says she tried cappuccinos for lunch, the Zone Diet, and personal trainers, all with little success. What was toughest of all was trying to ignore the catty remarks about "baby fat" she heard behind her back at fashion shows.

Here's what I believe about the weight obsession of media aimed at women. Any woman who watches a television health segment on losing weight (and who doesn't?) or buys a magazine because of a seductive cover line already knows, in her heart if not her mind, that the best way to diet is to eat less and exercise more. She also has probably figured out that some of us have a harder time than others getting or staying thin, that heredity plays a part in the way we look. Most of us can stay at a healthy weight. But most of us cannot stay at the weight that beauty and fashion magazines promote. Women in media—the editors, the celebs, the models, the advertisers—ignore this reality or sneer at it to peddle a false image that most of them believe is necessary to sell their products, a self-obsessed image to which they personally are dedicated and tell you that you should dedicate yourself, even if you can't.

Sure, it's a way to push your buttons and always make you feel down on yourself. Well, my advice to counteract the megamarketing of what is impossible for almost all of us is fairly simple: remember the poor frustrated greyhounds and the dog's life they lead, and stop chasing a weight that is neither attainable nor necessarily right for you or your lifestyle. That's good advice, as well, for dealing intelligently with another fascination of women's media: the terrible crime of— yikes!—getting older.

How to Stay Young Forever!

Ever wonder how much time we spend worrying about the wrinkles that seem to pop up daily like mushrooms after a rainstorm? Or the circles under our eyes or the saggy chin that just doesn't work with turtlenecks anymore? More than you probably realize, and it doesn't matter whether we are just out of our teens or nearing retirement, women's media is also relentless in telling us "You're looking older and if you don't listen to us, buy the creams and potions, and the plastic surgery we push, you won't be looking better." In fact, you'll be looking terrible, and to drive the point home, they hire models as beautiful as Barbie and almost young enough to still want to play with her. Like the fascination with superthin models, it wasn't always this way.

Over the past thirty years models have also become younger and younger, according to the same 2002 *Marketing to Women* study, even as our female population is getting older and even though older women have more money to spend on clothes and cosmetics. Doesn't it make sense that baby boomers would have more disposable income than their baby-sitters? Yet Chanel recently introduced its newest $60-an-ounce perfume called Chance with a $12 million advertising campaign based on the image of a sixteen-year-old Russian model[21] clinging to the perfume bottle. She looked as breakable as the glass. Apparently the fact that the average Chanel customer is not really a high school sophomore—she is, at least, in her mid-thirties—is irrelevant to the megawatt marketers who set the trends for women's advertising.

Very young models have become so much the standard that when you ask even professionals such as dermatologists and makeup artists to judge women's ages from photographs, they can't get them right. Because models, barely in their teens, are made to seem so glamorous and sophisticated, we assume that they are in their mid-twenties.

When we look at a woman who is really in her twenties, who may already have some darkness around her eyes or the beginning of laugh lines, we think she is older than she really is. That's when models and celebs start having a "little work" done by a plastic surgeon, a $200 power peel, a $1,000 chemical peel, a $5,000 laser peel, perhaps, or an eye lift and some liposuction under the chin. And it is not only their faces that are worked on. Twenty-seven-year-old actress Charlize Theron had her bottom buffed before she wore a backless gown to the Oscars one year.

If the preshoot peels and pampering aren't enough, models and celebrities get even more assistance after their pictures are taken from art directors and production specialists. Trust me, almost every photo you see in a magazine has been retouched to remove even the slightest imperfection. This was once done by airbrushing when the photograph was literally painted to make eyes brighter and teeth whiter and circles and blotches disappear. Now this is done by computer technology so advanced that a cover image can be and is created with a head from one photo and a body from another. For example, on its July 2003 cover *Redbook* put Julia Roberts's head from a one-year-old photo on a four-year-old picture of her body. The cover line was: "The Real Julia Roberts." Not exactly. The month before, Jennifer Aniston's publicist claimed *Redbook* had put together three different photos to make just one cover portrait of our friend.[24] Aniston, feeling manipulated, was mulling legal action.

Although Kate Winslet was all in one piece on a British magazine, she still was put on a drastic digital diet. Her Macintosh Makeover included: 1) adding to her hair and smoothing down the flyaway bits; 2) stretching her body so that she looked taller and, of course, thinner; 3) her cheekbones were sharpened, her eyes made whiter and the shadows under her eyes were removed (she's twenty-eight); 4) her hips were trimmed—her tummy was "literally sliced off, leaving her looking positively concave"; 5) her legs were stretched and her thighs made more taut.[23]

Kate, whose other nickname on the set of *Titanic* was Kate Whines-a-lot, complained about what had been done to her. "I do not look like that and more importantly I don't desire to look like that," she said. Even Real Kate didn't want to try to measure up to Cover Kate.

Once Madonna wanted her hair a different color on a *Vogue* magazine shoot but her schedule left no time for a dye job. The magazine's art director retouched her hair digitally. *Entertainment Weekly* once also fixed the gap in Madonna's teeth. The rest of us get to pay thousands to the orthodontist. Other famous photo manipulations: *Time* made O.J. darker; *Elle* removed Cindy Crawford's belly button; *Newsweek* straightened the crooked teeth of Bobbi McCaughey, the Iowa mother of the septuplets.

The *Journal* photographed the McCaugheys, too, and used some technical wizardry to get the seven rambunctious toddlers in one picture. That seemed to me pretty innocent and, believe me, necessary. Not like the time *TV Guide* put Oprah's head on Ann-Margret's body. "What were they thinking?" to borrow a phrase.

Once, I confess I did put an entire new outfit on Cher. What she wore in the photo she sent us for a cover was just too ridiculous. When we changed her vintage-style pea-green suit into a simple summer dress, we improved her body as well, though we did far less to Cher than she has probably done to herself. But she didn't like it and complained to anyone who would listen, which struck me as just the teeniest bit odd coming from a woman who always looks like she's just breezed in from auditioning for the latest episode of *Star Wars*. Like Joan Rivers, Cher seems to have totally lost the ability to "just say no" to her plastic surgeon.

So have a lot of other women. In 2001, women ponied up more than $6 billion for cosmetic surgery—that's a lot of liposuction and tummy tucks.[24] And the market for luxury skin-care products (the ones that go for fifty dollars or more) grew to $354 million in 2001.[25] That's a whopping 27 percent increase in just four years. And when it comes to cosmetics that "soften those fine lines," moisturize those "kissable lips," "get the lashes you lust after," "wash away the gray," we're spending more than $5 billion a year—all to look younger.

Here's why we're doing it, at least in part. Looking back over three years of magazines, we found twenty-three articles hyping plastic surgery, and one hundred more whose tone presumed or implied that their readers were unhappy with aging. What we couldn't find, not once, in the more than 300 issues we looked at were features that actively, positively portrayed beauty in a middle-aged or older woman. In fact, it was this very lack of appreciation for older women that prompted me to create *MORE* magazine, which is intended for women between forty and sixty. It was launched five years ago with a circulation of 350,000. The circulation now is a million.

Although baby boomers are the largest and richest of all demographics, *MORE* is still the only magazine focused directly on these women. Advertisers always target younger consumers between the ages of eighteen and thirty-four. That's why we can whiz through more than a hundred TV channels and still find little on but *The Bachelor* and *Bachelorette*. Marketing 101 maintains that if you get a consumer to try a product when she is young, she will be hooked for life. I say if baby boomers are the most divorced generation in history, if they can change husbands, they sure as hell can change their favorite brands of panty hose and perfume without therapy. But it remains a tough sell.

In the past, a couple of other magazines have been aimed at this demographic. One was called *Lear's*, and was started by Frances Lear, whose Hollywood honcho ex-husband, Norman Lear, produced *All in the Family* and *Maude*. Though he gave America its first lovable ultra-conservative spokesman, Archie Bunker, he is the founder and funder of the very liberal lobbying group People for the American Way. Frances had no experience in the magazine business and burned through $30 million of her more than $100 million divorce settlement to bankroll the magazine. The character Maude, bombastic, opinionated, and bipolar, was based on Frances, who laced the magazine's pages with feminist politics and man-hating messages. The magazine folded after six years.

Grace Mirabella, the former editor of *Vogue*, also tried to start a magazine for grown women. *Mirabella* was better edited than *Lear's* but still had problems trying to satisfy the desires of the readers to see women who looked like them on the magazine's fashion pages instead of the young, sexy models pushed by fashion advertisers who never met an anorexic they didn't like. The magazine was passed from hand to hand across various publishing companies before it, too, folded, after eleven years.

Still, I felt *MORE* could work when it was launched in 1998. So many baby boomers were now middle-aged, but they could remember the way it used to be for women in their forties and fifties, for their mothers and grandmothers, and how different and better it is today in their lives. That's why *MORE* only uses models over forty and is a lot more celebratory about a few gray hairs and a wrinkle here and there than most other women's magazines.

Hey, don't get me wrong. I'm all for looking good. You want a little plastic surgery to tighten up that chin or erase a wrinkle or two? That's fine with me. So are the cosmetics that can make us all feel better about ourselves and help us make the best of what God gave us. But while this obsession with the young and superthin has become the staple of most fashion magazines and can be traced in a direct line to their advertisers, it is leaving more and more women behind. Women who are just as happy to live with those "little lines" that come with "getting better" and dress in comfortable shoes and fashionable but hardly trendsetting clothes. Women who shrug off the negative messages aimed directly at them from the pages of fashion magazines and TV screens. That's not to say there aren't women who are very focused on their appearance. There are. But a growing majority are becoming less concerned about how they look.

That's a result of the extremes to which women's marketing has gone to sell us one fantastical image after another. And for many women, that disconnect is becoming an increasing turnoff. More than 60 percent of us say we don't care about clothes the way we used to, and only 33 percent feel the need to dress in the hottest fashions. Most women would rather take a nice vacation than buy a new

wardrobe, and the majority complain that shopping has become a dis-
appointing chore.[26]

Here's a thought. Maybe that's because women no longer see
clothes in fashion magazines they can wear. Even if they could, they
would have no place to wear them, with the possible exception of
Halloween or the center ring of the Big Apple Circus. As a matter of
fact, even the designer of the Big Apple Circus thinks exactly that.
"There isn't any real dividing line between fashion and costume anymore," she told *The New York Times*.[27] Most women agree they'd look
like a clown in many pricey high-fashion styles. They know as well
that the little tube tops, low-slung jeans, belly rings, and crocheted
vests worn over bra-free breasts only look "hot" on models and, of
course, J.Lo, who despite being a C cup manages not to need a bra.
Even Einstein would have trouble explaining the physics of this girl.
But then J.Lo has her very own "nipple tweaker," a man who pinches
them so they stand up and salute for the camera when she is making
a video.[28] Like the old joke, yes, she could pinch them for herself, but,
thank God, she's a superstar, she doesn't have to.

Fashion Victims

Most women probably wonder how the fashions that are shown on
the pages of high-fashion magazines are chosen. Well, they are picked
by the editors and stylists, of course, but there is, one might say, slav-
ish attention paid to advertisers. Writer Michael Gross counted the
number of credits certain fashion brands received on the fashion and
editorial pages in the September 2002 issues of five magazines: *Vogue,
Harper's Bazaar, InStyle, W,* and *Elle.* Then he compared the totals to
the number of ad pages placed by those big name brands in the same
five magazines during the eight months preceding the September
issue. What did he find? The most covered brand, Prada, got fifty-eight

credits, a few more than the fifty-two pages of advertising it bought. Dior came in second with fifty credits and forty-four pages of ads. Yves Saint Laurent got one fewer credit than the fifty-nine-plus pages it ran. Louis Vuitton, which scored thirty-one hits, ran thirty-four-and-a-half pages of ads.[29] As they say in the rag trade, are you beginning to see a pattern here?

Women have been encouraged to shop without dropping for the past decade. And magazines have helped turn them into shopaholics on nearly every page. That doesn't mean any of us are required to become spending robots. When it comes to buying that $300 Coach bag or putting the money into a 401(k), let's not forget that there is something called free will, and we all have it. We can all choose not to buy.

But once upon a time, women's magazines, like other print media, clearly separated advertising and editorial. The editors were editors who told things to their readers, not sold things. Not anymore. New magazines like *InStyle* and *Lucky* blend advertising and editorial almost seamlessly so it is hard for the reader to know where one ends and the other begins. Editors defend their symbiotic relationship with advertisers by claiming that they are providing a service to their readers by telling them where they can buy the clothes and makeup, shoes, and accessories splashed on their editorial pages. Right, and Winona Ryder was just helping Saks weed out its overstock!

InStyle magazine, which was launched in 1994 and has become the largest of all fashion magazines in terms of advertising, changed fashion reporting by focusing not on designers and models but on celebs and what they wear. But, of course, celebs not only don't look like ordinary women, they don't dress like us either. They don't go to offices. They don't drive the kids to the dentist. They go out in evening gowns after spending all morning in the gym, having their hair done, their makeup applied, and their eyebrows tweezed by Anastasia, "eyebrow designer to the stars" (yes, there really is such a person) so that paparazzi will take their pictures for *InStyle* and *People*.

What's more, it is only the very youngest celebs who go out, who wear revealing outfits and get their picture taken. Meryl Streep, who has four children, I'm sure hasn't bared her belly in years, and even if she did, most paparazzi would ignore her, and not just because they wanted to be tactful. She isn't the right age for magazines like *InStyle,* or *Us,* which is the current master at "anthropological celebratology," and devotes page after page in issue after issue to what the stars are and aren't wearing.[30] The competition for paparazzi pictures of celebrities has gotten so intense that magazines sometimes pay thousands of dollars for a special shot of J.Lo and Ben in each other's clutches.

More than forty hungry photographers waited outside Lenox Hill Hospital when Sarah Jessica Parker, her husband, Matthew Broderick, and her new baby, James, "wrapped in a stylish aqua-blue cashmere blanket," left to go home. There were more photographers there than in the basement of the Dallas police station when Lee Harvey Oswald was murdered. My husband was standing just a few feet behind Oswald when Jack Ruby shot him. And only two photographers took that now famous shot on a day that changed the world. Thirty-eight photographers fewer than those recording for posterity the details of James Wilkie Broderick's layette.

What fashion is at all today is a big confusing question. Even the magazines that claim to tell you what's in and what's out don't really know or have consistent standards. Model and former V-J Karen Duffy was picked as one of the worst-dressed people by *People* and as having great "Star Style" by *Us* wearing exactly the same outfit on exactly the same day. Karen says with a laugh, "My grandmother said, 'If you can't be perfect, be a horrible example.' In one night, with one outfit, I guess I managed to be both."[31]

As the reaction to the Jamie Lee Curtis story shows, what women are really hungry for is to feel good about themselves and the way they look. But the model images of women's magazines and the focus on celebrities as fashion icons makes it nearly impossible for most women to come near meeting the standards. And even though it is their job, it's even difficult for the rich and famous. Sarah Jessica Parker, who got back into shape within six months after having her cashmere-wrapped son, says, "I can afford a yoga teacher to come to my house. I can afford child care so I can work out an hour and a half a day. . . . We cling to this idea that celebrities look exciting. But not only is the standard too high for most normal women, it's too high even for us."[32]

Obviously, there is a fantasy factor in the way women are shown in movies, on TV, and in magazines that we enjoy. If we only wanted unvarnished, unmade-up reality, we can look in the mirror, can't we? But everyone craves a little glamour now and then. It was okay for us to envy Cybill and Cheryl and curvy Christie Brinkley when they were on the covers of magazines. They looked good. They still look good. But here's the difference as I see it. Today's top model Gisele Bündchen is six foot two (in stilettos) and weighs in at about 115 supertoned, fat-free pounds. Cybill and Christie had realistic, even attainable proportions. And don't forget Marilyn Monroe, still considered by most men the hottest woman ever, usually had trouble zipping up a size 12.

Let's face it. Marilyn was a woman. Gisele Bündchen is a giraffe. The more achievable ideals of the past have given way to a new race of Amazons roaming the jungles of Manhattan and Paris and Milan. They are so tall they look like NBA centers without the tattoos, or in some cases, with. And yet we're supposed to identify with these creatures who sprout wings at Christmas and flounce down runways in thongs that would make better dental floss than lingerie. *They* have nutritionists, manicurists, pedicurists, masseuses, plastic surgeons, and dermatologists on their speed dials. *We* have cleaners, babysitters, pediatricians, schools, friends, and family on ours.

Still, if all you had to do to get gorgeous was plunk down a few hundred dollars for a DKNY blouse or a pair of Ralph Lauren pants, if it were that easy, it would be worth it. If you could look as good or young or thin after a couple of visits to the drugstore or the cosmetic counter, the fantasy that women's media sells would be a bargain. But it just doesn't work that way, because what you see is not what you could ever possibly get. Even if you were that self-focused and could afford to spend enormous amounts of time and big bucks on yourself. That's because, today, models and celebrities are created and packaged like a product by people who live to pamper and promote, by expensive clothes, chemicals, and of course, by the trusty computer. It is an exhaustive, multilayered process of enhancements—hair, teeth, skin, body, makeup, clothes, and finally technology—which you could never, never replicate at your bathroom or bedroom mirror.

And here's one more disillusioning little secret. How many of us have raced out to buy J.Lo's mascara or Gisele's blusher after seeing the makeup brand credited under the glowing photo of a celeb or model in a magazine? Well, you can stop reading and racing. Makeup artists use what they want during a photo shoot, and the editors, long after the picture has been taken, write the credits to please the advertisers. The small type under each picture, which tells you the name of the foundation and lipstick that the model is supposedly wearing, is rarely accurate. Truth in beauty and fashion journalism? Not exactly.

The Makeover Myth

Francesco Scavullo was one of the world's most famous fashion photographers with a well-earned reputation for shooting glamorous pictures of unglamorous women. Can you think of a better subject for Scavullo's superexpensive, magical makeover treatment than Roseanne? I couldn't, and was willing to shell out $50,000, when you added it all up, to get him and his crew to shoot a cover for *Ladies'*

Home Journal with Roseanne when she was the hottest star on TV. She was so excited by the chance she flew to New York overnight in a chartered jet. Astonishingly, she only hit me up for the bill for the hotel room, which she didn't use and for the gym equipment she insisted be moved in to the hotel room, which she also didn't use. In that respect—not using the gym equipment—Roseanne was like the rest of us.

A makeup artist spent hours with her, followed by a hairdresser, and a stylist, and a couple of editors. Roseanne, another comedian known for her on-and-off-camera snarl, surprised us all by acting like a docile little girl through the whole excruciating seven-hour prep. Then Scavullo spent hours more lighting and photographing her. Her husband at that time, Tom Arnold, told me how important it was to her to try to look pretty, which struck me as poignant and a little sad. She adored the final result so much—a perfectly lit, heavily retouched, masklike photo of a slimmer, younger-looking Roseanne—that she must have hand carried it to a plastic surgeon and told him to copy it. And, poor thing, she's been having it copied ever since.

Roseanne wants something we all want—to look good. And we can look good; we just can't look like Gisele Bündchen. But neither can Gisele Bündchen without a lot of help that you never see or learn about. So women, especially young women, really shouldn't take seriously the way she appears on the pages of magazine. Or have any special faith in the makeup she is purported to be wearing. Or accept her manufactured image as any kind of standard to ever measure ourselves against. Just enjoy it as fantasy. Or ignore it as fantasy.

In truth, even the most knockout magazine makeovers we see in *Cosmo* and *Allure* last only a week or so before the woman who is so transformed goes back to looking much the way she did before her transformation. What *can* change is the way a woman can feel about her looks—and feeling good *inside* about the way we look *outside* is what women really need—far more than a new hairstyle or a new way of applying makeup. Women just want some encouragement to be basically satisfied with themselves. That's why women responded so enthusiastically to Jamie Lee's moment of honesty—her open acceptance and appreciation of herself. But that's a message that media for women gives out so rarely that when it does it makes really big news all over.

None of us probably will ever catch the rabbit, and truth be told, neither will any of the fashion and beauty editors who want their obsession with the perfect image to be ours, and care not at all how the negative messages they send and the unattainable standards they set impact the lives of average women. But I hope now that when you pass the newsstand and see a diet line that catches your eye and you buy it, you won't completely buy into it.

Now, don't be afraid, the next chapter is about fear.

CHAPTER 5

The Female Fear Factor

When Diane Sawyer looks me in the eye and tells me "sleeping on a conventional mattress is like sleeping on kerosene," she gets my attention—and that's the point. It was a March 30, 2000, *Good Morning America* segment.[1] I stopped making the bed, grabbed my coffee, and sat glued to the set watching a fairly typical and typically scary network report on the dangers of non-flame-resistant mattresses.

Watching with a pro's eye—hey, maybe this is a story for my magazine, too—I noted that the report had everything a woman needs . . . to start the day wrong. It had:

1. Fear—"This is a mattress study called 'The Big Burn' conducted by the California Bureau of Home Furnishings

back in 1991." Meaning nine whole years had passed before the show, but who's counting? "It was a test to see how long it would take for a fire to consume a mattress like the one you just spent the night on. Firefighters . . . say they are well aware of the risk," solemnly intoned reporter Greg Hunter.

2. **A threat that endangers children**—"Stacey Hernandez's son, Damon, set a polyurethane foam mattress on fire in California back in 1993 . . ." Seven years before the show. "Third-degree burns over half his body."

3. **A distraught mother**—"If I had known that that was so unsafe I would rather we had slept on the floor."

The story also featured a bit of a debate and a doubter or two, but any and all criticisms of the story's basic premise were passed over faster than a size 14 at a fashion shoot. "The Consumer Product Safety Commission and the mattress industry insist that the greater fire hazard is what's on the mattress, [namely] the bedclothes. Not the polyurethane on the inside . . ." Great. Now, what are the odds of finding a comforting little fire-resistant tag still on those sheets I've slept on through at least three presidents?

Then, as television is wont to do, we were given a chaser of reassurance after the scare session: "The federal government has required mattresses to be cigarette resistant since 1973," which I had already guessed is the cause of most bedroom fires.

Still, I sat there watching a terribly disfigured child, a weeping mom, and an incensed Diane. "This is really stunning," she said.

But what should be done about it? If I wanted to get a flame-retardant mattress right away, like before tonight when I might once again be "sleeping on kerosene," where do I find one?

"Only in some state prisons," Greg tells me.

Now, that's very helpful. Let me run right out and rob a bank.

That short *Good Morning America* piece was pretty standard fare, and a good illustration of the way editors and television producers construct human interest stories and consumer reports that are the bread and butter of media aimed at women. Next time you watch *48 Hours* or *Dateline NBC*, look at the way the story is told. They all tend to have the same format: High volume on the emotions, low volume on everything else (facts, balance, debate, assessment of risks, advice you can really use).

But even knowing how the media overdoes stories, my basic reaction to the *GMA* piece was probably just what yours would have been. How very sad about that child. And even though I know that most safety officials are neither uncaring nor unwise, I was left with the uneasy feeling that we are often in danger, even in our own beds.

And that's what *GMA, 20/20. Today, Dateline,* Lifetime, and other network series—all of them want you to feel. Afraid. Worried that the next victim might be you or your child. When it comes to selling fear, television and women's magazines live by one rule—there's no such thing as overkill, no pun intended.

Still not sure?

Let's take another look at the same *Good Morning America* program on that same day. Along with the "Can You Be Too Hot in Bed?" (that's how *Cosmo* might have titled it), there was also: a frightening report on two women who had been harmed by the herbal diet supplement ephedra; an ominous report on how stress may contribute to infertility; and a warning, in case you've been unstressed enough to get pregnant, that episiotomies may actually hurt new mothers. Ouch!

So *GMA* starts our day with four scary stories, and all before you drive the kids to the school bus, which we all already know is not as safe as it ought to be. TV mornings like this almost make one long for Barney—well, almost.

Danger, Girls! It's All Around Us!

For years, we have been warned and warned again about so many terrible things—benzene in our bottled water, Alar on our apples. Remember the well-known microbiologist Meryl Streep's dire warnings about this high-risk fruit? She sounded the alarm before Congress, in several women's magazines, and on talk shows. The apple hadn't taken this big a hit since Eve explained the food pyramid to Adam.

Funny, though, she seemed to be unusually camera shy when her claims were refuted, but not before almost single-handedly doing in the agricultural economies of several apple-producing states.

We may not have Alar to be afraid of anymore but never fear, there's always asbestos in our school buildings, secondhand smoke in our environment, the hole in the ozone layer, the ozone in the ozone layer, high-tension power lines, cell phones that cause brain cancer, and lead paint peeling off our walls. That old lead paint fear was recycled in a recent *Redbook* article that claimed that living in any house built before 1978—which means 40 percent of all homes in America—could be a serious danger to your children.[2] So now I know my kids spent their entire childhood in danger, not just when they came home after curfew.

We have also been warned by the Center for Science in the Public Interest, a.k.a. the food police, that popcorn, margarine, red meat, Chinese, Italian, French, and Mexican food along with McDonald's french fries contribute to heart disease. Still ordering fettuccine Alfredo? Heart attack on a plate, sister! Aluminum and zinc may contribute to Alzheimer's. And almost everything else including alcohol, birth control pills, bottled water, silicone breast implants, exhaust fumes, chlorine, caffeine, dairy products, diet soda, hot dogs, fluoridation, grilled meat, hair dyes, hydrogen peroxide, incense, jewelry, kissing, laxatives, low-fiber diets, magnetic fields, marijuana, olive oil, orange juice, peanut butter, playground equipment, salt, "sick" buildings, sun beds, sunlight, sunscreen, talc, testosterone, tight bras, toast, tooth fillings, vinyl toys, and wallpaper may cause cancer.[3]

And don't forget Lyme disease, which was the basis of three or four terrifying stories in the *Journal.* A medical editor once assured me Lyme would have been "the disease" of the '90s if it hadn't been for AIDS or the Hantavirus, another scary disease, this one carried by rodents. I'm still afraid to go into the shed next to our house, where I'm convinced there are hoards of furry little carriers skulking behind every bag of mulch ready to do me in.

Pollster Madelyn Hochstein told me a couple of years ago that a wealthy woman in a focus group in Beverly Hills said that she lay awake at night worried that "something was growing out there in the desert. Something bad. Something toxic." Sounds like the directions to Michael Jackson's ranch.

Madelyn was a bit taken aback by the woman's fear, but every other woman in the group understood perfectly. Now, *that* is scary, especially in a place where police protection is so good that the biggest threat most of these women face is an overly aggressive pool boy. Assuming that's a threat.

More than twenty years ago, political scientist Aaron Wildavsky looked around America and wrote, "How extraordinary! The richest, longest-lived, best-protected, most resourceful civilization with the highest degree of insight into its own technology is on its way to becoming the most frightened."[4] We have arrived.

And the media is largely to blame; even media reporters fess up to that. As David Shaw wrote in the *Los Angeles Times,* "The media, after all, pays the most attention to those substances, issues and situations that most frighten their readers and viewers. Thus, almost every day, we read and see and hear about a new purported threat to our health and safety."[5]

Of course, guys read and watch, too, but, let's be honest, women seem to take these emotion-laden stories more to heart. We just do.

According to University of Michigan psychology professor Susan Nolen-Hoeksema, women tend to ruminate, brood, and worry a lot more than men. Through an extensive twenty-year study, she found that many women spend countless hours thinking about negative ideas, feelings, and experiences.[6]

"Gender plays a powerful role in the perception of hazards," was the conclusion of Professor John Graham, founding director of the Harvard Center for Risk Analysis, after the center polled more than a thousand Americans to find out whether they believe in widely reported but unproven "hazards" like radon and pesticide residue on food. Graham found that women were more likely to believe such scares were true by a margin of ten percentage points or more.

"Some suggest that because women give birth, protect and care for their children, they may naturally tend to be more nurturing than men, therefore they may be more concerned about hazards that may harm their families," he noted. Probably true.

Graham also speculated, "Another possible explanation is that women are less familiar with science and technology than men and are generally more fearful of it." Possibly true. But he concluded that the role of gender in risk cannot be explained by simply noting that women are nurturers or less sophisticated than men about science. "More research is needed to understand why gender plays such a powerful role in perception of hazards," he said.[7]

Maybe we are more fearful because media aimed at women exposes us to so many stories about potential dangers. And while guys can slough it off, we tend to start worrying about yet another threat to our families. Maybe we're also confused because these stories aren't really about hazards as much as about outrage at *possible* hazards. On that little *Good Morning America* segment, we didn't get any real assessment on how dangerous the mattresses that millions of Americans sleep on every night really are. Nobody in authority told us to pitch our mattress out the nearest window. All we heard was that something bad could happen and once did. We saw the effect the hazard had on one family. But that was enough.

Says TV commentator Jeff Greenfield, "It's a basic rule of journalism—to get the human angle. But with a complicated technical story . . . the concerns, the worries, the fears of people . . . will always carry more weight than the disputes and the cautions of the experts."[8] In other words, let's not clutter up a perfectly good horror story with any mitigating facts.

Human drama, human emotions are what work. And pictures— dramatic pictures of a sobbing mother, an injured child, a disfigured teenager. Such pictures and the stories that go with them are easy for women to empathize with and understand. And that's the name of the game—attracting women. So why should we be surprised that so many of these pieces are for and about women. For example, on *20/20* there was a segment, in the early summer of 2001, introduced by Barbara Walters telling us:

> How do you like to be pampered? For millions . . . especially women, especially as summer approaches, the answer is a visit to a nail salon. Maybe you're headed there tomorrow. Well, we have to warn you, you may come home with more than beautiful fingers and toes because there is something ugly going on at some nail salons . . . Customers who don't know how to protect themselves are really getting nailed.[9]

"Getting Nailed" was about a California nail salon where a group of women were infected by tuberculosis-related bacteria that were found in the drain of the foot basin, which had not been carefully cleaned. The rest of the piece took us along as undercover inspectors raided other salons in various states. Many, owned by immigrants, were found to be violating local health codes, reusing emery boards and swabbing counters down with diluted disinfectant. Only the one salon was shown to have seriously injured any clients, but the legs of the women who had become infected did, I grant you, look quite gruesome.

At the end of the piece, Barbara Walters shared that "I wanted to have a pedicure this week," but she said she didn't. Why not? Did the *20/20* piece make her as fearful as it was supposed to make us? Not really. Barbara told us, "Once and again I've been too busy." She didn't say she would be sure to do a safety check the next time she hits Frederic Fekkai's exclusive salon as she advised her loyal viewers to do. Still, e-mails flew around my office and across the Internet—the world's biggest party line—as women warned their sister sandal wearers of the newly discovered dangers of the pedicure. This was *real* news we can use from one of television's most-respected women journalists warning us that pampering can be hazardous to your health.

And we do depend on media to tell us what's important in the world, good news and bad. Whether it's *Dateline NBC* or Peter Jennings or *Ladies' Home Journal*, the media is our information source, and we want the truth. And there's the rub. Although we might like to think so, journalists and editors don't just transmit the facts, ma'am. They select and shape it and make facts fit into emotional stories that tug at our heartstrings or send a chill up our spines. I've done it myself. That's because news is most effective when it tells a story that confirms our deep-seated beliefs and stokes our deep-seated fears. As psychology professor Paul Slovic of the University of Oregon says, "We trust people who tell us we're in danger more than people who tell us we're not in danger."[10] And when we hear someone is harmed we want a simple explanation for her pain. A very simple explanation. Editors and producers know that.

Look, I'm not telling you that all these "fear factor" pieces you read in magazines and see on the networks are untrue. Those women on *20/20* did get a nasty infection from their pedicures. Through the years I published many articles about wrongs against women and

families, and stories about health that were fair and honest. I believed
I was giving good sensible information. But there is always the temp-
tation to play gotcha! To simplify and dramatize in order to hold the
attention of the reader or viewer. And I can't deny that those of us in
media, like a little girl who keeps crying long after her stubbed toe
has stopped hurting, tend to exaggerate and do a lot of it for effect.

That's why even though women and men are safer and healthier
than we have ever been, we are also more afraid of what we eat, drink,
touch, and breathe. Eleanor Singer and Phyllis Endreny, two social scientists, did a study of risk coverage by the media and concluded, "A
direct comparison between hazards as topics of news stories and as
causes of death show essentially no relationship between the two."[11] So
we're really okay, but we are being told not to feel okay. That's because
the media, in order to attract readers and viewers, "often overplays
risks of dubious legitimacy. Scientific studies show that many of the
alleged hazards the media trumpet are either misstated, overstated,
nonexistent or there just is not enough scientific evidence yet to yield
reliable guidance on the true risk for the average American."[12] Which, I
admit, is a kind of shabby way to get readers or ratings.

Who Wrapped My Cheese?

Here's another typical example: A *20/20* show that warned us about
plastics. Yep, plastics. The kind we wrap and store our food in and
drink from every single day.[13]

Charlie Gibson, the show's co-host, gave the feature a very solemn,
very confusing introduction: "It has been shown that some plastics,
under certain conditions, release small amounts of chemicals. *Could*
these chemicals seep into the food we eat and *could* small amounts
be harmful to us or our children?" That's a lot of modifiers and a lot of
questions there, Charlie.

He continued, "The industry and the government say the plastics are perfectly safe." Well, that's reassuring. But don't relax just yet. Charlie went on to tell us that a couple of scientists don't agree. Danger lights begin to flash as reporter Brian Ross advises parents not to panic over plastic because "there is no proof of harm" and then spends twenty minutes implying just the opposite.

First Brian trots out a Dr. Groth of the Consumers Union, which publishes *Consumer Reports,* who scares the hell out of every mother who has ever gotten down on her knees and thanked God for plastic bottles and microwaves. And who among us has not? Dr. Groth tells us that their studies found that the chemical Bisphenol-A, or BPA, seeped into baby's milk at a rate of one part per billion after heating a bottle for thirty minutes. Hysteria sets in before we stop and think. Wait a minute. Did he say "one part per billion" with a *B*? Isn't that an infinitesimal amount? Even Brian has trouble with that one. "Well," Dr. Groth admits, "one part per billion is close, close enough to levels that have had effects in animals."

"It's not this close," he says as he puts his thumb and index finger about an inch apart, "it's this close." And holds his hands a foot apart. Well, that scientific explanation certainly clarified it for me. Dr. Kimberly Thompson of the Harvard Center for Risk Analysis says that by using toxicity tests—small numbers of animals given large amounts of a particular substance—"we can find adverse health effects for almost any substance, including water and the essential elements." Oh, and, by the way, she said "parents were scared unnecessarily" by the BPA stories.[14] Too bad Brian couldn't have squeezed her into his twenty-minute piece somewhere and saved a lot of women a lot of worry.

When we listen to a report like that, all we really hear is, "Chemical seeps into baby's milk." It's a little like one of my favorite Gary Larson cartoons. The one where a man is talking to his dog, Ginger, and says, "Okay Ginger, I've had it! You stay out of the garbage. Understand, Ginger? Stay out of the garbage or else." Then we see what the dog hears: "Blah blah Ginger, blah blah blah Ginger. Blah blah blah blah." We mainly hear the scary words, and we're meant to, because the story doesn't sell unless the risk is overblown. And because we are women, we are especially attuned to hear the scary words about baby's milk, brood about it, tell our friends, who brood about it and tell their friends, until we have thousands of unnecessarily panicky young moms.

Of course, something else got my attention about the doctor's claims that made me wonder about the report. How about heating a plastic bottle for thirty minutes, at least in a microwave? If your microwave is like mine, after thirty minutes, you could scoop up the bottle and serve it on crackers. Is he kidding?

Apparently Brian didn't think so, and the report went on. Dr. Groth has barely finished shredding the security blankets of plastic-bottle-heating moms everywhere when he polished off the rest of us with warnings of killer cheese. Well, not exactly the cheese but certain plastic wraps that can seep minute amounts of a chemical called DEHA into fatty foods like, well, cheese. Once again, the doctor tells us that he doesn't know if tiny amounts of the chemical are safe or unsafe (the federal government says it's safe) but warns us not to use the plastic wrap anyway. Thanks, Doc.

Some pieces strike me as even more irresponsible than the usual drill because they tend to frighten us—especially parents—about a trumped-up "risk" when there is absolutely nothing in the world you can do about what you are told. On "A Closer Look" segment on ABC's *World News Tonight* in 1998,[15] Diane Sawyer declared, "It is always startling to us when we learn that something we've done for a generation may turn out to be harmful. So we were stunned [yep, Diane was stunned again] that questions have been raised about how we vaccinate our children." What would these people do without the words "may" and "might" and "could"?

Alarming stories about vaccinations have been a staple of women's magazines for several years now with such anxiety-provoking blurbs as "Before your children are eighteen months old, they'll have routine immunizations against ten illnesses. Should they?"[16] There have been warnings about a vaccine against rotavirus that caused cases of bowel obstruction in some babies; about the DPT vaccine and anaphylaxis, an allergic reaction; and also about the belief among some parents that the onset of autism is somehow related to the way vaccines are given.

But this *World News Tonight* feature was not about these much-covered topics. Rather, it focused on a doctor who believed we give vaccines to babies at the wrong time; and if we gave them earlier, we could help prevent diabetes in later life.

To prove the point, reporter John McKenzie produced lots of confusing junk-science statistics like there are some "alarming details on the timing of vaccinations." In one study of mice, injected at two months of age with the common whooping cough vaccine, 23 percent developed diabetes. Of those vaccinated earlier, none developed the disease. And in Finland in the mid-1980s, scientists started giving children a common meningitis vaccine, then monitored their health for years. Remarkably, we were told, those who received the vaccine at two months of age or later developed diabetes at a rate 60 percent higher than those who were never vaccinated.

Huh? Even if you could follow what these statistics were supposed to prove, and I couldn't, what was the point? The expert in the report, who was supposed to advise parents, was every bit as confusing as the report itself. Her name was Barbara Loe Fisher, president and co-founder of the National Information Vaccine Center, which sounds like an official government organization but is, in reality, a nonprofit group founded by Ms. Fisher after her child suffered what she believes was a severe reaction to a DPT shot. She declared, we "have to find out whether or not vaccines are causing chronic diseases like diabetes."

But wasn't the original point of the piece about altering the timing of vaccines to *prevent* diabetes, not whether to vaccinate at all? Oh, never mind! In the five years since the piece was treated like hot breaking news, nothing has happened in pediatric land. Absolutely nothing. Kids are still getting vaccines according to the medical profession's currently accepted schedule. With malpractice insurance going through the roof and trial lawyers stalking potential clients like Glenn Close in *Fatal Attraction*, doctors aren't going to stray from established practices, and who can blame them? And who says the one doctor featured in ABC's story is right, anyway?

Still, if you were a young mother you were left worrying about something that may or may not be true and about which you could do nothing anyway.

It's not fair to blame television alone for our national case of the jitters. Women's magazines, I concede, are also filled with stories of small health risks writ large. The study of thirteen women's magazines done by the Media Research Center analyzed fifty-six articles on science and risk issues over the course of a year.[17] And what they found really was alarming. Thirty-five of the articles "educated" readers about potentially dangerous health effects from a variety of sources from pesticides to alcohol with headlines that would make you gulp—which I know from experience was the editors' intent. Chemicals of all kinds were a particularly popular scare topic. *Family Circle* had you shaking in your homes with its story "Danger in the House"—or as I would now call it, "The Attack of the Killer Cleansers." Yes, this article warned of a "chemical invasion" by cleaning products and garden pesticides that threaten everything from allergic reactions to cancer. Can't you imagine a small army of Comet and Mr. Clean goose-stepping to your doors—cleaning Nazis ready to strike if you don't pitch out everything nonorganic from under your sinks.

Two thirds of the articles reviewed in the study never mentioned that the actual risks from any of these threats were extremely small, and even more important, that the alarmist views in many of the articles actually disagreed with mainstream science.

One recent example was a *Good Housekeeping* story on the risks of food with the warning in the blurb "the most ordinary of meals can trigger a deadly allergy attack."[18] The magazine actually admitted it was warning readers against eating practically everything. Now we all know about *E. coli* in hamburgers, bean sprouts, and even cabbage; salmonella in chicken and eggs; and listeria in hot dogs and packaged meats. But in this piece, the secret stalker, the kitchen killer, the fatal food was . . . celery. That's right. Celery. When I saw that headline, every Bloody Mary I'd ever had flashed before my eyes.

The writer explained it this way: "It's hard to imagine a more innocuous food than this dieter's staple. [Well, yeah.] Indeed, it's mostly water. But, incredibly, some people can go into anaphylaxis if they exercise shortly after eating celery [I guess I can relax] . . . or in some bizarre cases, any meal can trigger such a reaction. Doctors don't know why this strange allergy occurs. . . ." Is that frightening enough for you? My guess is you have a better chance of being abducted by aliens than killed by celery.

Dr. Jekyll and Dr. Hyde

What women's magazines really specialize in are stories that make you afraid to cross the threshold of a hospital, trust your doctor, or take your medicine. In looking at ten years of cover lines—with all those exclamation points—one can see a dramatic acceleration of bad-doctor stories during the 1990s. The lovable and always trustworthy Dr. Welbys of the early '70s have morphed into greedy and/or incompetent Dr. Frankensteins today.

I've always said that health stories fall into two basic categories: There are good doctors who save your life and bad doctors who kill you. And even though they will deny it, most editors, reporters, and producers tend to divide medical stories into these two camps.

Coverage of health topics, which provide the best fodder for frightening stories, dramatically increased during the past decade both on television and in women's magazines. On TV the increase was part of the "feminization" of that media, the realization by executives that more and more often it was women out there watching—and watching everything—including the news. Media analyst Andrew Tyndall, of the Tyndall Report, a network news monitor, who tracked CBS news broadcasts in 1968 and 1998, saw the broadcasts shift from foreign policy, military, economic, and business issues to lifestyle topics like health, education, and sexuality. In fact, measuring coverage on all three networks, he found that the news time devoted to what he calls "news you can use" aimed at women quadrupled from sixteen minutes to seventy-one minutes a month and helped transform TV news in the process.[19]

Women, who are the gatekeepers of their family's health, visit doctors more, and who are, in general, less squeamish than men, are more interested in these types of stories. This may also explain the immense popularity of gruesome shows like *ER* and *CSI*. I have friends who actually watch these programs over dinner. Not me. Open-heart surgery and graphic autopsies may be their idea of the perfect side dish, but I'll stick with a green salad.

Women's magazines also package fear much like Dr. Groth's cheese—by "exposing" frightening and imminent threats to women, especially when it comes to health. Our survey of women's magazines found that when it comes to scare stories, the least substantiated ones were those about health. In fact, over the three years' worth of stories we reviewed, 258 health stories about everything from food contamination to mercury poisoning to rare diseases earned space in America's magazines for women—many overly dependent on anecdotal evidence and devoid of any valid risk assessment. Often, a hint of conspiracy was added ("10 Urgent Health Risks Doctors Don't Tell You About") to ratchet up the fear factor and make victims— usually just being a woman makes you a victim—even more appealing to readers.

In 1990, *Glamour* didn't have one cover line about health—let alone health scares. By 2002, it had one scare line on almost every issue. Like: "It's Common, It Can Kill. Why Aren't Doctors Telling Us about This Women-Only Disease?" (*Glamour,* April 2002),[20] a story about preeclampsia, a pregnancy-related condition that is not a common cause of death. There are over 4 million women who give birth in America each year. About 75 women die of preeclampsia. There are plenty of things to worry about when you're pregnant—how to get through an editorial board meeting without vomiting on the publisher or how to put on a pair of panty hose at eight and a half months, but worrying needlessly about dying from this condition isn't one of them.

Or: "The Female Health Threat 93% of Women Don't Know About" (*Glamour,* May 2002),[21] about five "down there" diseases. *Glamour* confesses that some of their readers, who they like to boast to advertisers are a lot brainier than *Cosmo's,* thought PID, pelvic inflammatory disease, was P. Diddy's initials. Or: "New Warning: The Hidden Threat to Every Woman's Breast Health" (June 2002),[22] a piece implying that many doctors would do a mastectomy rather than a breast-sparing procedure on a cancer patient because they receive $130 more in reimbursement fees when they perform the more invasive procedure. The writer of that article gives herself lots of wiggle room, since she neither cites statistics to back up her rather outrageous charge nor does she give us any specific anecdote as proof of such a claim. Instead, she simply opines, "I hate to suggest this, but decisions regarding patient treatment may sometimes be unduly influenced by physicians' financial concerns." Now that's rigorous reporting.

Not a month goes by without magazines sounding some kind of dire health warning, although the readers of *Glamour* are in their twenties and thirties, and one would presume are too young to be overly concerned about illness.

But there's a way to turn anything women do into a health threat— what about *Good Housekeeping*'s "The Health Hazard in Your Handbag" (May 2002)[23] that's about how all the junk you schlep around in your tote can make your shoulder hurt. It starts with a long anecdote about Carole Black, the head of Lifetime television who, in true Lifetime fashion, just may have been victimized by her very own handbag. What's next? "I was abused by a serial backpack?"

In 2000 alone, *Redbook* had six cover lines about bad doctors or doctors who miss an important symptom. *Ladies' Home Journal*, I must confess, had its share of scare headlines, too, like "Dangerous Medicine: When Cures Harm Instead of Heal," or "Foods that Can Kill." (They were the usual suspects. No celery.)

At the *Journal*, we did sometimes try to balance the negative with more positive features. One of the best and most serious pieces we ever published was by the dean of the School of Hygiene and Public Health at Johns Hopkins. Dr. Alfred Sommer tried to give readers information on how to realistically evaluate health claims—even those often featured in women's magazines, including ours. Maybe we should have taken some of our own medicine.

On television entertainment shows, it is not so much bad doctors that are ready to do you in, though God knows there are plenty of tough or unfeeling or incompetent doctors cast as a counterbalance to all those good, caring doctors like *ER*'s John Carter. No, TV's medical villains du jour are usually greedy HMOs or greedy hospitals or our whole greedy, uncaring, screwed-up health system. Translation: What do we want? Nationalized medicine. When do we want it? Now!

On the premiere of an ABC series called *MDs*, the writers seemed to imply that things are so bad, doctors can save your life only if the medical bureaucracy thinks you're dead. Just as "meeting cute" is a sitcom cliché, medical shows now cure "cute." Here is how the launch of *MDs*, a short-lived but not atypical series was promoted on the ABC Web site:

> It's day one for hospital administrator, Shelly Pangborn, whose former experience running theme parks may explain why she faints at the sight of blood. [Cute!] As Pangborn meets the dysfunctional staff, she notes their disdain for administrator Frank Coones and for Nurse Poole, who prefers profits to patients. [Boo!] Dr. Bruce Kellerman, head of cardio-thoracic surgery, and Dr. John Dalgety, a trauma surgeon, are an icon-oclastic duo who buck the system to save lives. [The Heroes!] Young intern Maggie Yang's unofficial first day on the job rounds out the insanity. She is coerced into assisting in an illegal "autopsy," a ruse that will allow Dalgety and Kellerman to perform a biopsy on a patient whom the hospital discharged earlier for lack of insurance.

In other words, those cheeky surgeons pretend a patient is dead in order to do a test that his HMO will pop for if he has departed this earth, but won't if he's still breathing. As fellow ABC-er John Stossel, who has been around a lot longer than *MDs*, says so often, give me a break.

Today on *Oprah*: Perimenopause

Another given in the coverage of women's health is the assumption that in one way or another you are always suffering from something. And just in case you're feeling fit as a fiddle, here's an insider's tip. The new "ailment of the decade" is going to be perimenopause, which sounds like something I'd plant in the backyard if all the shovels weren't in that damn shed with those toxic mice. I'm not predicting the rise of perimenopause because of any scientific research. No, this will be the next trendy "disease" because there are so many women who are the right age to experience this condition, which may or may not even exist. A year or so ago, Oprah Winfrey started a show by asking her audience of 8 million devoted viewers, "Are you in menopause . . . and don't even know it?"[24]

This question was answered by a building chorus of several anxious, anguished women telling Oprah:

"I feel like my body's going crazy on me."

"I had trouble sleeping."

"I have cold hands and feet."

"One minute I'm laughing and the next minute I'm crying."

"Why can't I concentrate?"

"Why am I so out of control?"

Oprah confided that when her symptoms hit, she thought she was having a heart attack. On the show, she was so excited because she found out she wasn't dying, and she wanted to share this good news along with a discussion of "premenopause" or what is more often termed perimenopause with her TV girlfriends who might be suffering unawares.

But then, listening to Oprah, it would be hard for almost any woman over thirty not to think she might be experiencing perimenopause, because it's such an equal-opportunity ailment. There's a symptom for everybody: cramps, hot flashes, night sweats, memory loss, sleeping problems, mood swings, anxiety, irritability, irregular menstrual periods, light periods, heavy periods, diminished libido, increased libido, vaginal dryness, frequent urination, migraines, bloating, breast tenderness, and heart palpitations, which particularly afflicted Oprah. Is there anyone who hasn't experienced some of these symptoms at one time or another? My husband would probably say I've been in peri-menopause since shortly after the arrival of our first child.

The United Nations' World Health Organization (WHO) kicked off the perimenopause boom by officially defining the condition at the end of the 1990s. Of course, this is the same crowd that voted to give Libya a seat on its human rights committee. The WHO doctors decided perimenopause begins two to eight years before a woman's final menstrual period. Other doctors say it can begin even twenty years before then. And some doctors just say, "Oh, please." Like Dr. Anthony Scialli, formerly of Georgetown University Medical Center, who doesn't want to offend but sounds as though he thinks, with all due respect, that the condition is a bit of a marketing scam. He says, "Women's health has been phenomenally overmedicalized and commercialized and to a large extent perimenopause is a manifestation of that overmedicalization."[25]

For its first foray into mass-media awareness, perimenopause could not have had a better platform than Oprah's show. So many women sent concerned e-mails that Oprah's heavily trafficked Web site crashed. In 2003, when I did a search on Google, there were 69,700 references to perimenopause, which, remember, did not exist as a condition just a few years ago. There are also now loads of books on the subject, including *What Your Doctor May Not Tell You About Perimenopause: Balance Your Hormones and Your Life From 30 to 50*, and *Before the Change*, which includes such quaint symptoms as "weeping" and "hysteria."

It does make me wonder just how far removed we really are from a Victorian doctor's description of females "as if the Almighty in creating the female sex, had taken the uterus and built up a woman around it."[26] Will our lives soon be subdivided by women health writers into micropassages? Prepuberty; periadolescence; and then for the boomers who survive perimenopause and menopause, there'll be post-menopause to look forward to—each with its own lists of symptoms, medications, self-help books, magazine articles, and television exposés. And, if they are lucky, an Oprah show of their very own.

Every Story Needs a Victim

Still, when it comes to scary medical reporting, there is no contest. Television newsmagazines seem to me to have the most impact. It's those pictures. It's their presumed authority. And even though you seem to get the facts about how high-tension power lines *may* cause cancer, what sticks with you isn't the fact that there is no conclusive scientific evidence that power lines are hazardous to you or your child's health. What you remember are the sad pictures of a sickly child who has lost his hair to chemotherapy curled up on his mother's lap as she blames the power lines next door for her child's condition. We wouldn't be human if we didn't feel for this poor woman, but do most of us get past the pictures to the facts? Not if the news producer can help it.

These shows are also able to layer on one story over another. On one *48 Hours* show, "The Silent Killers," Dan Rather started the broadcast with this provocative question: "If there were a hidden danger in your home or where you work or travel, would you know how to find it?" Gee, I don't, Dan, have you got a map? Then the grizzled and grumpy anchor, who has said publicly that he believes Bill Clinton is an honest man, asks us to believe that any one of us could be the next victim of four silent killers. What followed were segments on toxic mold, carbon monoxide poisoning from houseboats, a town with an abandoned asbestos mine, and a story of a woman who died of "economy-class syndrome" after a long plane ride. All on the same show. And the woman whose house was filled with toxic mold was none other than Erin Brockovich, the famous victims' protector who turned out to be a victim herself.[27] Obviously, nobody is safe.

When so many newsmagazine shows started copying women's

magazines' fear formula so directly, the editors who worked for me became frustrated and resentful. They were stealing our act, and they had a big advantage. A story that might be dull reading still had impact when you watched angry or grieving victims on TV. A long-time television producer friend, terrified of my even identifying the very successful magazine show for which she works, agrees that the appeal of the victim is the key. "There are only two rules when work-ing on these stories," she says. "Don't get the program into trouble but make it dramatic enough and sympathetic enough to get the ratings."

So it's no surprise then that women have been bombarded by lots of fear-inducing but false statistics about how vulnerable we are. As somebody—nobody is quite sure who—once said, "There are lies, damn lies, and statistics." Some are outright whoppers, like this one you've probably heard more than once. One hundred and fifty thou-sand females die of anorexia each year, claimed both Gloria Steinem in her best-seller *Revolution from Within* and Naomi Wolf in her best-seller *The Beauty Myth*.

Sure, we know that women worry about their weight. Some obsess over it. But that 150,000 death statistic would mean that almost three times as many women die every year from anorexia as in car acci-dents. Come on!

Still, it took Professor Christina Hoff Sommers to discover that less than a hundred women actually die from anorexia every year.[28] It makes you wonder why intelligent women like Steinem and Wolf, who were misquoting the findings of the American Anorexia and Bulimia Association that there may be 150,000 *sufferers* of anorexia, didn't question such an inflated mortality figure, a figure that com-mon sense tells you couldn't be accurate.

We now know that these charter members of the Girls' Club were dead wrong. Still, the statistic has been reprinted over and over again. But what's a slight exaggeration among friends, particularly if it helps promote their view of the world?—one in which, they believe, tens of thousands of women are manipulated by men into self-destructive behavior.

There are plenty of other terrifying but untrue factoids you've probably read or heard. Like this one: There are more visits to emergency rooms by women because of domestic abuse on Super Bowl Sunday than any other day of the year. That false but fairly irresistible tidbit—it's *such* a good story—was reported by our friends on *Good Morning America* and a whole slew of newspapers as well. *The New York Times* sportswriter Robert Lipsyte started referring playfully to the event as the Abuse Bowl. The report was never questioned until some real fact checking was done, this time by *The Washington Post*. But even then, it didn't die the sudden death it should have. It popped up over and over again in women's magazines. I am sure some diligent researcher can turn it up on the pages of *Ladies' Home Journal* and almost every other magazine for women. How does this happen? In general, you fact check against other sources and they can just be repeating the inaccurate story.

Even years after it was debunked, the executive director of the Milwaukee Task Force on Family Violence who was, oddly enough, planning a Super Bowl fund-raiser, told the *Milwaukee Journal Sentinel* there probably *is* a higher incidence of domestic abuse on that day because it is a weekend and the festivities involve alcohol. She offered no substantiation for her claim but just "believed" it was so.[29] And so the rumor starts all over again and reporters and news producers are always "ready for some football" and for the opportunity to bash America's fathers, husbands, and sons. Is that really how little we think of them?

Brill's Content was a short-lived magazine about the media, a self-appointed press watchdog. Unfortunately, the publication had lots of circulation problems because almost everyone who was interested in reading it was in the media and thought they should be sent copies free. (Like beauty and fashion editors who live life on the "comp," nobody in media ever wants to pay for magazines either. Many go to free movie screenings, too. And some get free books. Yet another reason they are distanced from their readers, who expect to pay for what they read.)

Brill's once did a comprehensive analysis of twenty features on NBC's *Dateline*, and ABC's *20/20* and *Primetime Live*, trying to assess how accurate and fair the reporting was on these very successful programs, which, by the way, generate huge profits for their networks.

So how good is the reporting? According to *Brill's* analysis, not so hot. The writers of the piece, two of whom had been producers of newsmagazine shows, declared, "After much debate, we found twelve of the twenty to be fair overall, despite a tendency, even in those segments, toward overplaying danger or heart-wrenching footage." They judged eight out of twenty unfair—about 40 percent, a significant amount, because "in these segments the hype just went too far. The unfair reports shared common flaws. When re-reported . . . the stories that seemed solid on their face proved to have distorted or omitted facts or interviews."[30] Can you imagine the outcry if 40 percent of the cars we buy were defective? Or if 40 percent of children's toys were dangerous, or 40 percent of the medical decisions in this country were wrong? I can, because *Dateline* and *20/20* and *Primetime* would be "stunned" and outraged and would tell us so in prime time.

The goal of these shows, as my producer friend admitted, is not as much to right wrongs as it is to make sure the viewers stay tuned. This is done by keeping the story as simple and dramatic as possible. The Victim is never asked tough questions. In fact, the Victim is always treated like the Expert on whatever problem he or she might have. The Villain does not get equal time. There is no subtlety here. Explains media critic Todd Gitlin, who has been burned himself by agreeing to appear on camera and then being shocked by the result, "If you tell the reporter what the reporter doesn't want to hear or try to carry the conversation in unexpected directions, you are apt to be left on the cutting room floor."[51]

Keep it simple, stupid, and keep the blood pumping. It is not very different from cable news shows when producers bark into the earpiece of a guest, "Interrupt! Go ahead, yell" to ensure a verbal food fight or when they cast for the most opposing points of view on a subject just so that the debate will be more rancorous. Potential Villains—corporations, government agencies, conservative scientists—often take a pass on these shows because they have been nailed in the past and know they will end up looking culpable, guilty or not. But not appearing on the shows doesn't protect them, either. Don't we all think when Brian Ross or Ed Bradley ends up saying something like, "We invited General Motors to appear but they did not respond to our request," the company must be hiding something? And that's exactly the effect they're after.

Some media consultants, who advise industrial clients, say don't waste your time giving reporters facts on why your product or service is not dangerous. Instead, get the compassionate stuff in because it is the only stuff that works. Others take a much tougher stance. Eric Dezenhall, who is the author of *Nail 'Em* (and it's not about pedicures), says his business is "defusing media-hyped attacks that seek to destroy someone." He has a simple analysis of fear-factor pieces. Look hard at the next one you watch and check out how on target he is. He points out, once again, that the narrative needs a victim and a villain. The villain could even be a car, "such as the Audi 5000, which was accused in the late 1980s of accelerating all by itself and running over children. As news becomes more like entertainment, the narrative must be spun into the entertainment formula that vaudeville respects. . . . The audience will not be satisfied until the target does the perp walk."[32]

And if the facts are wrong, so what? After Audi was completely demolished in the U.S. marketplace, the mother who ran over her own child acknowledged that her foot may have slipped off the brake. "But," Dezenhall notes, "vindication after Chapter 11 bankruptcy is not exactly strategically useful."

Have I Got a Story for You!

Where do these stories come from? How does an editor or producer find that special nugget of a story with a victim/villain combo that will have us breaking out the Kleenex or lying awake in bed fretting a few hours later? An entire cottage industry has grown up around the ability to feed fear-factor stories to women's media.

Let's examine one of the best-known female fear-factor stories of the past decade, the panic—and the lawsuits—over silicone breast implants. We all heard, during the mid-1990s, from women's magazines, the *Journal* included, from Connie Chung on television, from Ralph Nader's consumer group Public Citizen, that silicone implants were making women sick. It started with one suit by a woman from Boise, Idaho, who claimed that the implants had given her an autoimmune disease. And even though almost from the start there was no hard scientific evidence backing this claim, the assumption seemed credible and had great emotional impact. It was about a woman's breasts, after all, and no part of the body could be charged with more emotion. And it was about enhancing one's breasts, which was done most likely for the guy in her life or to *get* a guy in her life. Having done that and then getting sick, well, clearly it was a story every woman could empathize with, get upset about, and agree that if the "oozing gel" of the implants was dangerous (and how could it not be?), someone should pay and pay big.

Lawsuits proliferated until the FDA banned the use of the implants, and implant maker Dow Corning was forced into bankruptcy. As science writer Michael Fumento told John Stossel on a documentary called *Hype*, which traced the development and escalation of this scare, "There was talk of oozing gel spreading throughout women's bodies, and this was horrific to tell people. The media picked it up; and I think far more important, trial lawyers picked it up . . . because there was money in it."[33]

The lawyers used a simple but effective argument: "She was fine before she had the implants and now she's sick. Ladies and gentlemen of the jury, I ask you, what else could it be but the implants?" Most women still believe that silicone implants are dangerous.

Media coverage was so intense and so frightening that Dr. Marcia Angell, then executive editor of the *New England Journal of Medicine* noted, "Some of the women became so frightened that they actually tried to remove their breast implants themselves with razor blades. That's the measure of their desperation." Angell, both gutsy and rigorous, wrote a book about the implant scare and how the lawyers deftly used the media to frighten women.[34] Recently, after years of study, an FDA panel recommended silicone breast implants be "returned to the market."

Of course, trial lawyers usually can't plant stories directly promoting their point of view in magazines, newspapers, and on television, though the Association of Trial Lawyers of America Web site is full of potential fear-factor stories that freelance writers use as sources. They also do this indirectly by hiring media relations groups that put out press releases to "educate" reporters and editors. For example, Fenton Communications, headed by the former PR chief for *Rolling Stone*, was involved in both the anti-Alar campaign and the leaking breast implant story. Fenton currently represents dozens of liberal groups including Greenpeace, Rainforest Action Network, and the Sierra Club. When a freelance writer friend spoke with them about a story, they told her they were eager to help and that there were certain reporters they worked with all the time. They also asked if they could see her piece, if she didn't mind, before she submitted it for publication.

In the case of the breast implants, a Houston lawyer who made

$100 million from lawsuits was able to get one of his own employees on a TV program where she magnanimously offered to give women information they needed. Telling women to call for a helpful brochure, she gave out the number of the implant lawyer's firm. According to Stossel, the lawyer also paid the Fenton group to send a video news release about the dangers of implants that was used by over five hundred TV stations. Stossel noted on his program that Fenton Communications has also worked with groups that have demanded that ABC fire him, all the while getting that all-important publicity just for asking. When you start to look beneath the hype, you can often find the fingerprints of nonprofit groups with a partisan agenda, as well as the public relations firms they employ, often funded by trial lawyers.

For example, the piece about lead poisoning in *Redbook* quotes Eileen Quinn, deputy director of the Washington, D.C.–based Alliance to End Childhood Lead Poisoning (recently renamed Alliance for Healthy Homes): "The focus should be on government agencies and local groups to identify and fix properties. . . . It shouldn't be on parent's shoulders," she said. The piece continued, "Of course, finding lead and clearing it out of homes and public buildings takes money, so some local governments are trying to recover funds for lead abatement by bringing lawsuits against the lead industry including paint companies, such as Sherwin Williams. . . ."[35] The lead industry? I didn't know Sherwin Williams was in the lead industry. This piece also neglects to point out that the mother, who is its focus and who is described as having become an activist, was also on the board of the Alliance to End Childhood Lead Poisoning.

Another important point left out is that even though lead in paint was banned by the government in 1978, paint manufacturers stopped using it in the 1950s and were very up-front in publicizing the dangers. Still, that hasn't exactly stopped the same politically connected lawyers who made billions of dollars from tobacco settlements from representing Rhode Island, Chicago, San Francisco, St. Louis, and dozens of others in current lead paint lawsuits. Ronald Motley, a South Carolina trial lawyer who turned tobacco into a personal cash crop, has said, "If I don't bring the entire lead industry to its knees within three years, I will give them my boat."[36] I guess he knows he can always afford to buy another 120-foot yacht.

Now, if you are a mom who read that scary *Redbook* story, "The Poison That Hid in Our Home," and were concerned enough to want more information, and go to the Web, you'd find the Lead Poisoning Resource Center. And you would also find that the Lead Poisoning Resource Center was set up by (surprise, surprise) Motley's law firm.

But despite the trial lawyers' connections, there is no vast left-wing conspiracy to "sell" women fear. Low-level members of the Girls' Club, editors, and producers, don't swap scare stories with gazillionaire trial lawyers over expensive lunches at the Four Seasons. It's a far more convoluted course from a gleam in a greedy litigator's eye to an emotional feature in a women's magazine or a full-blown exposé hosted by a stunned Media Queen.

More likely, this symbiotic relationship between the media, interest groups, and trial lawyers exists because the writers and editors and producers are just so accustomed to getting their information from these sources and are naturally philosophically aligned with their thinking. Besides, these sources consistently produce the fodder they need to create good scary stories.

Believe me, a Media Queen or an editor-in-chief is usually too busy begging Julia Roberts's or Renée Zellweger's publicist for an interview with the superstar to be particularly rigorous about examining the trial lawyers–special interest groups'–media connections. And frankly, most editors know more about the ins and outs of Hollywood than of Washington. They don't realize that when an expert comes from a nonprofit group that doesn't mean the expert is unbiased. On the contrary, it usually means the source has a very definite ideological or political agenda, but the readers are rarely informed of that.

In the spring of 2003, both a *Family Circle* article on the dangers of pressure-treated wood and a *Parents* magazine feature on "sick" schools[37] used information from the Environmental Working Group. About this group, columnist Michelle Malkin wrote, "It is not just a humble 'nonprofit research outfit' as it is being described in the mainstream press." Rather "it is a savvy political animal funded by deep-pocketed foundations with a big government agenda of their own. . . . The group's main claim to fame is its anti-chemical fear mongering. It scares pregnant women about . . . chlorinated water and says that even one bite of fruit sprayed with pesticides could cause 'dizziness, nausea and blurred vision.' It has also declared war on different occasions on nail polish, hairspray, playgrounds, and portable classrooms."[38] Writer Sarah Foster has described the group's modus operandi as not targeting the public but rather "the news media who have the capacity to broadcast their message far and wide."[39]

Let's face it, fear makes trial lawyers rich, Nader's Raiders and others of similar ilk righteous and fulfilled, and gets media the ratings or the readers it wants and needs. Everybody's happy except, of course, us women, who now get to add "frightened," along with "frumpy and frazzled" to our repertoire.

Triumph over Tragedy

I suppose to some degree, in a roundabout way, we're all victims (if I may use the term) of that old saying, "Be careful what you wish for." I think we'd all admit that women love stories, even scary ones. We remember anecdotes, and we like to share them. We tell each other stories when we sit around the playground while the kids are on the jungle gym (by the way, we're now told that—five generations of healthy kids to the contrary—jungle gyms can be deadly, too). We trade our tales in the office when we are trying to avoid that boring spreadsheet waiting for us on our computer. Storytelling is as ingrained a female trait as worrying.

But there used to be many more heartwarming medical and health stories in women's media than there are now. A typical one would tell us about a woman who was hurt or sick and who bravely soldiered on. As bad as the accident or the illness might be, the victim in the story would usually say that it had made her stronger and more grateful about what was still good in her life.

We loved plucky heroines, and we loved miracle cures. Best of all, we loved miracles. One of my favorite stories in the *Journal* was about a man flying to visit a nephew who was injured in an accident and on life support. He got the last seat in the plane, next to a woman who was going to visit her very ill sister who was desperately in need of a liver transplant. They began to chat about the reason for their journeys. Using the phone on the plane, the two of them made it possible for the nephew's liver to be donated to the woman's sister. It was a wonderful piece, but stories like these—upbeat, uplifting, and "villainless"—are few and far between these days.

Once we read tales about strength and courage. Now, if there is a victim in a story, there must be a villain. The stories are less about bravery than about getting even. And to make the tale complete, women no longer triumph over tragedy, they sue after tragedy and try to get their revenge in court. Sometimes going on *Oprah* or being interviewed by Katie is part of the story, too. Instead of stories of inspiration, all become stories about blame and retribution. If the *Titanic* sank today, Molly Brown would have sued the White Star shipping line; Expedia, where she booked the trip; the girlfriend who recommended it; and probably the other girlfriend who introduced them in the first place. Then she would pour out the terrible details of her ordeal to an appropriately empathetic Katie or a "stunned" Diane, and finally start a foundation to create an iceberg-free world.

When it comes to media's obsession with the fear factor, don't we have enough to worry about today? Real things like 9/11 and the continued threat of terrorism that may impact all our lives. It's not that many of these stories aren't true to some extent and possibly even important. But I want you to stop letting yourself be manipulated so easily, and stop worrying about what you really don't have to worry about. Don't be cynical but do be skeptical. Learn to ask some of the tough questions that are often left out because the answers just might spoil a scary story. When you hear a claim qualified to the hilt with words like "*could* be dangerous," "*might* be harmful," or the classic "there's no scientific proof, *but*," think again.

I'm not finished with lawyers, but I hope your shots are up-to-date because you're about to meet the Victim Virus—and, believe me, from that danger, no woman is safe.

CHAPTER 6

The Victim Virus

The guys just didn't get it at first.

On the August night when Princess Diana died in a Paris tunnel, the ABC network had one sulky $10-million-a-year anchorman who didn't want his Labor Day weekend interrupted by the sudden, shocking death of the most famous woman in the world.

A female producer who was on the scene at ABC at the time told me that Peter Jennings, summoned to the studio from his home in the Hamptons, fumed that Diana wasn't even a head of state! So what was all the damn fuss about?

While the guys in the control room at CBS were so slow off the mark that many of the affiliates of that network, once so famous for its news coverage, continued to show a professional wrestling bout for an hour after its competitors reported the news of the princess's death and switched to appropriately mournful programming.

No, the guys just didn't get it. But any woman could have told them. Any woman who got that sick, kicked-in-the-stomach feeling of shock and horror and dismay at the awful news. Who felt she had lost a girlfriend she had known for years and really, really liked. Hey, she had stayed up all night to watch her spun-sugar fairy-tale wedding, hadn't she? She could have clued in the guys that we were all going to be absolutely obsessed for days and weeks and would want to hear reiterated again and again every single detail of her soap-opera life, every single detail of her horror-movie death.

For wasn't it so very terrible the way poor Diana died? A victim of the hideous, hounding paparazzi press who were relentlessly pursuing her, chasing her on motorbikes like bats out of hell, up and down the boulevards of Paris at ninety miles an hour. Of course, we learned later that Diana was more likely the victim of her own drunken, drugged-up driver, an employee of her playboy boyfriend, and had been somewhat neglectful herself in not buckling her seat belt during that insane final chase.

But any woman who had ever read a magazine with a picture of Diana on the cover—and who hadn't—knew that Diana was a victim of more than drunk driving. A child of divorce, filled with insecurities, she was the victim, as well, of her in-laws, the stiff and snooty Royals who didn't understand or appreciate her charm, her warmth, her instinctive genius for worldwide public relations. And of that sullen stick of a husband who had led her, a sweet and simple romantic like so many of us, into a chilly, loveless marriage. And who, during their engagement, had pinched her waist and told her she was getting chubby, which was enough, because of her insecurities, to cause her immediate descent into hellish years of bulimia. Hey, we had been given a laundry list of reasons to feel sorry for her over the years. So, despite her jet-set lifestyle, her million-dollar clothes budget, and her good looks, it was always "poor Diana."

Diana really didn't start out as an übervictim. She was a highborn, virginal Cinderella. That was the story that the press wanted to give their readers, at least at first. Diana, who had a job as a nursery school teacher, drove her own car and had given up wearing slips in hot weather—she was photographed in a sheer skirt with her long legs outlined against the sun—was held up as an example of youth, freshness, and modernity, exactly what the stodgy British Royal family desperately needed.

The first time I put Diana on a cover I had to choose between a good photo and a fairly rare interview with Jane Fonda or a not very good, soft-focus photo of the young princess and an even softer feature about how she was adjusting to royal life. Our allegedly in-the-know British women's writer on the scene gushed that there were a few bumps and bruises along the way, but Diana was doing very well, thank you. We didn't know then that, scarcely six months into their marriage, Charles was already back to canoodling with Camilla and that Diana, visibly shrinking before our eyes in paparazzi pictures, was spending a lot of time in the loo.

A researcher who was doing a survey of potential newsstand buyers to test covers for our magazine told me he thought Jane Fonda had more appeal, even though half of America still hated "Hanoi Jane" because of Vietnam and the other half had grown to loathe her for forcing her grueling aerobics on us all. I said to hell with research and went with Diana, and she sold very well. I was a new editor, and I needed that sale. Thank you, Diana! I used her again the following October, and she sold even better. I used her again in March, and she sold better yet. For the next nine years, whenever I needed a strong newsstand sale, we just called in pictures of Diana. Every other women's magazine in the world was catching on as well. It was a rare month when you could get through the grocery line without Diana smiling at you from the cover of one of your favorite magazines.

And Diana kept the endless soap opera going in various ways, including cooperating with writer Andrew Morton to help him produce his best-seller about her life, *Diana: Her True Story.* Max Hastings, the former editor of *The Daily Telegraph,* recalls, "I remember being at lunch and saying, 'Ma'am, I should let the other side make mistakes. Say nothing.' At the very moment we were having that conversation, while she was nodding away, they were setting up the television cameras upstairs"—for the interview in which Diana tearfully told the whole world her side of the story of the breakup of her marriage.

By the time an unhappy Diana met her tragic end, we had actually grown just a tad bored with her, turned off by her affair with the sleazoid Dodi Al-Fayed. But at the news of her death, millions of us were suddenly inconsolably bereft. Women in all circumstances once again identified with her and with the many different aspects of her megavictimhood. After all, a tragic early death is the most shocking victimizer of all.

The Rise of Global Mourning

At a memorial service in New York's Central Park attended by thousands—almost all of them women—a divorced mother told a reporter from *The New York Times,* "She had a bad marriage, she had to deal with questions of self-esteem, she had to share custody of her children, and I had the same problems."[1] Francine du Plessix Gray, an East Side intellectual and self-styled "progressive feminist," also felt close to the victimized Diana. "The disappointments, the humiliations of her experiences with men reflected the rage my friends and I still felt, decades later, toward all those fellows . . . who had jilted or deceived us," she wrote in her tribute in *The New Yorker,* a memorial

issue that was rushed into print by its British editor, Tina Brown.[2] The
issue enjoyed the largest newsstand sales ever for the magazine. In
the issue, Tina included her own off-the-record Four Seasons lunch
conversation with the divorced princess, uncertain about her future,
who was more to be pitied than envied for all her worldwide fame.
After all, Diana had ended up in Paris in August, and, according to
Tina, absolutely anybody who is anybody wouldn't be caught you-
know-what in a nearly empty Paris during the traditional French vacation month.

Maybe the TV guys didn't catch on at first because, during the
"Di-nasty" years, Diana had never been as much a story for television
as she had been for magazines. Something I, as a magazine editor,
was very grateful for at the time. There were no videos of the wacky
Waleses having one of their royal rows, of Diana throwing herself
down the stairs in Kensington Palace just to get a bit of attention, or
Charles having phone sex with his once and future squeeze, Camilla
Parker Bowles. There *was* an audiotape available of that overly inti-
mate conversation in which the Prince of Wales told his mistress he
wished he could be her Tampax. *Her Tampax?* What a romantic guy.

Magazines, daily newspapers, and the supermarket tabloids understood immediately what an enormous story the Death of a Princess
was—and how much they could profit from it. They knew that women,
especially, would want to read about Diana and look at all those gorgeous pictures of the most photographed woman in history (who was,
in reality, more photogenic and expressive than truly beautiful).

But TV caught up quickly enough and continued practically nonstop in its coverage of "The Final Farewell," "Good-bye to the People's Princess," and "The Death of Diana" (same story, different
channels) for much of the next week. A billion people around the
globe had watched Diana's wedding. I know I did. Two and a half billion people would watch the dark pageantry of her funeral.

Each morning, an appropriately sorrowful Katie Couric chatted with protocol pundits about etiquette at the royal funeral and with child-care experts on the effect on the young Princes of Diana's sudden death. On the day of the funeral, she stationed herself outside Westminster Abbey, celebrity spotting as if covering the red-carpet action outside the Golden Globes. "Cindy Crawford is arriving!" Katie exclaimed as a woman who wasn't Crawford entered the abbey.[3]

Walter Goodman, television critic of *The New York Times*, describing the coverage, wrote, "There was Barbara Walters revealing that she was a friend of the Princess, information that she said she had hoped to keep private. She revealed their friendship again on a two-hour special on Sunday night and then again on *Good Morning America*, when she read a letter from Diana promising her an interview. 'I'm almost embarrassed to talk about her as a friend,' Barbara said."[4] *Almost.*

Goodman also commented that on that same two-hour Sunday night special, Barbara Walters looked especially sad, while Diane Sawyer looked almost as sad, possibly because she didn't have a personal letter to show or a promise of an interview to reveal. Maybe she was just stunned, as Diane is wont to be, by the depth of her grief. But it was a chastened Peter Jennings who gave it all up. He turned to the dueling divas of despair at his side and acknowledged, "I'm learning from you both."

Right.

But Peter was slow on the uptake yet again. Or pretending he didn't know what had already been going on for years. How could he not have realized that the tabloidization and the feminization of the news, especially of television news, had been happening for quite a while. During the '90s, many news stories that had created tsunamis of coverage had centered on women—some victims, some villains, some both—and were high emotional dramas that riveted the audience.

Judy Milestone, a longtime CNN producer who went to work the night Diana died and "hardly got home for a week," said she could recall more than a decade of her career as a news producer by simply reeling off the names of women who had become the center of stories, "Diana, of course, but also Amy Fisher, Tonya Harding, Nancy Kerrigan, Lorena Bobbitt, Nicole [Brown] Simpson, Susan Smith, Louise Woodward, Paula Jones, Linda Tripp, Monica, Chandra . . ."[5] And the saga continued with Laci Peterson, who, both before and after the war in Iraq, became another favorite cable news victim.

Of course, tabloid journalism has been around since the mid-nineteenth century. It helped turn newly literate city dwellers into devoted newspaper readers and once or twice even nudged our country into a small war. But only in the last couple of decades has tabloidization gotten so, well, girlie.

Nowadays on TV, we watch a lot more stories than we once did that appeal to women and that women, primarily, want to know about, emotional stories, gossipy stories, juicy stories. Let's face it, millions of women were watching and weeping as the young Princes followed their mother's coffin up The Mall. Millions of guys were in the other room yelling, "Are you ever coming to bed?" The answer was no. We couldn't. We just couldn't give up on the fairy tale, even without the fairy-tale ending.

Millions of American women—in fact, women all over the world—had been infected by the victim virus and participated in a kind of global mourning. We had our villain—actually, we could choose from more than one—Charles, of course; Diana's mercenary brother; the paparazzi; or even the Queen, depending on your point of view.

And the tragedy featured more than one victim. There was Diana, but also her darling sons so clearly devastated by their mother's death, and the British public, too—the sad pictures of weeping women lining the streets of London ten deep as the somber funeral cars took Diana back to her girlhood home.

There were winners, too. American television, certainly, and women's magazines, plus Elton John, who had his first hit in years, the international tissue industry, and, last but not least, the florists of Great Britain. Like a bad case of flu racing through a kindergarten class, the Diana virus had evolved into a true celebrity pandemic.

Another British Invasion

How and why has the media become so obsessed with victimhood, in and of itself, as both news and entertainment? The victim virus started not from some primordial ooze or a lab accident or even a stressed-out mom who forgot to Clorox the cutting board. No, it was those pesky Brits again. Way back in the early 1970s, British journalists and their Australian cousins, who are the modern masters of tabloid journalism, began targeting female readership when their large-circulation national papers found themselves in financial trouble. At the time, David English, the new editor of the (London) *Daily Mail*, a money-losing tabloid, set out to edit a newspaper that would appeal primarily to women readers. His theory was not to add more pages of food coverage or fashion but to orient *all* news stories into "something that was attractive to women."[6] The advertising slogan for the paper became "Every woman needs her *Daily Mail*," and the shrewd editor proved to be so successful and so influential that he was subsequently knighted. Today, the *Daily Mail* is the paper with the second-largest circulation and second-largest female readership in Great Britain and is the engine of a vastly profitable media company. Since the '70s, David English's *Daily Mail* editing techniques have drifted across the Atlantic and are copied by many American magazines.

Oxford-educated Tina Brown, one of the stars of the Spin Sisters, whose husband had been a British newspaper editor, once lectured a group of staid American newsmen on how to make their papers girl-friendly. She was then at the height of her success as editor of *Vanity Fair* and lauded for her buzz-filled British-style editing skills. She defined her take on the female sensibility this way: "Men talk about what happened. Women talk about what *really* happened. Men talk about what they are supposed to talk about. Women talk about what *really* concerns *them* . . . Women are obsessed with the subtext, the meaning, the motive, the story behind the story . . . They also don't mind saying, 'I don't get this. I'm bored' . . . [They] refuse to be bored."[7]

Women's magazines, already knee-deep into emotional story-telling, instinctively were following her advice. In them, the victim virus had its first host, and before long, it had spread to the airwaves, infecting even more of us with stories of woebegone women, tales depressing or scary enough to send even fairly levelheaded readers screaming for Zoloft or the day spa.

The Project for Excellence in Journalism, the research arm of the Committee of Concerned Journalists, has carefully tracked the changes in television news over the past three decades. They report that nowadays there is a far greater emphasis on stories about people, as well as a new emphasis on gossip and scandal.[8] Coverage of celebrity and hard-luck tales almost doubled between 1980 and 1999, reports Harvard's Joan Shorenstein Center on the Press, Politics, and Public Policy.[9] And this interest in the "softer side" of news hasn't changed all that much even since 9/11.[10]

Nowadays, women are the primary audience for the evening news-magazine shows, the morning shows, and even the nightly network news. The producer of an evening news broadcast says his team decides on doing a feature based on whether it will appeal to the middle-aged woman they know is watching their program and the nonstop ads for Celebrex, calcium supplements, and Metamucil.

Tell Me a Story

As a women's magazine editor, I know that the stories that once would have appeared only in women's magazines are now snapped up by *20/20* and *Dateline* and *48 Hours*. Even Fox News, known for its testosterone-fueled reporting and commentary, had made its on-again, off-again magazine show, *The Pulse*, far more feminine than most of its other coverage. It relaunched the newsmagazine with a report on diets and an "exclusive" interview with the bemused parents of Evan Marriott, a.k.a. Joe Millionaire. That reality show, Fox's megahit with a hero who made Brad Pitt look plain, initially was watched by "18.6 million viewers, which breaks down roughly to 18,599,997 women and three men, all of whom happen also to be avid fans of Barbra Streisand, Madonna, and Saturday night marathons of *Trading Spaces*."[11]

At a Columbia School of Journalism First Amendment breakfast where media trends are discussed, Andrew Lack, at the time president of NBC and formerly president of NBC News, talked about the changes in news delivery. Lack declared that the news was once "what middle-aged guys thought middle-aged guys should hear about." Not anymore. "We are much more diverse," he said. "We know there are women out there."

Lack is credited—or blamed—as one of the major influences behind the blurring of the distinction between news and entertainment. He also explained that modern audiences are composed of "self-empowered readers and viewers" whom public media companies must attract in order to make the profits that will satisfy their shareholders. Which means it's the media's job to give the public what they will buy and ignore the fact that the public may have lost respect for media in part for doing exactly that. Recent polls by Pew[12] and Gallup[13] show that a vast majority of people think the media is biased, makes mistakes, and perhaps most significant of all, gets in the way of society solving its problems. Yet we watch—hours and hours a day.

Media researcher Dr. Valerie Crane, whose specialty is advising local TV stations on how to beef up their ratings, says, "Women even like issues framed as relatable stories."[14] So even news about serious topics like politics and the governing process have taken on, whenever possible, a highly personal, dramatic, and emotional slant. Did anybody here say "Monica"?

I have always known that women like to read about the problems other women face. Such stories have always been a staple of women's magazines, which, like tabloid newspapers, began publishing in the mid-nineteenth century. We like stories about another woman's troubles because it allows what psychology professors call emotional learning. That means that when we are reading or watching a story about a woman with a problem, it is as if we are learning about the problem from the inside out.[15] We identify and empathize with the woman involved because we often feel—and the media certainly wants to make us feel—that we could have the very same scary problem, whether it is killer stress or killer cheese. An emotional look is the easiest way to get our attention and keep us interested. As we read or watch, we assess how the woman with whom we empathize copes. We judge whether we would handle her troubles in the same way. If we believe we would, or if we consider the woman classy or attractive, someone we'd like to have as a friend, then we are highly sympathetic. Just think how we felt, most of the time, about our Diana.

If we don't like how she handled herself or if we don't empathize because we feel the woman is beneath us, we become highly judgmental and critical. And sometimes a story is set up just to make us snipe and sneer. Didn't plenty of women slam "trailer-trash" Paula Jones, whether or not she had a good sexual harassment case, and endlessly put down woefully ordinary Linda Tripp? But not Anita Hill, who propelled herself onto the national political stage in her prim little suits with her own set of seamy but far less serious charges, and with no more evidence than poor Paula. Even if you believe her story, is an off-color joke made to a co-worker really the moral equivalent of having the governor—your boss—invite you up to his hotel suite and then, with the breathtaking arrogance of someone who's always gotten a free pass on bad behavior, proceed to unpack "Mr. Happy and his luggage" for an afternoon delight?

Though there were differences of opinion between men and women about Anita Hill, polls taken at the time reported that more women across the country believed Thomas and were skeptical of Hill. *The New York Times* noted, "Americans still favor the Judge's confirmation by a ratio of 2 to 1. . . . Asked who they believed more . . . 58 percent of the respondents said Judge Thomas; 24 percent said Professor Hill. Women were only slightly more likely than men to side with Professor Hill; 26 percent of the women said they believed her more, as against 22 percent of the men."[16] But in New York women's media circles, one could not dare doubt even a single word of Hill's testimony. And if you thought she was not telling the truth, you might, if you were very brave, admit it only in an empty room with the door locked and the blinds drawn.

Unlike the hapless Paula, Anita Hill was taken very, very seriously. Why? Because feminists flocked to her side like a gaggle of outraged geese squawking for justice. The leading Spin Sisters of the time, who were very invested in pitting victimized women against dictatorial men and what they believe is a male-dominated culture, got a two-fer—a chance to portray a man as a predatory villain and get rid of a "right-wing extremist" in the bargain. At the time, Katie Couric and several other Media Queens made their sympathy clear, and it wasn't long before Anita Hill reached near saintly status. The editor of *Glamour* magazine at the time tore up an issue as it was going to press just to name Hill a "Woman of the Year."

All Victims, All the Time

Why do women like some victim stories so much? Let's be honest, sometimes just learning about another person's painful problem can make us feel better about our own lives. Or it can make us feel utterly superior. Heck, we think, we'd never be as dumb as the damsel-in-distress in the typical Lifetime movie, unaware she is being courted by a raging sociopath who has given her every possible clue that he is a raging sociopath. We'd probably figure out that the chainsaw under the new boyfriend's bed and the formaldehyde aromatherapy candles in the bath might be a teensy-weensy sign of some instability somewhere.

It is true women respond even to hard-news stories in an emotional way. And we respond most strongly to news stories that intrinsically have a high emotional content to start with. We just do. Maybe it's because of hormones or that we tend to rely on the right side of the brain more often, or the way we were raised by our moms. Or maybe it's because we're from Venus originally. . . . Lots of academics, and pop psychologists who write best-sellers, have their theories.

One study done by Turhan Canli, a State University of New York–Stony Brook psychology professor, found that women reacted to emotional scenes much more strongly than men. Canli says the study "shows that a woman's brain is better organized to perceive and remember emotions."[17] Maybe so.

"Women like to hear stories and women like to tell stories and to share experiences through storytelling" says researcher Cathy Chamberlain, who has been surveying women for years for Wirthlin Worldwide, a major international research firm. "Women find, from telling and hearing stories, what they have in common."[18] And there's the kicker. Today, the media still grabs our attention with storytelling, all right. But now the model is the The Perpetual Victim Story—all victims, all the time, as if victimhood is the one thing we must all have in common.

Yet the truth is that most of us actually have almost nothing in common with the abused and endangered women we see endlessly portrayed on television or in magazines. We weren't raped by our fathers. We haven't dated a serial killer. We didn't discover a long-lost twin with a homicidal chip on her shoulder in the checkout line at Target. And our children may be a pain in the derriere once in a while, but they're not out in the backyard setting Rover on fire. Yet turn on your TV or pick up a women's magazine, and the message is clear. If you were born female, from the first wail of life you are granted automatic membership in the victim sisterhood. Welcome to our world.

Back in the 1960s, the feminist movement told us that because we were women, we were all victims of institutionalized discrimination. At the time, that may have been true. But so much has improved for women since then. And life grows increasingly better and better for us. Today there are more women than men in colleges, young professional women earn as much as if not more than young men in comparable jobs, housework is easier and childbirth is safer, and all sorts of opportunities abound. Yet, media continues to send us one message loud and clear: Because we are women, we remain victims in our private lives, at work, in society as a whole.

Women bond by complaining, so what better way to get them to bond and pony up their NOW dues than to tell them about the victimization of women? Remember the has-it-all young editor I told you about who ended our first meeting with a whine-o-gram about her stressed-out, unhappy life? Like so many young women, she wears her victimhood like a status symbol and seems to assume it should garner her empathy, understanding, even respect.

Author and educator Charles J. Sykes wrote a terrific book, *A Nation of Victims: The Decay of the American Character,* saying "perhaps the most extraordinary phenomenon of our time has been the eagerness with which more and more groups and individuals . . . have defined themselves as victims of one sort or another."

Sykes explains the seductive triple attraction to being a victim. First, if you're a victim, you're free from personal responsibility for your actions or your problem. As long as you're a victim, whatever happens, however you behave, it can't really be your fault. There is always someone or something else to take the blame. You also gain moral authority and can take vengeance on an alleged oppressor. And who doesn't enjoy doing that? And because of your victimhood, you get special rights and compensations. Like filing a megamillion-dollar lawsuit or being courted by Katie and Diane and Barbara for a prime-time appearance to tell your story from your point of view. Sounds like a good deal.

Of course, bad things do happen to good women. There are many women who continue to be victims of abuse, illness, and misfortune, and who genuinely deserve sympathy and support. But in our current culture of complaint we have been made to believe that almost every woman can claim the crown of martyrdom as a victim of someone or something—even a bad hair day.

Part of the problem is the sheer volume of these self-defeating messages. In the last few years, dozens and dozens of new magazines for women have popped up on the newsstands, and with the advent of cable, we can choose from literally hundreds of channels including Oxygen and Lifetime, the mother network of all victim TV. That media explosion means many more magazine pages to create and hours of television to fill with stories, stories that appeal to women.

Are women really more victimized than they once were? Of course not. Everything in society confirms the increasing power and success of women. But because of the pervasiveness of a negative media, we think that women are more victimized than they once were even when it's a stretch to find reasons for their victimization. It's just like the summer of 2002 when we heard so much about kidnapped children that we believed more children were being taken. In truth, there were slightly fewer cases of child abductions than in an average year.

Or the summer of 2001 when cable and network news screamed the gory details of so many shark attacks that we assumed they were on the increase when, in reality, it was a typically sharky summer. The scariest thing on the beach that season was the introduction of the tankini.

But watch the network news or Lifetime or *Dateline*, and you'd think times have become so dangerous that women ought to pack up the kids, kennel the dog, throw the SUV into gear, and head for the hills. It's the only way to escape what seems to be an explosion of rape, spousal abuse, school violence, kidnappings, and child abuse. It must be so—it's on TV. The FBI tells a different story, however. Violent crime over the past ten years (1992–2001, the FBI's most recent comparative crime statistics) has actually gone down—a lot: 28 percent.[19] The murder rate, the single most reliable crime statistic, fell by 33 percent.[20] Rape, the favorite story line of so many shows and movies, is also down: almost 26 percent.[21]

And our kids? In that same ten-year period the *Today* show broadcast from Columbine and endless newsmagazine shows highlighted violent children, there has been a 46 percent decrease in violence against children at school. In fact, kids are safer at school than at home!

According to the Department of Justice's National Crime Victimization Survey the rates in 2001 in each crime category were the lowest since 1973. New York City—media central—where so many of these stories of murder and mayhem originate, is now the second-safest large city in the country.[22] But let's not allow a few facts to interfere with gut-wrenching story lines that draw women like a designer shoe sale at Filene's Basement.

When it comes to women-as-victim stories, television, whether on newsmagazine segments or movies of the week, tends to concentrate on the high drama of the victimization. Magazines, with a somewhat different focus, tend to celebrate the victim as "activist" who chooses to make being a victim her life's work by suing her victimizer, launching a campaign to inform others, or getting a law passed that no thinking legislator would dare oppose, fearing the deadly "uncaring, he doesn't feel our pain" label.

In my study of women's magazines, we found that over the past three years there were almost three hundred stories of victimized women and almost three hundred more of women who avenge some kind of victimization. That means at least a couple of stories and several references to victimization in every single issue. Traditional women's magazines make busy wives and mothers feel they are the stressed-out victims of their own full lives. Or they use an up-to-date take on the way women have been portrayed for centuries—as victims of their complex anatomy. Magazines for young women, however, find themselves in a bit of a schizophrenic state these days. On the one hand, they encourage women to be as sexually free and sexually skilled as possible to attract a man. Yet they warn young women at the same time that the allure they work so hard and spend so much money trying to achieve can be very dangerous.

"You're Too Sexy for Your Shirt!"

Two of the young women who helped me research this book were struck by the frequency of the mixed messages in *Cosmopolitan* and *Glamour,* the two largest-selling magazines for younger women. Both magazines seem to tell their readers that they owe it to themselves, as independent women, to be thin, trim, and toned, to use the right makeup and buy the hottest clothes. Both magazines constantly send the message that narcissism is an advanced evolutionary stage of female liberation. Me, me, me means you're finally free, free, free.

They also encourage young women to mimic men sexually, as if being predatory is the most important step in their personal liberation.

Issue after issue, cover line after cover line, they instruct their readers to "blow his mind" with daring sexual skill. They urge women to be self-confident enough to "put out on the first date," "ogle men openly," and "carry condoms all the time." Totally forgotten or ignored are the traditional concerns women have always had about men. Will he call to ask me out on Saturday? Will he call after Saturday? And after months or even years of Saturdays, when are we getting married? Are we getting married? These decidedly "nonliberated" questions are never addressed directly in women's magazines today. Rather, *Cosmo* advises that "dating is a sport" you should get good at, mainly through sexual experience. A kind of "Tour de Pants," I guess.

But then, without so much as a thought to a potential contradiction with this supersexed message, they issue scary warnings to their now wild, bikini-waxed readers in alarmist stories dressed up as advice to the "loveworn." Danger awaits! The next victim could be you—of stalkers or date-rape drugs, of predatory professors or groping gynecologists.

In *Glamour* and in *Cosmo,* amidst the beauty advice, the fashion layouts, and the sex tips, there is always a victim-of-the-month story, which I wager the editors privately characterize in exactly that way. For example, in the August 2002 issue of *Glamour,* you'll find "I Was Videotaped by My Landlord," followed in September with "Meet the Women Stalkers Love to Target." In the November 2002 issue of *Cosmopolitan,* there are no fewer than four cover lines about turning him on: 1) "Read His Dirty Mind—The Naughty Wishes All Men Have"; 2) "Sexposé: What His Favorite Mattress Move Reveals about His Feelings for You"; 3) "40 Sex Secrets of Women Who Are Great in the Sack"; 4) "Guy Special: 65 Pages on Boys, Love & Lust—Just Check Out the Size of This Package," as well as a fashion feature, "Tight Jeans & Sexy Tops: We've Put Together Your Hottest Party-All-Night Ensembles." But there is also a special *Cosmo* report on "The Surprising Thing That Can Make You a Target for Rape." Maybe reading *Cosmo.*

Yes, it *is* exactly your *Cosmo* girl great-in-the-sack sexiness, and your party-all-night availability that makes you such easy prey. "Women in their late teens through their twenties are at the most sexually attractive time of their lives," explains Robert Miller, M.D., a professor of forensic psychiatry at the University of Colorado, in the article. "Too many people assume that rape is only a crime of power and has nothing to do with sex. If that were true, men wouldn't be specifically targeting this age group."[23]

In other issues, we find *Cosmo* girls victims of their glamour jobs: "A Big Star Made Me Shave Her Pits"; of their moms: "My Mother Gave Me Anorexia"; of their usually mild-mannered boyfriends who suffer from "sleepsex" and turn into rapists in the middle of the night while apparently still fast asleep: "Her Boyfriend Did a Terrible Thing in His Sleep. Could Yours?" They're not talking about leaving the seat up.

It is a narrow world these *Cosmo* girls inhabit, issue after issue, focused on themselves and his body parts. Like this major international crisis: "Can Maggie Get Over the Small Size of the Sexy Frenchman's Baguette?" Ooh-la-la!

Or my favorite: "His Butt: What the Size, Shape and Pinchability of Those Sweet Cheeks Reveal About His True Self." When I was the age of most *Cosmo* girls, I didn't expect my boyfriend's behind to actually communicate with me. I'm a lot more liberated now, but I'd still be uncomfortable watching Deborah Kerr grab a handful of Yul Brynner's ass as she breaks into a rousing chorus of "Getting to Know You."

The knee-jerk victim saga combined with the sex-kitten story is so commonplace that a magazine like *Marie Claire* doesn't appear to find any dissonance running a story like "Get Gorgeous! 693 Sexy Buys at Every Price" near a long rant by radical feminist playwright Eve "all-women-are-victims" Ensler. Eve, who is the honorary poet laureate of the Spin Sisters, and wants violence against women all over the world stopped (she seems not very concerned about violence against men), details her own experiences with abuse for readers. Since she cannot claim genital mutilation or mistreatment by the Taliban, her confession instead is that she was "a woman who lost the ability to say no and so was . . . a witness as my own body was taken many times against my deepest will."[24] And even in her late thirties, when her bio says she was already an award-winning playwright, she was still "tiptoeing" around her apartment "for fear of waking the sleeping monster who might then beat me arbitrarily or lock me up."

These two totally incongruous pieces share the issue with another pair of stories on young women—"Gold Diggers Tell It Like It Is"— the digger girls who cheerfully declare, "I don't think of dating rich men as shallow; I look at it as getting what I deserve." Also a photo essay in which a sexy model wanders around town with a camera and asks guys to "bare their butts." Can you imagine the howls of protest by Eve and her merry band of pissed-off women if *GQ* or *Esquire* sent one of its male models out to shoot the bare bottoms of their sisters on the streets of New York? It wouldn't be pretty.

Lifetime Entertainment has just started publishing a new magazine that focuses, like the cable network, on "real life, real women." But a memo sent out to potential contributors makes reality sound like a hell of a place to be. For example, according to the memo, "Emotions Anonymous," a regular feature in the magazine, will deal with "an emotionally charged situation that ends happily. Such as "I Was Afraid to Leave My House for Two Years," "I Put Myself Through College as an Escort," and "My Father Was My Lover."[25] This is not reality for 99.9 percent of all women, but reality, Lifetime-style, extra grim or extra gamey.

I Want My VTV

Are you being manipulated by women's magazines? Absolutely, and to be frank, they've always done that to some degree. But who knew that television would follow our surging-hormones lead to a new level? Take one 20/20 episode that aired in 2001. Even John Stossel, who usually is a little more in touch with reality, got the bug. Introducing one segment, he said, "Suppose you're an older woman." (Okay, that's not too hard to imagine.) "You're alone and lonely, so you decide to take dance lessons and your instructor flatters you with flowers and phone calls. Could you be swept off your feet?" (Only if he looked like the original Joe Millionaire.)

Stossel continues ominously, "Some women said they were and before they'd realized it, they had spent small fortunes, in some cases practically all their life savings." On dance lessons.

Did he say dance lessons?

Reporter Arnold Diaz goes on to document the sad story of a group of elderly women in Florida suckered by a chain of dance studios into paying outrageous sums not just for the lessons but for "membership" in clubs, dinners out, and trips—all with a group of young, at least by their standards, dance instructors.

Of course, it was all a scam. The instructors, most in their thirties and forties and hardly a stud muffin among them I might point out, taught their clients to waltz and then waltzed off with tens of thousands of dollars in the form of dance lesson contracts. How did they bamboozle these lonely ladies? Diaz tells us they used the "Love Technique," phoning their dance partners to talk, going out to dinner with them, sending flowers with gushy notes. It wasn't long before all this attention began to pay off: as the objects of their affection began paying not only for the lessons but for the instructor's water and telephone bills and wardrobes. Some women even loaned them money.

One lonely widow, who is now suing the dance studio chain, cashed in her e-bonds and CDs, depleting almost all her life savings after being danced and romanced into signing contracts to the tune of nearly $100,000.

Incredulously, Diaz asks her, "When you were paying all this money out so quickly, did it occur to you that maybe you were just being used?"

"Not at the time. Not in the beginning," she says. "But towards the end, I realized they were taking me over."[26]

Hello? It took near poverty for that reality to break through?

Okay, this is a sad story, but come on, $100,000 for dance lessons? I don't care if Ricky Martin was doing the teaching, that's a lot of cash for a tango or two. Doesn't personal responsibility come into play here at some point?

Other news programs show women as victims of tobacco companies, victims of women scamming other women in pyramid investment schemes, victims of funeral scams, and even victims of themselves. One of the most incredible tales was a *Good Morning America* story about silicone parties that are popping up all over—kind of like the Pampered Chef with chemicals.[27] "Gypsy" injectors, mostly untrained women, travel from neighborhood to neighborhood injecting what I can only describe as truly dumb women with silicone and apparently whatever's handy to erase wrinkles or to get that just-hit-in-the-mouth swollen lip "trout pout" look that is all the rage.

The reporter portrayed these customers—some of whom had been permanently disfigured—as victims. But were they really? Are women who would let needle-wielding strangers inject them with unknown substances and no guarantees of any safety standards victims—or just downright stupid? But the interviews never include questions about personal responsibility for one's actions. Just once, I'd like to hear a reporter ask: "What were you thinking?"

As ridiculous as many of the "victim" stories we see on the network news, morning news, and the newsmagazines are, they can't hold a candle to entertainment programs. The Lifetime channel, Oxygen, Movies of the Week, *The Practice, Judging Amy, The Division, Any Day Now,* and many others all take aim at women with marathon victimfests morning, noon, and night. Most are dramas featuring a hapless female victimized by a spouse or the "system," terrorized by a crazy co-worker or a psycho boyfriend, threatened by disease or an evil corporation.

It's a race to find the most emotional victim story out there, but Lifetime, the home network of women, is in a league by itself. Take a look at one typical cheery Sunday night schedule: *Strong Medicine*: After Lu is raped by an acquaintance and reports the crime to the police, Dana performs a post-rape exam. *The Division*: Jinny and Magda investigate the case of an elderly victim of spousal abuse who is wary of coming forward. *Any Day Now*: Rene represents a group of women who were groped by drunken men during a business convention.

That's just one night. What about a whole season of that? *The Division*, a series, in just one season, entertained women with stories about killer liposuction, gigolos, child abuse, celebrity sex solicitation, a polluting chemical plant, and angst over a woman facing a "three-strikes" life sentence for holding drugs. Take a breath. That's half the season. Next, it was Internet baby brokers, identity theft, breast cancer, the rape of a female jockey, a male hostage taker, a child molester, police brutality, criminal brutality, guns, and whether a priest should be prosecuted when the exorcism of a young woman goes south. Makes your head spin, doesn't it?

But I think the series *Strong Medicine* may have even trumped its sister show. Some of the highlights of a couple of its seasons include heroin addiction (the pilot), a woman basketball star on drugs, a drug-addicted prostitute who wants her tubes tied, more drug addicts (episode seven), yet another drug addict (episode eleven). A faked hysterectomy, a former beauty queen who wants unnecessary surgery, a transvestite who's menopausal (Oprah would love this one), and a transgender mother in a custody battle. (Is this a man who's become a woman and wants to be the mom now or a woman who becomes a man but wants to be remembered as Mama?)

The story lines also covered ovarian cancer, birth defects, AIDS, pelvic inflammatory disease, brain disease, Tay-Sachs disease, breast cancer, ADD, cervical cancer, breast cancer again, flesh-eating bacteria, chicken pox, rheumatoid arthritis in a deaf woman who uses sign language, and even a woman who blushed too much.

And local news, especially during a sweeps month, tells some of the same stories as well. As the head of a group of network affiliates told me cheerfully, "We can't say we're trying to attract women viewers, but we're trying to attract women viewers eighteen to forty-nine. It's February. Of course, we are doing the old reliable, a series about rape."

Back at the beginning of the last century, the story that was the basis of countless women's novels and short features in women's magazines was about "a young girl who is deprived of the support she has rightly or wrongly depended on to sustain her throughout her life and is faced with the necessity of winning her own way in the world."

Getting on with it, being brave, taking responsibility for one's own life and overcoming obstacles rather than wallowing in misery was what once made heroines heroic. Sort of like the difference between Oprah's own gutsy, triumphant life story and her taste for "victim-centric" contemporary women's fiction that usually features a heroine who is more to be pitied for the hardships she faces than admired for the way she overcomes them.

If the most successful and admired woman in America, whose life would put a Horatio Alger hero to shame, is such a soft touch for the woman-as-victim story, can we be any different? Especially when a really clever "victim" can turn her hardships into an enormous advantage.

"First Victim" Hillary

Of all the woman-as-victim stories that have dominated the news, the one that continues to have the most far-reaching and long-lasting effect is Hillary Clinton's remarkable transformation from the "pariah in pink" to America's Most Unlikely Victim. Sounds like a reality show, doesn't it? It's almost as if she were born for the part.

Political operative Dick Morris, who knows Hillary's strengths and weaknesses so well, said, "In her victimhood, Hillary has achieved the popularity that proved elusive in her previous incarnations as an advocate, a policy maker, a campaigner . . . an administrator."[28] Only by so flawlessly playing the marital martyr when the role was thrust upon her, did Our Lady of Perpetual Conjugal Suffering achieve the personal power base she has always sought and that she is now using to gain increasing influence.

Maybe you remember the 1996 election campaign? Hillary was kept totally under wraps because her poll numbers were lower than any First Lady's in modern history. Back then, Hillary's likability ranked somewhere between that of a used-car salesman and a Sunday morning telemarketer. Tarred by Whitewater, tainted by Travelgate, tangled in a health care policy debacle, Hillary was practically radioactive at the time. I remember that Becky Cain, who was then the head of the League of Women Voters, and I interviewed the First Couple for a special election issue of the *Journal*. During the entire interview, the all-powerful Hillary, the policy diva of the West Wing who wielded clout the way her husband doled out charm, was as quiet as a schoolgirl on a first date.

She did not say one word. While Bill Clinton talked and talked, she just nodded her head, murmured her approval, and gave the president a look so sweetly adoring that it made the way Nancy Reagan looked at Ronnie seem, in contrast, almost shrewish. I remember thinking that I had finally figured out why Hollywood loves Hillary. She's a terrific actress.

At that time, in July 1996, a Pew Poll found that most Americans thought of Hillary as "strong, dishonest, intelligent, smart—and a word that rhymes with rich." Americans had decided that they did not like a two-for-the-price-of-one blue-light-special presidency. "We didn't elect her," was the frequent complaint of voters who didn't want a First Lady who yearned so openly and obviously to be the policy power behind the throne.[29] It was, well, conduct unbecoming.

Around that time, I gave Margaret Thatcher an award at a luncheon in Florida. Unfortunately, Lady Thatcher and I wore practically the same thing that day, a blue-and-white polka-dot power suit. Now I always wanted to be as smart as Margaret Thatcher, maybe half as powerful, but I never wanted to have her sense of style. Still, it was pretty funny. At the lunch, she really took off on Hillary in the way one iron lady can on another. "Doesn't she know what she is doing is *unconstitutional?*" Lady Thatcher thundered, practically rattling the china on the table. Now, there's a celebrity boxing match I would have paid to see.

After we heard nasty detail after detail about the president's sordid affair, from Monica snapping her jumbo-sized thong to the revelation that the stain on her blue Gap dress was not spinach dip, Hillary's poll numbers, for the first time ever, skyrocketed. Oh, what a difference being degraded makes. According to then congresswoman Cynthia McKinney (she lost her seat after suggesting President Bush knew of the September 11 attacks and kept quiet to help his corporate friends), "She [Hillary] exemplifies women all over the world. We have been in those circumstances. . . . Women definitely understand. . . ."[30]

Through all the embarrassment, Hillary kept her cool and said very little. It was the best way to ensure that she didn't lose the sympathy she was finally receiving. But she did talk directly to women who were now rapidly moving to her side, and she did it through women's magazines whose influence she well understood. Hillary claimed she had always read women's magazines, always been a fan, and respected their power. Still, I can't quite picture Hillary trying a jazzy new recipe for Thai chicken or searching *Cosmo* or *Marie Claire* for "25 Ways to Keep That Man of Yours—Yours!"

But she had become the perfect heroine for the *Journal's* classic column "Can This Marriage Be Saved?" I was in the White House on the late July day when Clinton's lawyer announced that the president would testify before Kenneth Starr's grand jury. I was there to interview Hillary for the 115th anniversary issue of the *Journal*. Frankly, I was surprised that she had agreed to the interview, but I was even more surprised to find in the pressroom another writer, for *Vogue,* who was interviewing her about her recent tour of historic sites in the Northeast. Hillary had spoken in Seneca Falls on the anniversary of the first women's rights convention. On a day when she knew her husband was finally going to have to tell the truth, you'd think she might have canceled these two interviews and stayed upstairs with the blinds drawn and a cold compress over her eyes. But according to her book, Hillary claims she, ignoring all reports in every major newspaper and newsmagazine nationwide, thought her husband was telling the truth all along. Duh!

When he finally did spill the beans a couple of weeks later she writes that she was furious, not because he cheated on her, but because he *lied* to her. She was "dumbfounded, heartbroken and outraged that I had believed him at all."[31] Maybe I'm just a stickler but don't you think a woman is usually "dumbfounded, heartbroken and outraged" because the sleazeball played around, not because he didn't admit it?

The writer of the *Vogue* piece was Ann Douglas, a Columbia University professor who wrote *The Feminization of American Culture,* a book that describes how Victorian women exploited the feminine image of powerlessness to gain their own kind of power. In her book, Douglas quotes a poem that appeared in the most popular women's magazine of that time. "A distraught but determined wife promises her criminal husband who has apparently asked (whether hopefully or despairingly we are not informed) if she is going to leave him":

Forsake thee? Never! Though the mark
Of Cain were stamped upon thy brow,
Though thy whole soul with guilt were dark,
Fear not that I will leave thee now.

Here's Douglas's take on the lamenting but loyal subject of the poem: "The wife has been (one assumes) unfairly treated; but, in a curious way, she is pledging to treat her sinful spouse equally unfairly. He has given less than what she has earned, she will pay him with more than he deserves, but the principle is the same. Each of them is self-involved; each is somehow impervious to outward influences and common sense. And her response is punitive in its mercy: he cannot shake her."[32]

Bump up the date 150 years and you've got a striking parallel with Hill and Bill, but Douglas didn't make the connection in her gushing mash note of an interview that appeared in the December 1998 *Vogue*. In five thousand words of nonstop adoration, she praises Hillary's "blue-eyed gaze, her erect, head-held-high carriage, the hum of authority that attends her, the confident air of wide intellectual command."[33] She admires her "wicked sense of humor" and "quick laugh," and if all this wasn't sappy enough, compares Hillary's humorous little book, *Dear Socks, Dear Buddy: Kids' Letters to the First Pets* to "early feminist writings." I guess that would be Socks in the role of Elizabeth Cady Stanton and Buddy in drag as Susan B. Anthony. As she croons and swoons, Douglas aims her claws only at those who might not agree with her observation about Hillary that "there is nothing cold or mechanical here." I suppose her impression could be accurate if one is also willing to believe that deep down the Terminator is just a big teddy bear with tech issues.

Douglas writes, "The press corps, skeptical by profession and currently caught up in what historians will surely consider the supremely irresponsible instance of media madness in the twentieth century, has not accurately presented Hillary Clinton to the public that has not directly encountered her." And why is that? "She is simply smarter than any press person she talks to, an experience that Washington officials do not routinely offer the media personnel who cover them."[34] Ouch!

Douglas's lush-and-gush piece turned into a cover for *Vogue*, the first time the wife of the president would be a cover girl for a fashion magazine. Anna Wintour, *Vogue*'s editor, knew instinctively the issue would sell. For the shoot, Hillary lost some weight ("She's aerobicizing like a gerbil," a friend noted) and, with *Vogue*'s help, finally found a flattering hairstyle which she decided, for once, to keep. For the cover shoot, she was styled with Cartier pearl-and-diamond drop earrings and dressed in a $4,000 burgundy velvet gown designed especially for her by Oscar de la Renta. Annie Leibowitz, the world's top female photographer, took a series of elegantly moody and highly flattering pictures for the piece. The total impression, if not quite Princess Di at her most attractively forlorn, was still definitely regal. Humiliation became Hillary.

Like the Victorian wife who got less than she earned, Hillary paid Bill back with more than he deserved. She may have shrewdly realized this payback would ultimately benefit her. She would make pity pay dividends, and this was a woman who knew something about making long shots pay big dividends. I'm talking about cattle futures, not Bill.

But the networks, led by chief cheerleader Katie Couric, did their share, too, in the rehabilitation of Hillary Clinton. According to the Center for Media and Public Affairs' Media Monitor, which tracked the networks' news broadcasts during that time, Hillary's behavior, for the first time during the Clinton presidency, was praised over 96 percent of the time.[35] "The sanctimonious, self-righteous, fire-breathing, know-it-all, obnoxious Hillary,"[36] a favorite punch line for Leno and Letterman, was forgiven and forgotten by the public at large, especially by her new female admirers. Bill's behavior, not surprisingly, was rated positively only 37 percent during the same time. But he bested Ken Starr, whose motives and actions were praised only 14 percent of the time, no better than Monica's. The winner? Hillary on points. Forced to play the victim, she saw the value in the role and in a moment of strategic brilliance, encouraged her husband to play the victim as well.

Although she might have been embarrassed by her declaration at the beginning of the scandal that her husband was innocent and the target of "a vast right-wing conspiracy," she has never backed away from the clearly baseless charge and, with a battery of spin doctors, ultimately made Bill-as-victim his greatest defense. And it all began on the *Today* show.

"I don't think there was a person in the White House who gave him a snowball's chance in hell, except Hillary," said a former official at the time. "Neither one of them is a quitter. He's a sniveler and a whiner, but when push comes to shove, he's got a backbone of steel—exceeded only by hers."[37] Most important of all, an energized Hillary became the doormat that just wouldn't lie still, barnstorming across the country for Democratic candidates for the House and the Senate during the midterm election in '98. She sensed the crowds would want to see how she was bearing up.

Liberals have always needed victims to enact their policies. In essence, liberals tend to see the world victim first because it helps them define themselves (and other liberals) as such obviously caring people. It also is a simplistic way to contrast themselves with others, especially those uncaring hard-hearted conservatives. Just as important, liberals need victims and encourage groups, especially women and minorities, to feel victimized because it gives them their power base. The Clintons were at their political best creating victims, sympathizing with victims, and ultimately becoming victims themselves. What could be more energizing to their supporters—as well as to many other women—than having Hillary herself star as "the most degraded wife in the history of the world."

Although some found her energy and effervescence on the campaign trail utterly cynical and manipulative, those whose profession is marketing to women understood completely. *Cosmopolitan's* then editor Helen Gurley Brown rated the First Lady's performance "absolutely flawless."[38] On election night, she and her girlfriends celebrated her success in keeping the Senate and decreasing the Republican's majority in the House by watching a private White House screening of Oprah Winfrey's ultimate victim movie, *Beloved.*

Was playing the victim Hillary's staging platform for her Senate run? Absolutely. And during that $69 million race, she played the victim card whenever she could, most effectively when she and her supporters complained that mild-mannered congressman Rick Lazio, her outclassed opponent, had invaded her "personal space" during a debate and attacked her too aggressively on a variety of issues. As most insiders knew, putting nice-guy Lazio up against Hillary Clinton was like Stuart Little taking on Cruella De Vil, and we all know where nice guys finish. Women bought Hillary's performance as Victim of the Year. So did a lot of men. After her supposedly rough treatment from the hapless Lazio, her poll numbers spiked and never dropped. She won with 60 percent of the women's vote.

Currently, Hillary's increasing importance as a senator, her top committee assignments, her role as head of the Democratic Senate Steering Committee and her big-bucks best-seller make it less and less likely that she can play the victim. Still, her first move at the helm of the steering committee, which crafts the party's message, was to complain that conservative commentators have too much influence. Next we may hear that they are unfairly victimizing the Democrats, a political tactic that she has proven better than anyone can be very effective. As I write this, Hillary is the top choice of Democratic liberal activists as the presidential candidate in 2004, though insiders expect her to wait until 2008. It wouldn't surprise me, however, to see Bill conveniently fall off the marital wagon publicly sometime in 2007 just in time for the long-suffering senator to publicly don a victim's rags one more time.

By the way, during my interview with Hillary on that long-ago August day, she did tell me she hoped that there would be a woman president within twenty years. "There are many women who are fully capable." And when it happens, "I really hope that women will feel good about that," she said, as if acknowledging it is still difficult for most women to be enthusiastic about a powerful female.

It was the mantle of victimhood more than her fancy Yale law degree, more than her years at the Rose law firm, or even her constant attempts to direct policy from her office in the West Wing, that led Hillary to her victory as the senator from New York and could propel her to the top.

In truth, Hillary is just one of a group of supremely powerful women, some of whom have learned to expertly play the victim card for their own benefit, others who peddle victimization and fear in order to influence you for ratings and readership.

Many of those powerful women were my fellow guests, the Spin Sisters Supreme, at that "mother of all baby showers" Hillary hosted. Some, like Barbara and Diane and Katie, you have heard of but others maybe not. Many are talented, and ambitious, and smart; and, I must admit, some are friends of mine. But, much as I like and admire many of these successful women, I also know they are elitist, liberal, parochial, and pampered, and all of them believe that if you're a woman, you should think like them.

The truth is you don't really think like them any more than you live like them. But Media Queens and their counterparts in publishing along with the junior court—the writers, editors, reporters, producers, and Media Queen wannabes—have far more cultural and political influence than you might imagine or they would admit.

They are the ones who tell you you're frazzled, frumpy, fearful victims. In response, you buy cosmetics and join health spas and light aromatherapy candles and worry endlessly about everything from your children's self-esteem to the dangers of celery.

The Spin Sisters sell adeptly, skillfully, and very successfully. But over the years I have realized that if media for women is so clever at selling a cultural view of the world, they are also promoting—sometimes consciously, sometimes naively—a political view as well, one they hold and assume you should hold as well. Remember how Rosie's attempt to change a Florida law was so slickly packaged, spun, and sold, girlfriend to girlfriend? Buying into a liberal viewpoint depends, in part, on your being unthinkingly sympathetic to all who are needy. And aren't you encouraged to do exactly that when you are so often made to feel like a victim yourself?

Why not really get to know the women who decide what stories you see and read, find out who they are and what motivates them? Then you can decide for yourself what and how much you want to believe. Even better, let's do lunch!

CHAPTER 7

Media Queens at Work and Play

Let me introduce you to some members of the Spin Sisterhood, the female media elite. I know just where to find them. We'll go to Michael's, a fashionable restaurant tucked beneath a wine-colored awning on Manhattan's 55th Street, west of Fifth Avenue. Across from the front door, Loreal Sherman, the pretty dark-haired mâitre d' who has worked at the restaurant for ten years, sits by the phone carefully checking her list of reservations. Sweet-tempered and unflappable, she has become an expert at placing the right people at the right table.

Since its opening in 1989, the restaurant has drawn a potent mix of high-strung media mavens, leading one critic with a particularly nasty sense of humor to compare it to a "dog run in Midtown filled with expensive poodles."[1] On this summer Wednesday, Loreal knows it will probably be

177

the busiest day of the week. In summer, Mondays and Fridays—even Tuesdays and Thursdays—can be light because so many of Michael's regulars are off on long weekends at their country homes in the Hamptons, on the outer reaches of Long Island, or in Litchfield County, a leafy enclave in northwest Connecticut. By one o'clock, the long bright front room, preferred by those in television and publishing, and the back garden room, where cosmetic and fashion executives hang out, are buzzing with the kind of chatter found in only two habitats in New York—Michael's and the Bronx Zoo aviary.

So who's here today? Although there are many male regulars, the restaurant, with its widely spaced tables, colorful David Hockney and Jasper Johns lithographs and flattering light, is a special favorite of the Spin Sisters. Tanned, but not by the sun (they use Clarins SP 45 sunblock followed by Chanel self-tanner), these sleek-looking women—mostly trim, mostly blond, mostly Botoxed—are dressed in tight little dresses or pants and silky shirts. They wave at each other, air kiss, then settle down with their bottles of Evian or Pellegrino to order Michael's signature $27 Cobb Salad, "mixed and not chopped," "chopped and not mixed," "mixed and chopped, please, but without the bacon, the egg, the avocado, and with the dressing, of course, on the side."

This is the high-toned hangout of that all-powerful collection of columnists, writers, producers, editors, anchors, and assorted hangers-on who flock to Michael's for lunch and before and after make decisions on what you will and won't see on television and what you will or won't read in women's magazines.

The Lunch Bunch

On a typical midsummer Wednesday, one just might find Katie Couric sitting at a coveted table in the front. Katie, who so much wants us to believe she's just like us, is probably nibbling her salad like a perky little rabbit in stylish sandals and a trim little suit. But that's hardly surprising. When you hire a personal trainer like High Voltage, whose fees, rumor has it, start at an amazing $7,500 a week, you stay on your diet.[2] That willpower alone sets her apart from the rest of us. You gotta admit, though, that Katie is looking great these days and with the new hairdo, she's doing wonders for the hopes of the post-forty set. Of course, most of us don't spend $550 to cut and color our hair as Katie has done, but when you make $16 million a year that's spare change.[3] As *Good Housekeeping* breathlessly described her, "Couric has never looked better. She is toned and tan and taking care of herself, projecting a new physical sexiness that . . . has attracted a legion of male TV fans in love with her legs. . . . But Couric's allure runs far deeper. Fueled in part by intense inner strength [she has] become a woman who has grown into her own beauty."[4]

Still, Katie loves to play up the fact that she is just a "typical frazzled working mom" with, I guess, a typical $3 million East Side Manhattan apartment. She likes to share anecdotes about her career with women's groups and magazine reporters and tells one particular story over and over again. It seems that when Reese Schonfeld, then the head of CNN, watched her first performance reading the news, he declared her to be so hopeless he never wanted to see her on-camera again. Success is the best revenge, huh, Katie?

She also talks about her personal life as well. She has told a variety of women's magazines about how she coped after the death of her husband from colon cancer and has shared how she has handled a return to dating. Like the time her older daughter, Elinor, said that it would be okay for Katie to marry again but not okay for her to have sex. Katie assured her daughter, not to worry, that married couples rarely had sex. (Okay, in this instance, she might be a little like us.)

Whenever possible, Katie shrewdly plays up her unique combination of being just like all the Soccer Moms out there and not being a bit like them. In a speech in Buffalo, she shared with her audience the fact that when she was in LaGuardia Airport on the way to make the speech, she 'was on the phone setting up a play date for her daughter (bet that's just like your life) when she was beeped. A tad annoyed, she took the second call. Her staff told her they had President Carter on the line for her. "President Carter, who just won the Nobel Peace Prize?" she asked. "Okay, put him on," she said somewhat reluctantly. She shared that President Carter just wanted to thank her for all she had done for him over the years[5] (bet that's not a bit like your life).

Marketing analyst Jill Montaigne told me she was surprised that when she asked a group of advertisers to characterize different media companies as celebrities every advertiser saw Condé Nast, the publishers of *Vogue* and *Vanity Fair, The New Yorker,* and *Architectural Digest,* as Katie Couric. "I think they saw her as the perfect Condé Nast reader, someone who has made herself very glamorous and with-it, and now had a big Hollywood power broker on her arm." Katie, as every female magazine reader knows, has had an on-again, off-again romance with multimillionaire California producer Tom Werner, who brought us *The Cosby Show* and *Roseanne.* That romance begat Katie's "no sex, please, we're married" conversation with her daughter.

Katie, who continues to be one of the most popular cover personalities on women's magazines, along with being the highest-paid woman on television, may be loved by millions of her female viewers, but she has been taken to task by conservatives for years for an obvious liberal bias in her interviewing style. I know Elizabeth Dole was so annoyed by Katie's hard-edged questions during the Dole campaign that she would not attend a *Ladies' Home Journal* event at the Republican Convention the year her husband ran for president because Katie was acting, somewhat reluctantly, as MC.

Katie, for all her friendly persona, is one of the most hard-driving forces in media. Her staff, behind her back, allegedly calls her Katie Dearest.[6] Even Andy Lack, the former president of NBC, describes her as the "fist in the velvet glove," and, believe me, it's her personal interests and politics that shape what you see over your morning coffee.

At another table at Michael's, also in the front, we might see Diane Sawyer, just in from a short break at her weekend home on Martha's Vineyard, the playground of Manhattan's rich and famous media/political elite where Carly Simon, Mike Wallace, Walter Cronkite, the Kennedys, and the Clintons sail and sun while they bemoan the state of affairs in Washington over chilled martinis and Long Island iced tea. Diane is married to director Mike Nichols, and the sophisticated news and entertainment power couple are favorites of the New York media elite. In one story, a reporter drooled, "Sawyer is an American phenomena—a television blond whose beauty is said to be matched by her intelligence. The dimples. The low soothing voice. The impeccable clothes."[7] Diane likes to portray herself as an intellectual, uninterested in her looks, uninterested in fashion, though she is famous for running through airports in Manolo Blahniks (which means she might actually be superhuman—not a bit like us) and wearing Armani and Valentino.

Diane appears to have a special attraction for journalists who have been giving her adoring coverage for years. In one story early in her career, she is described as "brilliant, magnetic, industrious, inquisitive, disciplined, witty, gracious, charming and loyal."[8] With those kinds of accolades, she sounds more like a Boy Scout than a Media Queen ... except that Boy Scouts are politically incorrect today—something Diane would never be.

Diane has a tough streak, however. Once she characterized her pairing with reporter Sam Donaldson during the early days of the newsmagazine *Primetime Live* as "Emily Dickinson and the Terminator." One ABC insider at the time cracked, "I didn't know Sam wrote poetry."

While no Katie when it comes to putting on a happy face, Diane seems intent on creating a friendlier image these days, but the high priestess of the hidden camera (the weapon of choice on news-magazines) apparently has a strange way of showing it—to her own staff. For a 20/20 segment on lying, Diane invited six ABC producers to lunch for a gabfest and her homemade chili. What they didn't know was that Diane had dumped enough salt into the pot to preserve Liz Taylor and planted hidden cameras to record the reactions.

After she left the room, the producers, who were nicey-nice with Diane at the table—one vegetarian even felt compelled to dig in—started to complain, all of which was filmed for her later consumption. When the producers were let in on Diane's little "joke," few were laughing, especially, I would guess, those unlucky souls who had taken the opportunity to do some general trashtalking. Ironically, the piece never ran after one of those who had a serious Maalox moment supposedly talked to a lawyer.[9]

Diane, also politically shrewd, was a onetime Nixon staffer. But nowadays she appears in politically correct mode most of the time. Her husband, Mike Nichols, was an enthusiastic defender of Bill Clinton, at one point telling *Time* magazine, "We've often thought about our leaders. 'He's a great man and has a real gift with people.' . . . But the very gift that makes him a great leader is the same thing that keeps him jumping on a lot of women."

In a *Good Morning America* exchange, Diane was chatting about education with co-host Charlie Gibson, whose daughter was a Clinton staffer. He declared, "My wife has a sign on her office wall, and it says, 'Won't it be a great day when the Air Force has to hold bake sales to get a new bomber and the schools have all the money they need?'"

Sawyer grinned back. "I love your wife! I love her for many reasons. Love that sign!"[10] What neither Charlie nor Diane mentioned was that his wife, who you might have thought struggled to run P.S. 90

in the Bronx, is actually head of the Spence School, one of Manhattan's most exclusive, expensive, and well-endowed private schools for girls.

ABC's other reigning diva, Barbara Walters, is also lunching at Michael's today, though not with Katie and certainly not with Diane. For the past three decades, Barbara has always been near the top of the Most Admired Women lists. I have always thought of her affectionately as the Rabbi's Wife of television, both smart enough and assertive enough to ask precisely the questions you want answered. But, thank God, you don't have to ask them, as long as Barbara is around. Barbara reveals a more casual side these days on her girl talk show, *The View*. Her long career, which started as a writer on the *Today* show in 1961, reflects the history of women's achievements both as a pioneer of change and a beneficiary of such change.

Barbara's probably at a table in the corner in a tête-a-tête with her good friend Liz Smith, the most popular gossip columnist in America. Liz is over eighty and still going strong, and while not technically a Media Queen, she has enormous influence in both television and print circles. Genial and down-to-earth, philanthropic, and a good old Texas gal, she is not above asking, when sent a pair of inexpensive slippers as a token Christmas gift from a publication, for another pair in a larger size. Most often, she peppers her daily column with kisses and hugs in the form of complimentary items about her media pals Diane Sawyer, Helen Gurley Brown, Tina Brown, and, of course, Barbara Walters. Liz also has a six-figure writing contract with *Good Housekeeping* to interview some of the celebrities she writes about in her column.

The satirical magazine *Spy* used to do a monthly count of how many times Liz adoringly mentioned her friends. But she has a sharp tone now and again, and nowadays, even though she is a fan of almost all Texans, including Barbara Bush, her barbs are most often aimed directly at the president and the current administration. She started one column by quoting from playwright Tony Kushner's Vassar graduation address. Liz wrote, "Kushner equates President George W. Bush with evil; in fact he refers to the chief executive as 'Evil,' saying he's 'chewing pretzels and fondly flipping through the scrapbook reminiscing about the 152 people he executed when he was governor.'" Liz called Kushner's ramblings "hilarious."[11] That same week, she editorialized in her column, "See if you think we are maybe being taken for a big ride on many fronts by a presidency that wants unending powers to raise money, detain the suspected without civil rights, create bureaucracies and 'wage war' while also raising infinite amounts of money for politics without end."[12]

In the past, if Liz was ever called on the carpet about her political views, she always pooh-poohed the importance of her column, which appears in newspapers throughout the country, saying it is just gossip and that, heck, nobody takes an old gal like her very seriously. Yeah, right. And Tony Soprano is just a businessman with an attitude.

Nowadays Liz has been a lot more defensive about her political opinions, and has started harrumphing, "I am really fed up with people telling me to write 'gossip' and leave the serious stuff to the experts. . . . Why shouldn't someone like me . . . have political opinions?"[13]

At the next table, we might find another of Liz's pals, Tina Brown, the Madonna of modern editing, who invented "buzz" as a necessary magazine marketing tool. A longtime fan of both Clintons, her career as editor of *Vanity Fair* and *The New Yorker* thrived during the years of the Clinton presidency. When she was its editor, Tina once wrote an adoring mash note to Clinton for *The New Yorker* after attending a White House party for Tony Blair: "See him as his guests do," she cooed, "a man in a dinner jacket with more heat than any star in the room. His height, his sleekness, his newly cropped iron filing hair, and the intensity of his blue eyes. . . . He is vividly in the present tense and dares you to join him there."[14] Tina may have tried to cover up her obvious crush with a bit of literary flair but, really, it was nothing more than the stuff of teen diaries, all gushy and adoring. But it paid off. Tina spent part of Election Night 2000 with the Clintons celebrating Hillary's senatorial victory.

Her Clinton connections came back to haunt her, however, when she became editor of the now defunct *Talk* magazine, a $50 million media disaster. She lost all access to the Bush White House when she ran a satirical photo essay showing models made up to look like the Bush teenage twin daughters behind prison bars. Many of *Talk's* editors thought the photo spread was in bad taste and warned Tina about publishing it. But Harvey Weinstein, who was *Talk's* principal backer along with the Hearst Corporation, just so happens to be a top Democratic fund-raiser. Funny how these coincidences pop up.

On any given day at Michael's, you might also see Cathie Black, the attractive president of Hearst Magazines, at a table near the wall. *Crain's New York Business* has proclaimed, "Nobody in New York embodies the magazine business like Cathleen Black,"[15] who is smart, capable, and extremely personable and is acknowledged to have done a superb job at the helm of the Hearst billion-dollar magazine empire. Hearst publishes many of America's largest and most successful magazines, including *Cosmopolitan, Good Housekeeping, Redbook, House Beautiful, Esquire,* and *Harper's Bazaar,* as well as 112 other magazines in over 100 countries around the world.

Cathie is credited with overseeing the very successful launch of *O,* the Oprah magazine, which is now, after *Cosmopolitan,* the second most profitable of all Hearst publications, even outdistancing the century-old *Good Housekeeping.* Hearst, usually considered a fairly conservative company, is a funder of one of the country's most powerful left-of-center feminist groups, NOW's Legal Defense Fund. The Ms. Foundation gets contributions from Diane Sawyer.[16] These groups attract donors saying, "By contributing to us, you are supporting women and women's issues." But only *some* women and their issues.

A Cause to Believe In

At Michael's, Cathie is most likely to be lunching with one of the Hearst editors who report to her, such as Glenda Bailey, the current editor of *Harper's Bazaar,* who was formerly the editor of *Marie Claire,* another Hearst magazine. Glenda is a flame-haired Brit with a broad, almost unintelligible east Midlands accent. She is extremely liberal politically and so outspoken that she once proclaimed that what America needed was a Department of Women like State or Treasury with a Secretary of Women to redress the many wrongs done to the female population in this country. Of course, she told this to a group of female overachievers who all made six- and seven-figure salaries with large expense accounts to sweeten the deal. For most of these women, losing their car and driver or their lavish wardrobe allowance is the closest they'd come to discrimination. Unfortunately, the 1964 Civil Rights Act doesn't guarantee chauffeurs and Chanels.

Glenda's left-wing politics constantly spilled over into *Marie Claire,* most notably when she championed the cause of a woman named "Adelaide Abankwah" who "left her homeland" of Ghana "to escape genital mutilation."

The piece about "Adelaide" appeared in the magazine under the alarming headline: "Why Are Women Who Escape Genital Mutilation Being Jailed in America?"[17] The story recounted Adelaide's supposedly tragic plight. She told the *Marie Claire* reporter, "My mother was the Queen of our tribe. She had been sick, but was strong, and I did not expect her to die. I thought I was safe to marry my boyfriend. But she did die, and it was the tradition that her firstborn become the Queen. To succeed the Queen, you must be holy—a virgin. My grandmother planned a marriage for me. I told her I had a boyfriend and that when they tested me before marriage they would find out I wasn't a virgin.

They wanted to punish me by cutting my genitals. . . . Escape was [my] only option."[18] How tragic! How gruesome! How perfect for *Marie Claire*. A woman being punished for being sexually liberated. But when she arrived in America, the immigration authorities noted Adelaide's phony passport and didn't buy her "I must be holy or else" lament. She was packed off to a detention center. The lawyers who interviewed her didn't buy her full-of-"holy" story either, but Glenda did, and made freeing Adelaide "a personal mission" and a *"Marie Claire* campaign."

Glenda visited Adelaide frequently at the detention center, went to court with her, and enlisted the aid of liberal leading ladies including Gloria Steinem, Congresswoman Carolyn Maloney, Julia Roberts, and finally First Lady Hillary Clinton. Their combined clout got Adelaide sprung and even had *The New York Times* bewailing her ordeal: "When asked by a reporter to describe the genital cutting process that she might have faced in her homeland, Ms. Abankwah paused and her eyes filled with tears."[19] *Media Industry News* also praised Glenda's spunky championing of Adelaide's cause.[20]

Now what's the Ghanian word for baloney? The problem—I bet you guessed—was that Adelaide was a royal phony. "Princess Abankwah" was in fact a hotel worker named Regina Danson, who had allegedly stolen the real Abankwah's identity and cooked up her persecution story to gain asylum. *Marie Claire* should have titled the story, "Made Up in Manhattan." Her "Queen" mother was still alive, and there was no tradition of female mutilation in the area of Ghana where Danson lived and worked. According to the real Abankwah's lawyer, "Danson ruined my client's life, embarrassed her family, and ruined the credibility of all bona-fide asylum seekers."[21]

Although Glenda's politics are a lot more out front than most, she is a fairly typical Spin Sister. Most women editors, producers, and writers may be more discreet, but they tend privately to share the same attitudes, opinions, and allegiances. And they are not shy about voicing them around other media types whom they assume agree with them. Believe me, Michael's would not be fertile ground for a Republican women's recruitment drive.

Jane Chesnutt is the longtime and very capable editor of *Woman's Day*, whose readers, by and large, tend to be middle-aged, middle income, and middle American. But she wasn't the least bit wary of sharing her opinion of President Bush during a Magazine Publisher Association's day-long series of briefings by various figures in the administration. Among them was Secretary of State Colin Powell, one of the Republicans who gets the Girls' Club Seal of Approval because they've convinced each other anyone that reasonable couldn't really be a Republican. Over lunch, Jane commented to the other editors at her table, "I like Laura Bush. Women like Laura Bush. She's reassuring. She makes women feel, well, if she can stand George, he can't be such an idiot. . . . Oh, whoops, I guess my politics are showing."

Kind of. But politically correct sniping, a criteria for membership in the Spin Sorority, is as expected as Susan Sarandon at an anti-war rally. In recent years, poll after poll, including ones done by the *Los Angeles Times*, Gallup, the Kaiser Family Foundation, the American Society of Newspaper Editors, the Freedom Forum, and the Pew Research Center have shown that editors and journalists tend to be politically liberal and that women in media tend to be even more liberal than men.[22] Just looking around Michael's, one can see many women who, like Katie and Tina and Liz, have made their Democratic party enthusiasm clear through the years. Like Ellen Levine, the very talented and elegant silver-haired editor of *Good Housekeeping*, who friends say might once have hoped to become Senator Bill Bradley's presidential press secretary. Or Esther Newberg, a top literary agent at ICM, a powerhouse New York and Los Angeles talent and literary agency. Esther, who represents many best-selling authors, takes extra special care of a favorite client, Caroline Kennedy Schlossberg, who has started producing a series of books, including

The Best Loved Poems of Jacqueline Kennedy Onassis, which takes advantage of her mother's name to climb the best-seller list but, at the same time, remains primly discreet. Caroline also writes about American history.

Esther, who once was Congresswoman Bella Abzug's administrative assistant, has had a long and special relationship with the Kennedy family. She was one of the "boiler room girls" partying with Ted Kennedy and his cousin Joe Gargan on that fateful night in Chappaquiddick when Mary Jo Kopechne died. In fact, Esther was Mary Jo's motel roommate for that weekend.[23]

Today nobody would ever dare to mention Chappaquiddick to Esther or ask about Mary Jo's death from one of the few people who might be able to add more details to the story of that night. Funny, the biggest book she could ever publish might be her own, but we're more likely to see Janeane Garofalo gobbling a Cobb with Bill O'Reilly at Michael's before Esther Newberg spills the Kennedy beans.

Esther has a fierce temper and likes to slam down telephones in the middle of business discussions that don't go her way. She once had a waiter at Michael's deliver a silver platter stacked with coins to an editor who had dared rush out a book in advance of one that a client of hers was writing on the same subject.[24] Now that, to Esther—forget Chappaquiddick—was unethical.

Other Michael lunchers include Bonnie Fuller, the recently appointed editorial director of American Media Inc., which owns the supermarket tabloids, *The National Enquirer* and *The Star,* and the former editor of *Us, Glamour, Cosmopolitan, Marie Claire,* and *YM.* Bonnie, a Canadian, is the only editor who gets almost as much attention as Tina Brown in the columns about media in the New York papers and the media gossip Web sites that producers and editors surf to the point of addiction. Nobody but nobody is as interested in the media as the media. With all those hours sitting at the computer I'm surprised the club hasn't had a victim of Economy Class syndrome.

But if it did, *The New York Times* obit would relabel it First Class syndrome or nobody would show up for the funeral.

Bonnie, shrewd and extraordinarily hardworking, has for the past fifteen years ricocheted from one women's magazine to another, vastly increasing her salary and, many say, dumbing down whatever publication she was editing by increasing its focus on sex and shopping. Bonnie was the first to add fart jokes to the teenage magazines—certainly a journalistic milestone—and then coy locker room sex language to *Cosmo* and *Glamour*. Also outspokenly liberal, she endorsed Gore in the 2000 election, warning *Glamour* girls not to be "Bush-whacked" by an administration that would "take away your rights." Doesn't this hyperbole seem vaguely familiar to you? It should, because it's just a political version of the victim virus and the fear factor, playing on the same emotions that send you screaming from the nail salon or dumping plastic-wrapped cheese the way J.Lo dumps husbands.

Holding court at a side table, we might find the whippet-thin Anna Wintour, who is reputed to earn more than $1 million a year and have a $50,000-a-year clothes allowance. When Anna, at a Women in Communications lunch, received an award, she proudly announced, in her crisp British accent and with a totally straight face, that *Vogue*, in response to 9/11, was launching a historic new fashion industry initiative to help the recently liberated but still downtrodden women of Afghanistan. And what was this grand humanitarian effort? Was it modern obstetrical care that was sorely needed in this country where a woman dies from complications during pregnancy and childbirth every twenty minutes? Or maybe better access to the education forbidden to women under the Taliban? No, Anna proudly announced that *Vogue* was going to lead an effort to bring beauty salons to Afghanistan. I'm serious—and so was she. Anna, who has her own hair and makeup done each day by professionals in her office, said she was sure beauty parlors were absolutely critical to the building of self-esteem for Afghan women. Call me crazy, but doesn't a women's hospital seem a little more useful? At least she didn't suggest day spas.

Anna is a woman of her word and has great power in the fashion world. She promptly put the squeeze on various cosmetics companies to donate products and create a curriculum for a beauty school in Kabul. L'Oréal Matrix agreed to support Anna's initiative and provide training on how to color and texturize hair as well as provide "salon-business-building skills."[25] *Vanity Fair* lauded Anna's efforts, thrilled that there was now a place where aid workers could "get their roots done."[26] Ignored was the fact that the average woman in Afghanistan has a few more problems than bad hair days.

Before she went on maternity leave we might also find Lisa Caputo, a regular, at lunch, possibly with Ann Richards, the witty former Democratic governor of Texas. After leaving the White House, Lisa landed at CBS, then Disney, before becoming the head of Citibank's financial advisory service for women called Women & Co. Both Disney and Citibank have big-name Democrats at the helm. Democratic contributor Michael Eisner is the head of Disney and former Treasury Secretary Robert Rubin is a top Citibank executive. Now Lisa holds a luncheon for women each year with Rubin as the speaker. Rubin, who always appears modest, gets his chance to modestly trash the current administration's economic policies and to modestly reminisce favorably about his own.

Ann Richards, who is also one of Liz Smith's best friends, now heads the New York office of a political public relations firm. She also recently wrote a book about osteoporosis with Dr. Richard U. Levine, who is the husband of Ellen Levine, the editor-in-chief of *Good Housekeeping*, where Liz Smith is a frequent contributor. A wave distance away, at the table across from Ann's, we might find Kati Marton, the author of *Hidden Power* about presidential marriages, which Tina excerpted in *Talk*. Kati, who is very pretty with great style, used to be married to Peter Jennings and now is married to Richard Holbrooke, who was Bill Clinton's ambassador to the U.N. and was assumed to be the top candidate for Secretary of State in a Gore administration.

Forget six degrees of separation. These women, just a few of New York's reigning queens of print and TV, are practically joined at the hip—professionally, socially, and politically. They know each other, lunch with each other frequently, eat dinner at each other's weekend homes, attend each other's parties and fund-raisers, envy each other, do favors for each other when it means they are also helping themselves, and agree with each other, especially about anything that has to do with social issues and politics. To do so is so very comfortable, convenient, and, often, as it turns out, profitable. As Don Forst, the editor-in-chief of New York's *The Village Voice,* a Manhattan weekly, says, of the media elite, "The people who hang out together . . . have the smoothest cheeks in the world because they kiss each other so much. . . . They all read the same papers . . . they all endorse each other's books; and they all think they're wonderful."[27]

They hang out with each other unless, of course, one of them has a problem like their friend Martha Stewart, who celebrated the launch of her IPO on the New York Stock Exchange with a party at Tina Brown's elegant East Side town house, which, according to *The New York Observer,* includes "a library, six baths and three maid's rooms" and cost a cool $4 million. One "loo, designed for a captive audience," is covered in carefully preserved press clippings about Tina and her husband, editor Harry Evans.[28]

When Tina asked Martha solicitously how she felt that day, when Martha's stock had soared from $18 to $35, Martha's smug reply was: "Rich." In a more recent and less smug time (her stock is now way down), Martha had to cancel the Democratic senatorial fund-raiser she was hosting when the embarrassing ImClone insider trading scandal broke.[29] Not a good thing.

Agreeing with each other about practically everything keeps these women in the social and professional loop and helps them get the celebrities they need for the covers of the magazines they edit or for the TV talk shows they anchor or produce and for the exclusive gossipy little items they need for their columns and for the articles they write. And that translates into the enormous media power they enjoy and the mind-boggling salaries they earn.

Grrrrl Power

It's really not surprising to see that lists of important or powerful women almost always include the television Media Queens, with Oprah usually near the very top.[30] Although you won't find her at Michael's; it's a long cab ride from Chicago. Interestingly, when it comes to the Most Powerful Men in America lists, the same just isn't true about the male media stars, no matter how successful they may be.

When it comes to television, the network anchors and cable commentators may be guys at the very top of their journalistic profession, but there are other men in government and industry who are more powerful or highly paid and are considered even more successful. And though Sean and Bill have great influence with their fans, they are usually preaching to the converted.

But women media stars, who are part of our daily lives, with their combination of fame and familiarity, intelligence, and glamour magnified by the power of media, which gives them access to everyone and everything, makes them a force like no other; one that is uniquely influential. Right there in our living rooms, morning and night, like our most sophisticated girlfriends, they combine relaxed girl talk with discussions of serious issues, share the latest diets along with the latest political polls, act as impressed by celebrities as the viewers may be themselves yet seem all-knowing when important news breaks.

Oprah, Katie, and Diane, according to a Pew Poll on the Press in 2002 about the public's attitude toward the media, are respected and trusted by their audiences.[31] And, along with Barbara Walters, they have become symbols of the increasing achievement of women. Yet for all their superstar appeal and role-model accomplishments, day in and day out, our Spin Sisters Supreme market themselves as ordinary women and always seem so concerned about the problems and needs of women, in general. Male media stars are just not like that. Maybe, that's why, we may listen to Tom and Peter and Dan at night, but we respect Katie in the morning.

But should we? Should we listen to Katie or Barbara, or Diane or Glenda or Tina or the rest of the Spin Sisters more skeptically when they tell their tales of fear and victimhood, sell us their view of what's hot and what's not, and sometimes push their own left-of-center political agendas? I'll report. You decide. Don't get me wrong. In many ways, I admire these women. Getting to where they are isn't easy. They are all very smart, very hardworking, very talented women who have reached the top of their profession. Good for them! But good for you? Maybe not.

When most of us have a problem, we seek and get advice from family, friends, and colleagues. We know them; we trust them; we tend to share the same values. Okay, everybody has a crazy cousin out there who still has a poster of Che on her wall and thinks doffing her clothes in a PETA fur protest is a serious political statement. But for the most part, we want advice from people who understand our lives. But most of the members of the Girls' Club, $16-million-a-year Katie included, no matter how much they try to act like girlfriends, don't share your problems or your lifestyle and probably not many of your political or moral views either.

Do we have a disconnect here? You bet. By definition, Girls' Clubbies are no more in touch with you and the reality of your life than Anna Wintour is with the poor women of Afghanistan. Well, maybe a little. Still, you shouldn't be surprised because what our Queens of Media are focused on isn't your life exactly, no matter how much they may seem like pals. They are concerned with getting big ratings or increasing newsstand sales or pleasing their important advertisers. They are wildly competitive, especially with one another, and the pressures of their jobs can make them behave in ways that may surprise and even disappoint you. Not only do these women not live like you or think like you, they do things you probably wouldn't do either. And there is no better example of just how far out or even how low down a Media Queen must go to get ahead than what she'll do to "get the get." What's the "get?" It's *the* interview everybody wants with the headline newsmaker of the moment or the hottest celebrity or even the latest serial killer. It gets you ratings, readers, and most important, it gets you noticed.

So let's finish the cappuccino, get our check, wave Michael's goodbye, and see what really goes on behind the scenes when the Media Queens go to work. And that starts, as it usually does, in Mediaville, with a party.

CHAPTER 8

Getting the "Get" (and Other Adventures)

It was a big-buzz pour at 21, one of New York's fanciest restaurants, for Connie Chung, who had just signed a $2 million annual contract with CNN for what turned out to be her short-lived interview show. At the party Connie got up and sang to the tune of "Get Me to the Church on Time" her own chirpy version called "Get Me to the 'Get' on Time." She warbled how she'd "outmaneuver Barbara Walters," and "trip Diane Sawyer," in pursuit of a hot interview, and ended by crooning, "That's right, Osama, come talk to Mama! Just get me to the 'get' on time."

Almost everyone at the party cheered and applauded, believing that Connie was truly telling it like it is. Though I must admit that stodgy old me wondered if Osama Bin Laden should ever be a comic punch line even in a clever parody.

Still, Connie, like Barbara and Diane and Katie, like all ferocious competitors, understands the power of the "gets"—the big, exclusive, headline-grabbing interviews that will get them and their shows the megawatt ratings that determine life and death in TV land. It was probably Connie's unexpected big ratings "get" with Congressman Gary Condit at the height of the Chandra Levy hysteria that led directly to her prime-time CNN contract. Her tour of duty there lasted nine months.

But then, Connie has had her ups and downs before. She even wrote a tell-all paper, "The Business of Getting 'The Get'—Nailing an Exclusive Interview in Prime Time," when she was at Harvard's Joan Shorenstein Center on Press, Politics and Public Policy after the bitter breakup of her co-anchor "marriage" with Dan Rather at CBS.

Remember that star-crossed media coupling? Dan told Bill Clinton just after he and Connie got it together that, "If we could be one-hundredth as great as you and Hillary Rodham Clinton have been in the White House, we'd take it right now and walk away winners."[1] But then I guess you can never believe what a guy says on the honeymoon, now can you?

Connie's also made a few other memorable stumbles along the way. She was at her most shameless when she asked Newt Gingrich's elderly mother what "Newtie" said in private about Hillary. When the older woman tried to duck answering, Connie sweetly coaxed, "Why don't you just whisper it to me. Just between you and me."

And about 18 million other people.

But those big "gets" are super important, a serious cutthroat stress-inducing business for our Media Queens and those who work for them. Neal Shapiro, the president of NBC News, explained, "It's the big interview that causes viewers to find you and watch. It's the difference between a twelve share and a twenty share"[2]—the yardstick of success in TV viewing. Mostly, the "get" game is played by women, starting with young women, the bookers and producers who work for network news divisions, the junior Spin Sisters. Usually ambitious and hyperactive, focused on their work, they compete with each other like tryouts for *Survivor,* and, in a way, that's exactly what they're doing. Trying to survive the cut in one of the most competitive businesses around; and so, for these young women, virtually nothing is out-of-bounds when trying to land a trophy guest. On the phone hour after hour, they plead and beg, telling potential interviewees, "It will make my career," or "I'll get a raise—and I need it desperately to pay my bills," or even, "If you don't come on, I know I'm gonna lose my job."

Amy Rosenblum, now executive producer for Maury Povich, remembers her first "get" for *CBS Morning News.* "The guest wanted to back out at the last minute. He called around five in the afternoon the day before the show. I started to sweat and thought fast. I told him nobody was allowed to cancel after four-thirty. It was just *not allowed!* He believed me. I realized that you needed street smarts, chutzpah, the ability to connect with people and be able to say anything to do the job. I knew I could do it."[3]

The competition between bookers currently may be fiercest on the morning television shows that are cash cows for the networks. Occasionally this has led to nasty name-calling dustups. A case in point— *Good Morning America* and the *Today* show's battle over an exclusive with the Antelope Valley girls, those California teenagers who had been kidnapped, raped, and ultimately saved by the Amber Alert system in the summer of 2002. That time, *Today* got the interview, but the *GMA* staffers squealed that their competitors over at Rockefeller Center had used dirty tricks to bag the two unsuspecting teenagers.

Rumors flew that one determined producer, in pursuit of the "gets," had swerved her car into another producer's on the highway. One, employing a creative "ratting" strategy, called the police to complain that the competition was stalking the girls, and they needed protection. But the award for most offensive "go-getter" of the week goes to the producer who sobbed to the girls that she would get fired unless she got the interview. So, the two high schoolers, who had just been raped and nearly killed, were supposed to feel sorry for *her?*

NBC finally admitted that one of their *Today* producers did buy one of the girls $80 worth of clothes, which is against NBC policy and pretty cheap, at that. But, according to the network, the producer did it only because she "felt bad for someone going through such an emotional time." I'm sure that was the only reason.

And even though ABC and CBS expected to do their own interviews later with the girls, the NBC producers told the teens, after they had talked to Katie, that "they shouldn't do those interviews" and whisked them away in a limousine.[4] All's fair in love and television.

But then maybe *Today* felt it was payback time since, a few days earlier, Katie lost an interview with Dennis Hall, one of the nine coal miners rescued after three days trapped in a mine in Pennsylvania. Katie thought she had the interview when the "get" got away and decided, at the last minute, to talk to Diane instead. *Good Morning America*'s chief, Shelly Ross, said that a producer had "spent many hours" with the Hall family while rescuers worked to free him and the others.[5] News alert! Embedded journalism didn't start with the Iraq war.

Producers have inserted themselves into tragic situations for years, brimming over with empathy and comfort for the grief-stricken and the scandal-plagued in the hopes of snaring that first big interview with sobbing parents or spouses or the next Monica. It certainly paid off for ABC. When Katie learned that Diane was getting the miner, and she was getting the shaft, she allegedly blew up at *Today*'s executive producer, Jonathan Wald. A few months later, Wald was quietly replaced because industry sources said he just "did not play well with Katie."[6]

Making Nice

It's not just the junior leaguers who are willing to do some high-powered groveling to get the big interview. Sometimes the competition makes our high-salaried Media Queens sink to a pretty low level, too. Yes, these women, who have their multimillion-dollar paychecks partly because of the trust and respect we invest in them, can behave in ways that we and they surely know are simply wrong. Ways we wouldn't want our real friends to behave.

Take Katie, for example. Four boys had just drowned in a tragic accident in Lawrence, Massachusetts, plunging through thin ice on the Merrimack River. Katie Couric interviewed two boys who survived the same freezing water. She peppered them with questions, asking, "How did all this happen?" "What was that like for you?" To the nine-year-old boy who had tried and failed to hold on to his friend, she said, "Francis, I know that for a period of time you were holding on to a little seven-year-old boy [and] trying to keep him afloat. Can you describe what you were going through when you were trying to do that?"

When little Francis, overcome with weeping, could only reply, "It's a little hard for me," Katie persisted, milking the moment for every drop of melodrama. "Can you describe, at least, what you felt like in the water, Francis?"[7]

Dr. David Fassler, a child psychiatrist associated with the University of Vermont, says, "It can actually exacerbate the impact of a trauma to push kids to tell their story or to encourage extensive media contact with them."[8] Now, you can wonder why the boys' family allowed the interview. But you can also wonder why it was conducted at all. I would imagine that if Katie's own seven-year-old daughter had been in that little boy's shoes, she would not have wanted her to be prodded by a television interviewer—by *anybody*—to stop crying and speak up about what was clearly an emotionally devastating experience.

Still we watch. We do. Partly because this wholesome girl-next-door whom we are supposed to admire for her achievements and success and like for her good deeds and perkiness is leading the way, encouraging us to look and listen, implicitly assuring us that our voyeurism is not only permissible but appropriate. And, after all, getting the interview with the two young survivors was another competitive coup for the *Today* show, though the program's executive producer declared that getting the Merrimack River interview had nothing to do with beating out *Good Morning America*. "I just want to put on the air the best show that we can put on," he insisted.[9] But does being the best mean having one of the highest-paid, best-known, most popular women in our country using her star power to make a grief-stricken little boy tell us how his friend slipped from his grasp?

There is no situation too tragic to be exploited any more than there is no celebrity Media Queens won't butter up, no matter how awful the "gets" behavior. Remember Barbara Walters being oh-so-respectful during her interview with eccentric Sharon Osbourne? The interview was such a rating bonanza that ABC broadcast it twice. At one point during the interview, Barbara asked Sharon, "Is it true you once sent someone you didn't like a box full of feces?"

Sharon sheepishly admitted, "Yeah, I have done it. A few times. In a Tiffany box."

"You're nothing if not elegant," Barbara quipped.[10]

Elegant? Audrey Hepburn was elegant. Jackie O. was elegant. Yet, from this award-winning journalist whom we respect and admire, we get a touch of sarcasm, not an honest reaction to this utterly despicable, crude way of behaving. There's the problem. It's not that journalists haven't always interviewed celebrities. They have, and we have always wanted to read or see those interviews. But now even top journalists seem so grateful when they get their big interview that they are often blandly sympathetic and accepting no matter how the celebrity misbehaves. If Barbara Walters doesn't murmur the obvious,

"Sharon, that's disgusting," doesn't it make setting standards of behavior, or even believing there *should* be standards, a lot tougher for us all?

In recent years, Barbara has moved farther away from the hard news interviews that began her career and more into that foggy half news/half gossip format that defines her celebrity specials. In fact, Neal Gabler, author of *Life the Movie: How Entertainment Conquered Reality*, said, "Barbara Walters is a remarkable phenomenon because she helped answer a very difficult question for television: How can we devise a format to get in on the celebrity action? . . . Walters, who was by all appearances a newswoman, smuggled celebrity interviews into her newsmagazine programs and specials. . . . Suddenly there were stars on television answering the most personal questions under the aegis of a respectable news organization, namely ABC. Once these interviews were sanctioned as some sort of news, every other network news organization had to follow suit or lose the entertainment war."[11]

Nowadays when Barbara does go back to basics with a head of state, she tends to treat a dictator almost as gently as the wife of a rock star. In 2002 she earned the Media Research Center's "And They Call it Puppy Love Award," a tongue-in-cheek "honor," for her follow-up interview with Fidel Castro, twenty-five years after last talking with him. Narrating the feature, she gushed, "For Castro, freedom starts with education. And if literacy alone were the yardstick, Cuba would rank as one of the freest nations on Earth. The literacy rate is 96 percent."[12] Just a few months after that interview, "Professor" Castro taught Barbara and the other television and Hollywood celebrities who had made similar pilgrimages to Cuba in recent years a lesson by summarily executing three boat people and throwing most of the Cuban dissident community, including many journalists, into prison. According to Reporters Without Borders, an organization that reports on freedom of the press worldwide, Cuba has more journalists in prison than any other country. The only country more restrictive to the press is North Korea.

Perhaps Barbara's ultimate performance, however, came in her annual Academy Awards special in 2003 with nominee Julianne Moore. Since Moore had kissed a woman in *The Hours,* one of the films for which she was nominated, Barbara proposed that the forty-ish actress do the same to her. Obviously, Barbara had decided to try what seemed to be the season's trendy ratings booster—girl-on-girl kissing. Moore was clearly taken aback, but Barbara pushed on; and in the end, Moore, who should have won an Oscar just for being such a good sport, humored Barbara with a quick peck. I guess it was the way to get some buzz for the special.

Diane also has conducted interviews high on promotion values and short on substance, short even on basic journalism. Remember, it was Diane Sawyer who managed to keep a straight face during her Michael Jackson interview when then wife, Lisa Marie Presley, declared, "Yes, yes, yes!" they did have sex. And the Queen of Cool didn't even try to probe further when Jackson said he had "Never, ever," molested a young boy though he paid a boy's family $20 million to drop a case against him.

During that interview Lisa Marie, sounding like a witness for the prosecution, offered this defense, "[The kids] they jump into bed with him. . . . I know he has a thing for kids." Diane didn't explore that virgin territory, either.

Of course, the battles are fiercest when the Media Queens themselves are directly involved in "getting those gets." When Katie signed her new megabucks contract and said that she was going to start doing an occasional evening interview show, Barbara Walters complained jokingly to her pals on *The View,* "Of course, I love Katie, but there just aren't enough celebrities to go around." Still, Barbara remains the master at securing the big interview. She does this by writing notes, sending elegant gifts, extending invitations to her antique-laden apartment for tea and cookies, and being, according to one interviewee she was courting, "the most charming person in the entire nation." This, even though she told Connie Chung, "The least pleasant part of the job is the competition. All of us hate booking. I hate talking to people when friends and colleagues are going after them. It's debilitating."[13] Maybe so, but not enough to stop doing it.

Other Media Queens use their own techniques. To reel in her "gets," Diane Sawyer makes the most of her languid glamour, her intellectual appeal, and the double-whammy power of her perch on *Good Morning America* as well as her evening interview show. Like Barbara, Diane also protests, methinks too loudly, the demeaning aspects of "getting the get." When competing, "Lawyers show you other people's letters," she said, "and [have you listen] to their phone calls. . . . The ritual has everybody by the throat."[14] Still, Diane wasn't above penning her own letter to the mother of Samantha Runnion, a five-year-old who was abducted and murdered. The note was delivered to the mother's neighbor by an ABC employee who said that Diane was on her way to Los Angeles and wanted to put the mother on her show and that such interviews could be "cathartic."[15] Diane also sent a locket as a get-well gift to Private Jessica Lynch when she was in the hospital. Katie sent the Iraqi war veteran a stack of patriotic books as part of her pitch.[16] Diane got the interview.

But then the 2003 fall sweeps period was one of intense competition among these divas of dish. After a three-way tussle with *Good Morning America* and Oprah, Katie won crowing rights to the "first, exclusive interview" with Utah's Elizabeth Smart and her family. Katie's hour-long prime-time Smart-talk turned into a bland informercial for the family's book about the kidnap ordeal. And though Katie's few on-camera moments with Elizabeth were highly promoted, the blond teenager gave monosyllabic answers to Katie's relentlessly cheery questions. Barbara's "gets" during the same period were Diana's blabbermouth butler Paul Burrell and a previously closemouthed Martha Stewart. And Katie, in advance, scored an exclusive with reporter Jayson Blair, whose faked stories led to a shake-up at *The New York Times.* *Times* columnist Maureen Dowd, for once indirectly criticizing a Spin Sister, sniffed, "The seriously creepy Jayson Blair is riding his con to fame and bucks. He has now replaced Elizabeth Smart as the carnival 'get' who should be got."

Ironically, the world's most famous interviewers, Diane and Barbara and Katie, rarely reveal much about themselves in interviews they give. And when they do, they go into spasms of media paranoia for weeks afterward. Whenever we interviewed either Diane or Barbara for the *Journal*, both would always call back to change quotes, explain further, try to find out exactly what photo was going to be used on the cover. For years, Barbara was particularly circumspect about her private life and the problems she had during her adopted daughter's difficult adolescence. "I didn't know whether to kill her or kill myself," she says, recalling that time. They are now close, and her daughter now runs a "tough love" school for troubled adolescents in Maine.

When we did a piece on Katie for the *Journal*, she was annoyed by my decision not to use a picture that included her nanny at the time. No perky Katie here, she threatened to pull out of the interview if we didn't feature the nanny as part of the family. We didn't relent, and she finally acquiesced—lucky for her, as it turned out. The nanny left shortly afterward and started trying to peddle "insider" stories on Katie and family.[17]

When in "get-the-get" mode, Katie, no surprise, can be very cute. Like the time she sent Tonya Harding's lawyer a cake with an inscription in frosting, "We Refuse to Stop Sucking Up."[18] The sentiment was actually closer to the truth than you will ever get Katie or any other Media Queen to admit. Katie used that same friendly tone when trying to curry favor with enviro-terrorist Ted Kaczynski, the Unabomber. In her cheery pitch letter to a man who murdered three people and injured twenty-two others, she said she would like to give him the chance to explain his experiences "to our huge audience," "to share your views," and would be more than "happy to just come and meet" with him if he thought "it would be helpful."[19] To hear Katie chirp, one might think this lunatic was going to share his favorite Montana trail walk with us, not the psychotic logic behind his twenty-five-year career in murder and mayhem. By the way, Kaczynski disdainfully turned over Katie's letter as well as letters from producers at *20/20* and *Good Morning America* to the University of Michigan library in a seemingly nonviolent protest against tabloid TV.

Clearly, Barbara's most memorable "get" was that Gap-buying, thong-wearing, poetry-spouting presidential intern of preference, Monica Lewinsky. To get that exclusive, everyone but *everyone* groveled. I've already told you Barbara hand-carried a high-fiber lunch from New York to Washington for Monica's lawyer, William Ginsburg, while Diane Sawyer, it was rumored, invited Ginsburg to her luxurious Martha's Vineyard home for the weekend. Fortunately for Diane, before he could board the ferry, Ginsburg had been replaced as Monica's lawyer and was sent packing back to Fresno.[20]

Of course, Monica's chat with a sympathetic, motherly Walters was primarily promotion for The Portly Pepperpot's (as she was always affectionately described by the *New York Post*'s Page Six gossip column) gushingly girlish book, which was written by Andrew Morton, Princess Di's stealth biographer.

I was at a meeting at ABC the day Walters's coup with Monica was announced. I remember the head of advertising chortling with delight, knowing he could charge a premium for the commercials on such a "must-see" special. Not a bit subtle, one of the ads turned out to be for Victoria's Secret lingerie, and another promoted an upcoming ABC dramatic series with these words, "When she was only twenty, she seduced the most powerful man in the world." And who could that be? Actually, Julius Caesar. The miniseries was about Cleopatra.

Do any of us remember what Monica said or didn't say during Walters's cotton-candy questioning? Of course not. Though I bet a lot of us still have half-used tubes of the lipstick shade she was wearing that night lost somewhere in our makeup drawer. It was Club Monaco's Glaze, and it sold out all over the country the next day.

Meanwhile, Monica, who tells anyone and everyone who'll listen that what she really yearns for is privacy, hit the airwaves recently as a hostess of her own extremely stupid reality show, *Mr. Personality*. Maybe her manager got her the gig so she would have an alternative answer to "What's the single most degrading thing you've ever done?"

Let's Stay in Touch

For Barbara, keeping up with past interviewees—staying "friends"—is all part of "getting the get" and maybe "getting the same get" again. A while back, talking to her cohorts on *The View*, she inadvertently offered a little insight into how she operates so successfully. The "gals" were having a typical laugh-filled chat, this time about Bill Clinton hiring interns for his New York office. Joy Behar asked the audience, "Clap if you would have your daughter be an intern for Bill Clinton."

Over light audience applause, Barbara said, "I think that's so unfair."

Behar asked, "Why?"

Walters: "Because the man was the president. He does need people to work in that office, and come on, I mean let it go already."

Behar quipped, "Barbara, you're not interviewing Monica Lewinsky anymore, so forget about it."

Walters: "No, but I might want to interview Bill Clinton!"[21]

And even Monica was back when her reality show debuted, taking her place as guest co-host for a special edition of *The View* appropriately named "Real Life Hot Topics." Keeping one's options open is a vital part of winning the "get" game. That means being nice enough during the interview so that the "get" will come back again, and Katie and Diane and Barbara, like Rosie, are, at least on-camera, the Queens of Nice.

When it comes to staying in good graces with hot celebrities and their agents, what the celebrity wants promoted is the big thing, and the Media Queens have helped celebs promote everything from anti-war hysteria to an overpromising, underproducing exercise device to the star's latest movie, TV show, autobiography, charity, CD, diet, clothing line, children's book, cosmetics line, current spouse, cook-book, or the latest lefty political cause.

Sometimes they are just willing accomplices in selling a celebrity's latest image—realistic or not. Diane Sawyer's interview with a spacey, strung-out Whitney Houston was a ratings smash, especially with younger viewers, that all-important demographic. Whitney told Diane that she drank, popped pills, smoked pot, and used coke but that she was never addicted to any of the substances. Right.

"I like to think . . . I had a bad habit . . . which can be broken," Whitney declared, and Diane amiably didn't disagree. In fact, Whitney got ticked only when Diane mentioned crack cocaine. "First of all, let's get one thing straight . . . crack is cheap. I make too much money to ever smoke crack!" Whitney whined, making it clear that, after all, she had some standards.

Diane had taped the interview in November, during sweeps month, but the much-promoted show did not air until December to coincide with the release of Houston's frequently postponed new album. Could there be a connection? Was Diane helping Whitney pro-mote the new CD? Absolutely not, claimed an ABC spokesperson, who said Sawyer was just "too busy" with *Good Morning America* and other commitments to get the package finished any sooner.[22] And if you believe that you must be smoking something, too.

Cover Stories

Getting the "get" isn't limited to television. Not hardly. Magazine edi-tors, queens and otherwise, at all the women's and fashion and teen magazines fight each other every single day to get celebrities to appear on their covers rather than their competitors'. Battles between the editors and writers of *People* and *Us*, *Marie Claire* and *Cosmo*, *Ladies' Home Journal* and *Redbook* for the big interview and cover photo are just as vicious as they are in TV land. Having the right celebrity on the cover at the right time can mean, at least sometimes, an increase of hundreds of thousands of copies in newsstand sales, which is extraordinarily important to an editor because it translates into big bucks straight to the bottom line for the publisher.

Editors spend much of their time on the celebrity chase worrying about their covers and bargaining for the famous—unlike in television, they rarely court the infamous. Many magazines now have celebrity "wranglers" who are called editors but neither write nor assign articles nor lay a blue pencil on copy. They earn their pay by tracking and landing a star any way they can. Because of their unquenchable need for celebrities, editors of almost all major magazines, especially those aimed at women, have given over some of their editorial decision-making to the publicists and PR agencies of the stars they seek, though most would probably deny it.

They don't want their readers to know what goes on, but I doubt that there is an editor of any magazine that uses celebrities on the cover who hasn't made some kind of compromise he or she would be ashamed to admit. Or maybe they are so inured to the deals they make that they now consider kowtowing to publicists accepted standard practice. Believe me, I know how easy it is for that to happen. I wish I didn't.

Here's how the game is played. First, the celebrity must want to be in your magazine. And that rarely happens. As temperamental as most stars are today, many no longer feel you are doing them a favor by writing about them. Just the opposite. So their agents, the Access Police—powerful women like Cindi Berger, Rosie's publicist, and Pat Kingsley, who is known as Dr. No for the many turndowns she gives editors—play one magazine against the other. Getting these members of the Spin Sorority—yes, publicists also belong—to choose your magazine takes a lot of elbowing and begging coupled with some good old-fashioned butt-kissing blandishments like flowers, candy, perfume, gift baskets filled with potpourri and aromatherapy sent first and foremost to the publicist and then to the star (if you can get to her).

It goes without saying that, as you are making nice, you have to reassure the publicist (if and when he or she calls you back on their cell phone—a big if) that the story about the celebrity in your publication will be one both the star client and the witch of a publicist will like. "Our readers adore Michelle, or Jennifer, or Julia," you say. "They only want to hear good things about her." Just as Barbara keeps the questions safe and soft in her interviews to keep the celebs and their publicists happy, magazine editors rarely take on powerful publicists either. Too much is at stake to let the small matter of old-fashioned journalistic ethics get in the way of getting the "get."

Another negotiation: Celebrities only want to do cover stories. An inside story, even a flattering one, just won't do. But just *any* cover won't do, either. The agents always want a *specific* month's cover, agreed to in advance, often in writing, and sometimes with the agreement vetted by a lawyer, to coincide with the opening of the new movie, TV show, or CD the star wants to promote. Once you agree to that cover, the state of California could fall into the Pacific and that celebrity still had better be on the front of your magazine. Or you will face the wrath of the agent, who will descend upon you like an apocalyptic Lucifer breathing fire.

After Jackie Kennedy Onassis's death, I dropped a piece about Susan Sarandon and instead ran one about how women cope with the death of their mothers as the cover story. It was timely and sold well, far better, I thought, than another bland self-promoting celebrity interview. (I think Sarandon had a part that summer in the forgettable Grisham movie, *The Client*.) But her publicist, the ubiquitous Cindi Berger, shrieked at me, "stunned" that I could be so "totally unethical."

My crime? Putting on the cover of the magazine I edited what I thought was a better, more news-related story for my magazine's readers. Horrors!

Getting the celebrity, of course, is just the beginning of this fun-filled process, which rates somewhere between a root canal and the last stages of labor. The star's publicist will also want to approve the photographer, the makeup artist, the stylist, and the hairdresser, plus make certain demands for the day of the shoot that must be met as well. During a photo session, stars and their publicists insist on creating a certain atmosphere, and they don't care, not one bit, how much it costs. Jennifer Lopez expects that a magazine provide her entourage with Diptyque scented candles, a large buffet, and bottles of expensive Cristal champagne just in case anyone feels thirsty. All this just to make her smile for the camera or talk the talk. When it comes to celebrity whims, nobody dares to say no.

It doesn't end with a little caviar or the right French bottled water. No, there is also almost always a major negotiation over the writer of the piece. Publicists ask for previous clips of the writer and certain writers who have dared to be too frank or too funny can be black-balled, sometimes for years.

Says publicist Stephen Rivers, "Putting a celebrity on the cover is a commercial decision, not a journalistic decision. You're using my client to sell your magazine: Why shouldn't I have a role in picking the photographer and everything else?"[23] So much for any notion of journalistic independence you might have been laboring under when it comes to women's magazines, or really when it comes to any magazine at all that uses celebrities on the cover.

Melina Gerosa Bellows, a vivacious, smart brunette, spent years as the entertainment editor of *Ladies' Home Journal,* wining and dining publicists, chasing after celebrities, and being occasionally hit upon by them in the process. Everyone wanted to hear what the stars she interviewed—Julia Roberts, Nicole Kidman, Cher, Oprah (with whom she worked out), Mel Gibson (with whom she smoked cigars)—were really like.

Here's what they were like: They were guarded, stayed on message flacking a film or a CD, or pushing a cause they wanted promoted. Or, more often than not, they were just plain dull. Melina says, "Trying to get an interview, to get the publicist to agree, to set it up, arrange the photo shoot, and then finally get the star to say something memorable or substantive is so exhausting that when you come back you have to convince yourself and your editor that what they said is important even if you know it isn't."

And it is partly this enormous effort to soothe publicists, to make the ethically questionable deals that celebrity journalism requires that makes the final story seem more important than it is even if the end result is hardly worth publishing. I have seen it happen over and over again: that moment when you realize there is nothing more unique or profound in the interview you have worked so hard to get than Jennifer Aniston saying, about her parents' divorce, "It was awful."

Well, that's when the real scam begins, finding ways to convince you, the reader, that there is something worth reading there between those glossy covers, something worth buying. Melina now works for *National Geographic Kids* and finds stalking pandas such a relief. And they don't expect gift baskets, either.

So now you know that magazines, like television shows, write similar flattering pieces about celebrities in order not to alienate the star's agent or the star (almost equally important), or the studio or network, all of whom the editor will need again. And why do stars finally agree? Because publicity is cheaper than advertising, and journalism is now part of marketing. Women's magazines have become the bedside companion to the multichannel TV publicity campaigns that are geared up by the Access Police when it's in their client's or the studio's or the network's interest. So when Diane interviews Whitney or Jennifer about their latest projects, you'll likely see their beautifully made-up faces on *Marie Claire* or *Redbook* or *People* or *InStyle* that same month along with whatever buzz has been cooked up to spin the media and you.

Believe me, I have been part of this action, part of the chase, more times than I'd like to admit. Over the years, I've made "getting the get" more important than I should have, coddling celebrities for my covers and finding myself grateful for the "gets" I got. My worst-case scenario? Who else but the Woman of a Thousand Causes, Susan Sarandon. Here's how I did my sucking up.

A couple of years ago, I asked this talented actress, who had her last child at forty-five, to write the foreword for a *MORE* magazine book, *Fifty Celebrate Fifty,* about women approaching or having recently celebrated their fiftieth birthday. She had a new publicist and so was willing to take requests from me. We needed her because, no surprise, a celebrity helps a book get noticed. We understand promotion, too. Also, we thought she would come to the launch party, which would help get attention for the book. And maybe even go on television to talk about the book because you need a star to go on television for the daytime shows. See how it works? But to get her to agree, Sarandon cut a deal that would have made Don Corleone proud. First we said we would donate to one of her causes in her name. We would also pay the writer who would ghost the foreword for her.

Truth be told, a *MORE* editor virtually wrote the less-than-a-thousand-word foreword, but we paid up anyway. To get her to publicize the book, Susan also wanted us to give another donation to a charity that provided therapy to young mothers, teaching them how to be better parents. And the charity wanted us to host a big fundraising party for them. No party, no donation, no Susan. No publicity for the book, the book people moaned. No place to entertain our advertisers, the advertising people groaned. So we paid up. And do you think Susan was grateful? Not really. She kind of dissed us . . .

and not privately but to *The New York Times*. As the *Times* gossip columnist, James Barron, wrote,

> This interview began in unpreparedness. The interviewer could not put his hands on the book he and the interviewee were to talk about. Not to worry: "I don't have the book here, either," the interviewee, Susan Sarandon, said, "and I'm in it." . . .
>
> The interview turned out to be an improbable prelude to a benefit tomorrow featuring Ms. Sarandon . . . Money is involved: "They wanted to do an event and they seduced me into doing it on the basis of giving a large donation to a group that I work with," Ms. Sarandon said, apparently referring to the editors at *MORE* on the one hand and a nonprofit group called Help a Parent, Save a Child on the other. [Wait a minute. Who seduced whom?] How large a donation can Help a Parent, Save a Child expect to get, she was asked. "We started out at $10,000," she said. "I'm not sure what we're up to now, the more I've stepped in to do more press."[24]

A lot more than $10,000, Susan! At the event, the therapists who ran the charity all got up and talked nonstop for an hour about how their years and years of therapy had helped them. I don't know how much the therapy helped the young mothers who were the supposed beneficiaries. Personally, I think getting them a job might have been a slightly bigger help. By the way, less than a year later, Sarandon was on to other things, leading anti-war rallies and debating foreign policy on *Meet the Press*.

Now I'd like to tell you that celebrity groveling is as bad as it gets in women's publishing today. I'd also like to tell you I've been frequently mistaken for Catherine Deneuve, but, sadly, neither is true. But this is. Many Spin Sisters, who work one of the most important "beats" in women's magazines, may fudge even the most basic principle of reporting: simply telling the truth.

Talking Dirty for Fun and Profit

In the fall of 2001, the Web site Mediabistro.com, a networking organization, hosted a panel on what's good and what's bad about women's magazines at Obeca Li, a trendy Manhattan nouvelle Asian restaurant. On the panel, Laurie Abraham, then executive editor of *Elle*, was unusually outspoken and direct. She told the audience what she found most troubling in magazines for women: "We lie about sex."

Now, under normal circumstances, a roomful of experienced journalists might be outraged that they were being called liars. Wouldn't you be? But that wasn't the reaction that evening. Most just sipped their Chardonnay and Merlot, shrugged a little, giggled a lot, and agreed with her.

Jane magazine once ran an article called "15 Ways Sex Makes You Prettier." It told readers, whose average age is twenty-four, that sex improves your skin, makes you thin, and smoothes your wrinkles. Was it true? Probably no more than most of the sex articles that appear each month in all the other magazines for young women.

Magazines for older women have practically given up on sex advice these days. So, alas, no further revelations of the power of clitoral orgasm and the search for the mysterious G-spot appear in *Ladies' Home Journal* or *Family Circle*. Once upon a time, staid, big-circulation women's magazines were called the Pious Pornographers, and, in a pseudoscientific manner, published descriptions of Masters and Johnson's laboratory experiments on curing impotence or premature ejaculation with paid sex surrogates.

Now, once in a while the traditional magazines do serve up articles about sex, but, like the bland leading the bland, it is usually about the lack of desire for it. Newer magazines like *Real Simple* or Oprah's *O* that are targeted at the too-tired-for-sex working mom are downright prissy. These are magazines for women who prefer meditating or organizing their closets, and only sweat in a Hot Yoga session instead of the bedroom.

But others, like *Cosmopolitan, Glamour,* and *Marie Claire,* overflow with how-to articles in the no-holes-barred style of *Debbie Does Dallas.* For example, in a September 2002 *Cosmo,* "Lisa, 28" breathlessly reveals: "I was sleeping with this older man named Tom who was sweet, but there was no spark between us. After seeing each other for a few months, he invited me to a party at his place where he introduced me to his very handsome nineteen-year-old son. Later that night after Tom went to bed, his son and I started talking, and he told me he was a virgin. After a few more drinks, I couldn't help putting the moves on him, and we sneaked out to the guest house where we had sex. For a first-timer, he was even better than his old man."[25]

These soft-core scenarios are presented with a straight face, as if they were fact-checked reportage meant to be believed by readers. What's more, the editors seem not to care one whit that such stories, in which any kind of behavior is tolerated and even hyped, could have significant cultural force, shaping and reinforcing young women's attitudes about sexuality and relationships.

So how come the editors, writers, and fact checkers who work on them seem unconcerned by half-truths and rewritten quotes? When Liza Featherstone of *Columbia Journalism Review,* reporting on the panel, tried to find out, those she talked to "asked that their identities be protected with the top secrecy accorded to Seymour Hersh's CIA sources."[26] But what she found was that *Elle* editor Abraham's assessment was remarkably honest.

"These stories were so tweaked," said a fact checker from the now defunct *Mademoiselle,* "that fact checking them was not a priority." A *Glamour* employee acknowledged that quotes are routinely rewritten. "They get people to interview people—or purport to interview people, but quotes are rephrased to sound as perky as the magazine's copy. No one talks like that," she admitted. Anecdotes are routinely exaggerated. The worst abuses occur in articles that relate to sex and health, always encouraging readers to believe that sex has health benefits that are often arbitrary or unproven. As one writer explained, "It may be something you do sometimes to pay your bills."[27]

So why does a little white lying about sex really matter? I mean, everybody lies about sex, don't they? It's just entertainment, right? And maybe that serves a purpose at least some of the time. During the war in Iraq, *The Washington Post* staff writer Peter Carlson declared he could understand that after watching war news, we all might crave something "utterly mindless. You want stupidity and you want it now," he wrote. "Fortunately, you're in luck. The American magazine industry—one of the world's foremost purveyors of mindless drivel—has thoughtfully provided for all your stupidity needs. . . . Admit that it's reassuring to know that [with] a billion Muslims mad at us . . . editors at *Cosmopolitan* are worried about the fifteen things you do that creep him out in bed."[28]

If you want to know the truth, that issue of *Cosmo* was far, far stupider than merely the bone-dumb advice about the things that "creep him out," which included no-no's like staring into his eyes for more than thirty seconds because "he can feel scrutinized and examined like he's being evaluated." And "when he's trying to relax and get his love groove on, being judged will do anything but jack up his lust."[29] The poor dear.

And then there are these instructions, a couple of pages later in "Flirting Moves That No Man Can Resist." "Grin and hold his gaze for three seconds. Then bite the corner of your lip and look down."[30] And how about this Stepford Wife bromide: "When a man is watching the game don't start talking unless it directly pertains to the game or if you want to have sex."[31] And if you want to have sex, try Number 39 in "50 Ways to Make Great Sack Sessions Sex-traordinary." "Glide [an ice cube] between his upper thighs letting it melt along his shaft. Then trace your hot tongue along the icy trail."[32]

Of course, first heat your tongue in the microwave.

Okay. I'm kidding, I'm kidding.

But *Cosmo* claims it isn't. And their editors would insist such quasi-advice, which ricochets between soft core and ploys that Scarlett O'Hara's grandmother would have thought old-fashioned, is both a helpful service to their readers and as serious as the quasi-reporting about sex found in all the magazines for young women. Just like the series *Sex and the City* and a half dozen other TV sitcoms and reality shows that seem to imply that nowadays young women never leave home without an ice cube and a condom.

Is this a totally accurate picture or, once again, just spin? Spin about an important part of young women's lives?

A couple of years ago, the Institute for American Values conducted a survey of a thousand college women. None attended schools with religious affiliations. Yet the survey found that 31 percent of the seniors were still virgins.[33] Now just think of the anguished *Cosmo* cover line editor Kate White could write: "We Thought You Had Tried Everything, and, Gulp, We Found You Had Tried *Nothing!*"

The survey did find that "hooking up," casual sex without any kind of commitment, is "widespread and often associated with drinking." When the researchers conducted sixty-two in-depth interviews on eleven campuses, the students told them that hooking up, though prevalent, was not an appealing or satisfying experience for most women.

A New York University student was typical. She said, "I don't think women deal well with [hooking up] . . . the next day they're upset and they regret what they did and [they ask themselves] 'Why did I do it?'"[34]

But is this alternative view ever reported? A reality that just isn't like all those giddy, no-regrets tall tales about always rapturous sex without commitment. The reality would acknowledge that young women assess their sexual behavior in a variety of ways. And that, for most, sex is still not that casual or emotion-free. Even more important for many young women, even today, sex and moral beliefs remain intertwined. But let's not go there. That wouldn't seem hot or hip. That would remind readers of stodgy old notions about values and complicate the message that being good in bed is all that should matter. And that is part of my point. If media for women is willing to shave the edges on stories about sex, and endorse only one view of sexual behavior, what else isn't accurately reflected about women's lives, opinions, or values?

Women want to trust the magazines they read, even if the trust may be misplaced. So whether it is *Cosmo*'s sex fantasies, *Redbook*'s insistence that you are always, *always* stressed, or *Marie Claire*'s partisan campaigns and lobbying efforts, millions of women are affected by what they are being told, just as they would be in a conversation with a more sophisticated, better-informed friend whom they really respect.

The editors who control women's magazines may be lesser known, but they are no less influential than the Media Queens of television. I am sorry to say that nowadays these magazines are often less honest and just plain sillier than much of what we see on television. Not to mention that some of them are far more politically biased. And that's saying something.

The Spin Sisters of print and broadcast have tremendous impact both culturally and politically. But how they play and work, the morals they seem to promote, and the biases they comfortably share may have little to do with the audiences they say they serve. And what they tell women every morning and month after month may be what they think you want to hear.

Or, what they think you *should* hear.

Need proof? Tune in to *The West Wing* on Wednesday night. Or just read on.

CHAPTER 9

"If Only Women Voted"

In an episode of *The West Wing*, the liberal feminist-activist Amy Gardner, played by the husky-voiced Mary-Louise Parker, moans to her off-again, on-again love interest, Deputy Chief of Staff Josh Lyman: "If only women voted, Democrats couldn't lose." Amy's supposed credentials include "a year and a half as issues director for NOW, two years as political director of Emily's List, founder of the Democratic Women's Forum, and director of the Women's Leadership Coalition." On *The West Wing* it's the perfect résumé for a woman who President Bartlet and company think accurately represents the political opinions of nearly all women in this country.

Of course she doesn't, but who's there to argue the point? Toby? C.J.? Abby, who plays the role of First Feminist with the gusto of Patton heading to Berlin? Not likely.

Josh agrees with his occasional sleep-over pal, but points out to the perennially sulky, perennially snotty Amy that until that day comes, women will just have to deal with men. And men (darn 'em) are not quite as easy to persuade as every woman in America who, Amy is absolutely convinced, she speaks for. (Well, of course, except for those religious nuts and the rest of the right wingers, but they're not worth talking about or talking to, are they?)

Pretty outrageous and pretty uninformed, isn't she? But then why shouldn't she feel this way? In the political and media circles in which someone like Amy would inevitably travel in real life, almost every woman *does* think the same way. And if she doesn't, believe me, she is very, very quiet about it. I know—I've been literally snarled at when I've even suggested that another possible point of view on an issue might exist.

Snooty Amy accurately reflects the belief of much of the media elite that women, if they are smart, if they know what's good for them, must, first of all, share the feminist liberal agenda (though they would never call it feminist because most women don't like the term). And, secondly, agree with them on any and all political issues. Of course, conservative media spins its point of view as well. But it isn't assumed that even though some men tend to be conservatives, all men, just because they *are* men, should automatically be conservatives. And if they are not, they are somehow letting down the rest of the guys.

Yet, I've come to see that many Spin Sisters seem incapable of independent political thought, though they would be horrified to hear me say that. But it's true. When the political bell rings, most salivate like expensive Pavlov poodles over Bill and Hill, abortion and gun control, Streisand and Sheen, gay rights and saving the spotted owl, or, at least, an African "princess."

If what I say is true, why should any of us be shocked that, just as media for women sells you one-sided notions about stress, about the way you should want to look, about what should make you feel sorry for yourself or fearful, much of media for women is peddling a one-sided message about politics, too? A message that in many ways is the culmination of all the other stories it sells about how tough life is for women today, even middle-class women.

Deep down, most of our Spin Sisters are just good old-fashioned left wingers, wired for a liberal response to every issue. They tend to see the world and the women in it as the poor inhabitants of a desolate land called victimhood and believe government is the great hero destined to solve all the problems of those who feel victimized. Kind of like a federal Fabio ready to sweep you off your feet into aromatherapy baths and Hillarycare.

For the last two decades, we've been told over and over again that if we are women, we are, de facto, victims—because of the stress in our lives, because of the dangers in our environment, because of our need to be attractive in order to please men, and because of the inherently dangerous, violent nature of men. We, who are certainly the most fortunate women the world has ever known, remain a victim class. Forget the gains we have made in almost every significant area, from health to education to economics. Forget the opportunities that are available to us. Forget our personal strength and resiliency. According to Amy and her real-life cohorts, our political attitudes should be based on redressing the accumulated wrongs we continue to experience because as women we are a victimized group. And if, by chance, you don't buy their political line, well then, there must be something wrong with *you.*

Amy would snarl, as she is always snarling at poor dumb, liberal (but not sensitive enough, never sensitive enough) Josh, *"You just don't get it!"*

That's how for-women-only political bias operates. It implies that if by chance you don't happen to support the liberal agenda in every detail, then you are the one who is out of step. Or rigid. Or crazy. Or a traitor to your sisters. And we are all sisters—unless you disagree.

In his best-seller *Bias*, Bernard Goldberg writes about media elites: "Their friends are liberals, just as they are. They share the same values. Almost all of them think the same way on the big social issues of our time. . . . After a while they start to believe that all civilized people think the same way they and their friends do. That's why they don't simply disagree with conservatives. They see them as morally deficient."[1]

So Tell Us How You *Really* Feel

At a party for women journalists from the Vietnam era that Lesley Stahl hosted a few months before the Iraq war, ABC reporter Lynn Sherr (remember her from the *20/20* piece, "There's No Place Like the Office"?) spoke to a media-elite crowd that included Dan Rather, declaring that she just hoped that the president understood what he was doing. Everyone in the room nodded and applauded. In most media circles, there's no safer bet for an applause line than a slam at the intellectual shortcomings of George W.

Yet when asked about liberal bias in the media, Lesley Stahl declared, "I'm not saying we don't have opinions, but I'm saying we try to cleanse our stories of them."[2] That approach works about as well as Woolite on a ten-year-old's soccer socks. As Dr. S. Robert Lichter, president of the Center for Media and Public Affairs, notes, "The essential argument by the media is that, yes, most mainstream journalists may be left of center, but they operate in the tradition of objectivity so this doesn't affect their coverage of news. . . . What this argument fails to grasp is the way bias works in people. Yes, journalists tell the truth—but like everyone else, they tell the truth as they see it."[3]

And nobody does it better than Katie Couric. The Media Research Center, which painstakingly tracks "liberal bias" on television, cites what it considers over five hundred examples of Katie's left-leaning point of view, from her frequent defense of the Clintons to her lauding of Senator Jim Jeffords when he left the Republican party. Conservatives have taken Katie to task for describing President Reagan as an "airhead." Ann Coulter and Katie took on that charge in their explosive on-air snarlfest after Ann published *Slander.*

Many conservatives also complained about her comments, after the beating death of gay student Matthew Shepard, that "some say" there is a climate of anti-gay hate that's been fostered by a provocative advertising campaign by the political right in this country.[4] She also lectured Oliver North about the dangers of conservative talk show hosts: "The rap that some people give them is that they reflect the views of a very vocal minority, the extremists in this country, and don't really reflect the true nature of political debate in the United States. And, as a matter of fact, they tend to be quite divisive and sort of have a bad, a negative impact on the country."[5] By the way, using "some people say" is often Katie code for "I believe" when, as Lesley Stahl put it, trying to "cleanse" a story of personal bias.

In truth, Katie does not so much state her views as imply them with a look, a gesture, or by asking tough questions to some, usually conservatives and even moderate Republicans, and tossing softballs to others like her friend Hillary. Katie makes her likes and dislikes very obvious even if you are watching with only one eye while making breakfast or getting dressed. In an interview with writer Gail Sheehy, who wrote an enthusiastic piece for *Vanity Fair* about Hillary Clinton, Katie was even more positive about Hillary's skills than Sheehy. When the writer called Hillary a "co-scoundrel," Katie chastised her, "That's pretty harsh." Not if you're Paula Jones or Kathleen Willey or Gennifer Flowers, it's not.

Katie waxed on: "She's also won a great deal of respect by working very, very hard. . . . And by not pulling any kind of prima donna act. . . . It's been quite remarkable . . . the conservative Republicans speak with her . . . I mean, many of them said, 'Oh, my constituents will kill me but I really like her.'"[6]

Tell us how you really feel, Katie.

Again, in a friendly, sympathetic interview with liberal legal writer Jeffrey Toobin about his book *Too Close to Call,* which concluded that the "wrong man was inaugurated on January 20, 2001," Katie commented that, while the Supreme Court decided the election, "Ruth Bader Ginsburg . . . and Scalia were butting heads. Justice Scalia, I [shouldn't] call him [Scalia]." Toobin replied, somewhat coyly, "Justice Scalia, just a little respect, Katie."[7] The pair sounded like a couple of high schoolers dissing the brainy class nerd: "He's just not one of us (snicker, snicker)."

Katie's greatest influence may be in making women feel as though they should be as enthusiastic as she is about the women she admires. Just before Mother's Day in May 2001, Katie saluted three women who made "a special contribution to motherhood and to all mankind."[8] One was Donna Dees-Thomases, founder of the Million Mom March; the second was Marie Wilson, the head of the Ms. Foundation. The woman who created "Barney" rounded out the group, although even Katie didn't know whether she should thank the woman or blame her for the annoying purple dinosaur. It was a perfect Katie moment—she could focus on the accomplishments of three women in a way that seemed innocuous. But was it?

Katie gushed especially over Dees-Thomases, who, she said, had organized a "grass-roots movement of stroller moms" to take on (in Dees-Thomases's words) the "mean gun lobby." What a perfect Lifetime movie moment. Listening to Katie coo over Dees-Thomases, I thought I was about to meet an average woman who decided to take on the big boys. And thirty seconds into the interview, you could see that Dees-Thomases certainly had the "I'm just a mom like you" routine down pat. She always claimed that before organizing the march she didn't know "the Brady Bill from the Brady Bunch."[9]

Clever line. *Too* clever. Actually, Dees-Thomases is a sophisticated political/PR operative who worked in Congress as an assistant press secretary to two Democratic senators, was a spokesperson for CBS News (for Dan Rather, actually), and is the sister-in-law of Hillary's tough-as-nails lawyer pal Susan Thomases, who was a top advisor in the 1992 Clinton Presidential campaign and remains a close Clinton friend. Donna's not exactly a typical Soccer Mom, but neither is Marie Wilson, who heads not only the Ms. Foundation but the White House Project, which aims to get a woman elected president.

Are you thinking that it might be a little difficult to head one group that is unabashedly feminist and be objective while running another that is allegedly nonpartisan? One look below the surface at the White House Project, and its agenda is clear. Many White House Project meetings highlight Democratic, gay, or liberal activists. One meeting I attended just after September 11 featured retired Army General Claudia Kennedy, who gave her stump speech for an aborted Senate run against Virginia's Republican John Warner. She also decried the bombing campaign in Afghanistan and wondered what the Joint Chiefs would do "after the bombing campaign fails." She didn't have to wonder long.

White House Project award winners and presenters include that noted nonpartisan Marlo Thomas, gay activist and Bush basher Melissa Etheridge, former Democratic VP candidate Geraldine Ferraro, PETA and gay activist Kathy Najimy. But on the *Today* show the politics of Ms. Wilson were never mentioned, as Katie extolled her virtues.

All of this wouldn't matter except that Katie's implied opinions and her outspoken enthusiasm for certain people and causes influence millions of women who start the day with her five times a week. She seems like a friend, and it's a natural inclination to want to agree with your friends.

Still, Media Queens like Katie and Diane, network producers and magazine editors, maintain that they are able to see the world free of their own prejudices because of their training and discipline. But as the late columnist and award-winning editor Michael Kelly noted, most journalists really don't have any professional training or discipline to help temper their beliefs.

He wrote in his syndicated column, "Journalism is not a profession in the sense of medicine and law or science. Journalists do not go through years of brutal academic apprenticeship designed to inculcate adherence to an agreed-upon code of ethics (such as the Hippocratic Oath) or an agreed-upon method of truth determining (such as a method of scientific inquiry)."[10] *The New York Times* scandal provoked by reporter Jayson Blair dramatically proved Kelly's point.

Bernard Goldberg also wrote, "The sophisticated media elites don't categorize their beliefs as liberal but as simply the correct way to look at things. They think they're middle of the road—raging moderates—while everyone else (the people who live in the 'red states' that George W. Bush carried) is on the fringe."[11]

Television producer Av Westin told me that he thought that since people in media often come from similar backgrounds and attend similar schools, it's not surprising that they tend to share the same political views. "You want to employ and be around people who agree with you," he said. "There's nothing so surprising about that."[12] And Susan Winston, a former executive producer of *Good Morning America* and a longtime independent producer of TV programming, also agreed that women, especially those behind the camera, tended to be liberals.

"Most women in top positions in television today went to college in the seventies," she said. "We were feminists. We were liberals, and most of us still are."[13]

CNN *Capital Gang* regular Kate O'Beirne puts it this way: "The younger women behind the camera, the young producers who are so important on the news programs, may not be old-style feminists, but many of them attended elite eastern colleges and were influenced by the very liberal attitudes of the professors in their women's studies departments."[14]

Recently, columnist David Shaw declared "many big-city journalists—especially those who set the agenda for what gets covered in the rest of media—have moved away from much of the largely middle- and working-class audience they purportedly serve. At best, they're out of touch. At worst, they've become elitist." Okay, so it turns out they're not like you. Does this really influence their choice of stories? I don't know. Is Katie Couric perky?

Shaw continues, "The natural sympathy most journalists feel for the underdog and for the downtrodden prevents the media from ignoring the poor. The fascination that the American public has with the rich and famous prevents the media from ignoring the upper strata of society."[15]

And who does that elitist attitude leave out? You—the middle class, most American women. So instead of articles that reflect your values and real interests, you read about Adelaide Abankwah and hear about Hillary and Rosie and Susan Sarandon, the reigning Queens of the Liberal Left. But women like the deeply devout Lisa Beamer before 9/11? Forget about it.

Women Who Pray Too Much

Here's an example of what I mean. In the early 1990s, I thought we should do a piece for *Ladies' Home Journal*'s longtime series, "How America Lives" on what seemed to be an important new trend in the country. I realized that many families were once again focusing on what Republicans had begun to call family values and were, in record numbers, sending their children to religious schools or home schooling their kids.

My suggestion was not exactly a radical idea for a story even then. Finding a way to teach traditional values was becoming an important issue in the lives of many middle-class women—probably many of you reading this book—yet one that media for women rarely covered. Let me put it this way. If you asked a women's magazine editor back then if she had ever published a story about a conservative woman or even *read* one, she'd probably, first, take at least twenty minutes racking her brain. Then, with the kind of satisfaction usually relegated to a Ben and Jerry's binge, she would cite a *Redbook* feature that caused a stir at the time about the wives of a polygamist Mormon. And she would be deadly serious.

Even at the *Journal*, none of the other editors thought the family values trend was important and they argued with me that what I was proposing was an uninteresting feature about a dull, uptight midwestern family. That's another standard reaction—not only are conservative women dumb, but they are dull and uptight, too. I insisted, and we did the piece on a devout family in Montana. Guess what? Readers loved it. I think that, unlike my colleagues, you're not surprised.

In November that year, Republicans won the Congress, buoyed by Newt Gingrich's Contract with America. Listening to the wailing and keening in editorial meetings, and at Michael's, you'd have thought Lucifer himself had been elected. Shortly afterward, Hillary Clinton, concerned by the loss (it was the first time Republicans had won control of the House in forty years, thanks in large part to her health-care initiative) invited a group of women's magazine editors and a few trusted New York columnists to the White House for a cozy upstairs-in-the-living quarters, off-the-record, girls-only lunch.

Lisa Caputo, Hillary's press secretary at the time, explained when she sent out the invitations that the First Lady felt that she was being misunderstood and wanted some advice on how she could more effectively reveal her "true self" to our readers. Somehow, I didn't think true self meant the lamp-throwing, epithet-screaming, staff-firing Hillary.

No, assuming we were all on her side, what Hillary wanted was our help in boosting her image with mainstream women, whose votes Clinton needed most. Most of my colleagues were happy to oblige.

A pack of us flew down to Washington on an early morning shuttle. I shared a cab to the White House with three other top editors. On the way, they started to trash Newt Gingrich and his vote-winning Contract with America. Besides agreeing it was just a PR stunt to fool gullible voters (there's that dumb and dumber thing again), they were especially enraged that the Contract endorsed prayer in the schools. "Doesn't that idiot understand the concept of separation between church and state?" one of them snapped. "It is sooooo inappropriate," another declared. The third dutifully nodded her head in total agreement. And then it was my turn.

I said that as I understood it a child wouldn't have to pray if he or she didn't want to. "I mean, nobody would be *forced* to say a prayer," I offered.

"Oh, no, no, no, no," they shrieked, amazed that I didn't share their view. How dumb could I be? Pretty dumb, but smart enough to catch the undercurrent. Everyone who's anyone knows that the only people who support prayer in schools are those poor, misguided evangelical Christians who really aren't very well educated, you know.

But my colleagues were even more amazed when our African-American taxi driver turned around, and said, "Prayers in school? It would do the kids good. I'm all for it."

The car went awkwardly silent as we rolled up to the gates of the White House. When one editor climbed out, she turned and whispered reassuringly to her pals, "I'm sure he can't really mean that. He just doesn't understand."

There was no discussion, no debate. Never a thought as to why someone would not agree with them. They didn't want to examine or understand our driver's reasoning. It made them far more comfortable and certainly superior to dismiss him as uninformed. It never occurred to them that this man's children probably went to a tough, inner-city school, not the elite havens their little darlings attend, and that he might just possibly have a better insight into the benefits a little prayer might provide.

But then, nobody says grace at Michael's. In fact, talking about religion makes many people in the media world uncomfortable. So uncomfortable that they try to avoid the subject entirely. As one freelance producer, who insists on being nameless, told me, "We have problems with using hicks. Unless it's after a tornado in a trailer park, and she's crying about the Tupperware blowing away. And we especially have trouble with religious hicks." Nice, huh?

David Corvo, executive producer of *Dateline*, agreed that dealing with the devoutly religious is usually a newsmagazine no-no. For example, he said that the only way *Dateline* would do a feature on Heather Mercer and Dayna Curry, the missionary girls who had been imprisoned by the Taliban, during the bombing of Afghanistan, was in the form of a *Family Feud* story, in this case "mother versus daughter."[16]

On that *Dateline* segment, Heather's mother criticized her daughter for going to Afghanistan. Her humanitarian activities were merely a cover and the girls had misled the president and the nation. According to the mom, they were really "out there proselytizing" and "breaking the law."[17]

Although the Taliban's total lack of religious tolerance was never decried during the twenty-minute segment, missionary activities were characterized as "deceptive" and "demeaning." But then, this is the same crowd that has little tolerance for anyone or anything religious right here at home.

Dr. Samir Husni, an ebullient Lebanese who teaches journalism at the University of Mississippi, is known as Mr. Magazine because he keeps track of and reports on every new magazine published in America. Samir told me, "When I first came to America to go to graduate school in the 1980s, when I read magazines I thought, *This is America.* They really reflected Americans and American life. I think I loved magazines so much because I could learn about America; I could understand America from popular magazines. I don't feel that way anymore."[18]

His female students, he says, read *Cosmopolitan*; but he shakes his head, "They are absolutely not *Cosmo* girls and don't want to be." He lives in Oxford, Mississippi.

"People there are very conservative, very religious. A lot of America is like this." He shrugs. "You don't see these people in our magazines anymore." Or on our TV screens.

It's not just writers and editors who are made uncomfortable by religion: It's also advertisers, especially the biggest ones. In 2002, for example, I tested a magazine called *Women's Faith & Spirit*, which had promising newsstand sales and circulation potential. Selling the idea to the corporate brass was no small feat. But I knew a religious-based magazine would have even more trouble appealing to advertisers. Believe me, advertisers are not exactly profiles in courage.

When I described the magazine, which was aimed at devout women, to a marketing team from Proctor & Gamble, they became closemouthed and obviously uncomfortable. Yet they have no trouble advertising Cover Girl, one of their leading cosmetic brands, in *Cosmopolitan*, in an issue hyping "The Toy Women Can't Keep Their Hands Off"—the Rabbit vibrator, touted by the insatiable Samantha on *Sex and the City*.[19] Certainly, advertising in *Cosmo* is a no-brainer for a lipstick manufacturer. But nowadays, putting a Cover Girl ad in a magazine for women who want to be as open about their faith as *Cosmo* assumes they are about the intensity of their orgasms, appears to be just *too* risky.

The expected argument might be that religious women are older and thus less likely to need several tubes of eight-hour lip color, but, in this case, it simply wasn't so. Thousands of readers responded enthusiastically to a survey that was part of the magazine's test issue. The average age of our readers was mid-thirties, and more than a quarter of them had family incomes of over $100,000—dream consumers by magazine standards . . . if only they weren't so religious.

Although college-age men and women have similar goals of raising a family and being well off, young women, more than men, want spirituality to be an important part of their lives. Over the past decade women of all ages have grown increasingly religious. All the leading pollsters have reported the renewed importance of religion in American life, especially for women. Ninety percent of Americans believe in God. As *The New York Times* commented in an introduction to a photo essay about prayer, America, far from being a secular nation, is a profoundly faithful one.[20] Seventy-one percent say that their faith rewards them with a sense of purpose. Sixty-four percent say their congregations care about them personally, and 74 percent say that faith, and only faith, gives them that most elusive of modern grails—a sense of inner peace.[21]

These figures can appear surprising, astonishing even, because they are rarely noted by our media. Religion and religious women, who they like to think are a small, slightly wacky minority, make the Girls' Club uncomfortable. Yes, we all know women think about their bodies a lot. That's why we have scads of diet and weight-loss cover lines shouting out at us each month. Women also think about attracting men, being better in bed, flattening our bellies, firming our butts, cutting our hair, zapping our wrinkles, decorating our bedrooms, renovating our kitchens, cooking fast, cooking healthy, entertaining extravagantly, entertaining easily, getting organized, getting confident, saving money, saving time, and buying the latest and best makeup, dresses, pants, shoes, bags, and swimsuits whenever we can find them. And women's media reflects all this—in five hundred magazines and on a hundred chattering channels. And women giggle about the latest doings of J.Lo and Madonna or Meg and Julia or Brad and Jennifer or Ryan and Trista or Diane and Katie and any and every celebrity who is in the spotlight for fifteen minutes or less. And women's magazines and entertainment shows report breathlessly on their every insignificant twitch and turn. And all that's okay up to a point.

But something's wrong when 65 percent of American women pray at least once every single day,[22] and the media they consume is far more comfortable telling us about the Rabbit vibrator than the deeply felt religious faith that is so important to so many women. In fact, many editors, writers, and producers might even shake their heads and look down their perfectly sculpted noses at such behavior.

But would women really want to read more about prayer and less about vibrators? In truth, nobody knows because media today is far more skittish about confirming traditional values than promoting the new, and the sensational. Several years ago, Todd Gitlin described media as a funhouse mirror that we look into and see reflected back a distorted image of ourselves. Nowadays media tends to be more like a filter that only lets certain images through. Currently, it is so self-referential, copying itself and what it deems interesting over and over, that we rarely see important aspects of our attitudes and beliefs reflected back at all.

TV critic Michael Giltz writes that while most of America is religious, "Only a tiny handful of good-for-you prime-time . . . shows ever mention the word 'prayer' let alone make it a plot point."[23] Sitcoms or dramas are so up-to-the-minute about every other happening in American life that the most popular shows are always "based on a true event" or "ripped from the headlines." But not about religion, never religion. Unless, of course, it's a child-molesting priest or a born-again who goes bad and takes out the Sunday choir with him.

When Joy Behar on *The View* exclaims, "Thank you, Jesus," because it is the last day of one of her many diets, the politically correct ABC censors deleted her thanks before rebroadcasting the show.[24] Oh, TV of little faith.

Personally, I am not religious, though I wish I were. I believe that faith is a gift, and I truly respect those who have it. Unfortunately, too many in my business dismiss those with religion as both dumb and bigoted. Still, women's magazines, great little marketers that they are, knew something was going on out there with women besides "curbing your carbo munchies" or "reading his mind in bed." Oprah especially, both personally and professionally, understood this new interest in "spirituality." But magazines, including hers, are very, very careful to separate "spirituality," which is soft, warm, fuzzy, and "me-centered," from religion, which is not—and isn't supposed to be. Spirituality, shot with a soft-focus lens, has morphed in women's media into another form of stress reduction, a fresh and modern self-help technique. Lulling and inoffensive, spirituality is more about taking long walks and buying $65 Jo Malone scented candles than making ethical decisions or moral judgments. It is another way to calm ourselves, refresh ourselves, or applaud ourselves. As a Catholic girlfriend of mine says, choosing between Origins Fretnot tangerine bath bar or L'Occitane lavender bath salts is just not the same thing as facing confession.

Jill Montaigne of the Sullivan Group, who advises media companies on attracting advertisers, says today's marketers are interested primarily in being associated with what they call the cultural dialogue—what's new, what's hot, and often, what's a little outrageous. "They want to be part of the magazines and television shows that are part of this cultural dialogue. They see America as coastal and care what is happening on the East and the West Coast." And they see the rest of the country, as Jill says, "as empty."[25]

This antipathy toward anyone or anything outside New York and L.A. is not limited to the religious. Carol Story of *The Early Show* agreed that small-town folks are rarely seen on television because they are often just not articulate enough in a one-minute sound bite. Mary Knowles, who has produced shows for Lifetime, says that women with regional accents just can't be the lead in a program, even if they are saying exactly the right thing. And if you are from the South, no chance. "Once I was doing a show on discrimination against pregnant women. I found a woman from northern Florida. She had been discriminated against when she was pregnant, and she said it very clearly and very directly but with a strong Southern accent. The executive producer just didn't want her to lead the piece. She said she would put viewers off."[26]

Pollster Kellyanne Conway has said, "You just don't see many women on television from the 'red states,' the states that voted for George Bush. You don't hear about their beliefs. They are almost invisible."[27]

Playing at Politics

The women who control the media may be a bit skittish about religion and standoffish about small-town "girls," but they are also remarkably uninterested and uninformed personally about how our government works or the hardball tactics of politics today. And that's important, too, because so much of what you see and read has a political undertone or consequence to it. Yet many of these women deal with issues only on a superficial level—and always with a liberal bent.

For example, I was surprised when I asked Barbara Walters, who worked so hard to get the first interview with Monica Lewinsky after Clinton's impeachment, what she thought of Congressman Bob Barr. The Georgia congressman was certainly the most outspoken and abrasive of the House managers during the impeachment process. Barbara told me matter-of-factly she didn't know who he was! On a segment of *The View* in May 2002, Jane Fonda appeared to promote an anti-war play she had produced. Co-host Star Jones declared she was absolutely baffled that Vietnam veterans were still enraged by Fonda. She said, "I've been floored by the number of e-mails this show has received from Vietnam veterans and their families . . . I know that you've moved past it and our country has moved past it."

Fonda disagreed. "I will never move past it, we should not move past it. We need to learn the lessons. . . . It's much harder to realize that people we elected to office lied to us, put our men in danger and killed them in order to save their own egos."[28]

When Fonda was included in the *Journal*'s book *100 Most Important Women of the Twentieth Century*, I got many letters, too, from angry vets reminding me that Fonda had said that our POWs shouldn't be hailed as heroes because they were "war criminals." I pointed out that our list included not only heroines but Hitler's moviemaker propagandist Leni Riefenstahl and Argentina's Eva Peron. Unlike Star, however, I did understand why some people were so enraged by our choices.

But when it comes to politics, subtle or not, most of the female media elite get their opinions from the editorial page of *The New York Times*, now edited by Spin Sister Gail Collins who, for years, wrote for women's magazines including *McCall's* and *Rosie*. Their favorite columnists are Maureen Dowd in the *Times* and Anna Quindlen in *Newsweek*, who also wrote frequently in the past for *Good Housekeeping* and occasionally for *Family Circle* and whose middlebrow novels are bought largely by the readers of women's magazines. Collins and Quindlen, like Dowd, can be counted on to blast the administration with the fervor of true believers. They did not write about politics directly when they were freelancing for traditional women's magazines. Neither, for example, did conservative Peggy Noonan when she was writing for these magazines. But I'm sure that Quindlen, especially, felt most readers must naturally and unquestioningly share her liberal views when it comes to politics.

Nancy Pfotenhauer, the soft-spoken head of the Independent Women's Forum, a conservative women's think tank, says one of the reasons the Forum began its *Women's Quarterly* was to provide an outlet for opinion pieces and features aimed at women with an alternate point of view. For example, Nancy told me, we rarely see writing by women for women that promotes personal responsibility.[29] Today, whether it's *Marie Claire* or a Lifetime movie script, it's all government, all the time.

Editors might scoff at the notion that a magazine for middle-of-the-road or more conservative women is even necessary because, they'd insist, there is no liberal women-in-media conspiracy. Besides, they would say, they are famously tolerant of different opinions because being tolerant is a basic tenet of their belief system. That is, unless you don't agree with them, like Gloria Steinem, who oozes tolerance but has no problem calling Texas senator Kay Bailey Hutchison "a female impersonator" because she disagrees on "women's issues."[30] Consider the monumental hatchet job that was done on Florida recount official Katherine Harris, who is now a congresswoman. About Harris, *The Washington Post* Style reporter Robin Givhan snidely commented that Harris looked as if she "applied her makeup with a trowel," "can't even use restraint when she's wielding a mascara wand," and concluded, "why should anyone trust her?"[31] Real insightful political commentary.

There have been several best-selling books decrying media bias on television news programs and in newspapers. On TV, that bias may be more understated since it can be expressed through a word, a gesture, a well-timed comment, by Katie and Diane.

Not so with women's magazines: Whether it's *Marie Claire* or *Cosmopolitan* or *Redbook* or more than a dozen others—nearly all of whose takes on cultural or political issues are far more brazen than television in expressing their one-sided political preferences. If you are a reader of any of these magazines, how could you not be influenced? How could you not be impressed by being told over and over about the obvious good-heartedness and right-mindedness of a parade of Hollywood hot shots celebrated in laudatory articles along with their inevitably liberal causes? Talented, popular, successful, famous women like Susan Sarandon (who looks so great for her age) and Rosie O'Donnell (who has been so generous to kids) or Sheryl Crow or Barbra Streisand or Julianne Moore or Meryl Streep. Who wouldn't be at least a little swayed to support the views of these women that you have been told over and over you should admire?

Women of the Year

In my analysis of nine major women's magazines over a three-year period, there were seventy-five articles slanted toward a left point of view or sympathetic to women on the left like the sainted Marian Wright Edelman, head of the Children's Defense Fund. The same pantheon of women are featured over and over and allowed to express their political opinions as if they are the only ones worth having. Women's media needs celebrity. And celebrities with a cause are often the most available of all, at least for positive interviews and profiles.

For example, between 2000 and 2002, Susan Sarandon was featured in *Glamour, Good Housekeeping, McCall's, Rosie,* as well as celebrated in *Redbook* as a "Mother and Shaker."[32] I've already shared the details of *MORE's* pricey sucking-up salute to Susan in February 2002. And I don't doubt that I've missed a few other laudatory articles about Sarandon in other publications mostly read by women. And every time Susan ("passionate on the subject of injustice")[33] is featured, every time she speaks out for her causes, the magazines praise her like Mother Teresa with a makeover, enthusing in equal measure about how good she looks and how wonderful her cause is. Sarandon, a shrewd, experienced operative, knows exactly how valuable this access and exposure is to her career *and* her cause du jour.

Sarandon told *Redbook,* when they honored her, that celebrity makes speaking out a lot easier. "When I have an opportunity to pass on information, I do. That's how we bring about change."[34]

Right.

Though one gutsy woman who isn't about to change her views because of Sarandon is her own crusty, seventy-nine-year-old mother. While Sarandon was one of the leaders of the Hollywood campaign against the war in Iraq, her mom, Lenora Tomalin, told Lloyd Grove of *The Washington Post,* "I am a conservative. I voted for George W. Bush, and I simply agree with most everything he has said." Of her daughter's anti-administration activism, Tomalin said, "That's a given. That's the way she thinks. That's what Hollywood thinks. We don't agree, but I respect her. More than she does me."[35]

But surely her eldest child can respect her mother's opinion without agreeing with her?

Lenora's response: "*Wanna bet.* . . . When I visit Susan I tread on eggs. . . . The most difficult time was during the presidential election. . . . I live in Florida and I was a Republican poll-watcher. . . . I was sitting at the breakfast table [and my thirteen-year-old grandson said] 'I hear you voted for Bush.' . . . Susan said, 'All he wants to know is how could you have voted for Bush?' And I thought, I'm not going to discuss my politics with a thirteen-year-old who has been brainwashed, and just let it go."

A few days later at a party at the Academy Awards where Susan had coyly flashed a *V* as a peace symbol for the cameras, free-speech, anti-war advocate actor Tim Robbins, Saradon's longtime companion, threatened the *Post* reporter. "If you ever write about my family again I will [bleeping] find you and I will [bleeping] hurt you."[36]

Don't you wonder what Thanksgiving dinner must be like at their house? I'd just send flowers and stay home.

Though it sometimes seems like the Sarandon/Robbins hit squad are media darlings (and they are), they're not alone. Look at Jane Fonda, another perennial favorite of women's media. While Sarandon, at least, can promote a movie she is starring in along with her "opportunities to pass on information," Jane has not made a movie in years.

Doesn't matter. She was still featured in *O, Vogue, Marie Claire,* and in *Good Housekeeping* in the issue that appeared just before the 2000 election.[37] (The always objective Katie Couric and Democratic political operative Susan Estrich were also featured in that November 2000 *Good Housekeeping* issue, a particularly one-sided grouping.)[38]

In the *Vogue* article, titled "Super Jane," the blurb declares, "Jane Fonda has re-dedicated herself to political activism . . . And she's as radical as ever." When Jane told the *Vogue* interviewer "toward the end of the sixties . . . I went through a personal profound transformation. I saw that when people united around an ideal that is right and noble and speaks to justice and democracy, it could change the world,"[39] her words went unchallenged. Nobody mentions Jane's activities in Vietnam in that *Vogue* article or recalls the fact that while she smiled next to a Vietcong anti-aircraft gun in Hanoi, it was the daily torture of our POWs that was changed. They were beaten more severely on the day she was posing sexily for the cameras. Quite a noble idea there, Jane.

She also told *Vogue,* "The forces of darkness that are now in Washington are absolutely opposed to the empowerment of women."[40] The forces of darkness? Tell that to Condi Rice. The *Vogue* article was full of glamorous photos of Jane and laudatory comments about her goodness from the executive director of the nonprofit that Fonda founded, not exactly an impartial appraisal.

The same softball interviewing style goes for other political activists, too, those without an Oscar on the shelf but with a Democratic party membership card in their wallets. When you read over and over again about tough, shrewd activists like Eve Ensler and Million Mom March Donna Dees-Thomases in one of your favorite magazines, they're not portrayed as having very specific, well-financed agendas but rather as selfless supporters of causes that, it is implied, would benefit all women and with which all women, inevitably, should agree.

Besides being praised by Katie on *Today's* Special Mother's Day edition, Donna and her Million Mom March got enthusiastic treatment from a variety of magazines, including *Marie Claire*, which raised money for her cause. Dees-Thomases was featured in *Parents*, *Parenting*, and *Glamour* as well. She was honored as one of "25 Mothers We Love" by *Working Mother* and as a "Mother and Shaker" by *Redbook*, and honored again by *Glamour* as a Woman of the Year.[41]

Although there was no mention of her political ties, *Redbook* did tell their readers in an issue a month before the election that Dees-Thomases's next goal was: "Getting out the vote in November."

"The most important thing now," she says, "is to vote for congressmen, state legislators, and senators who are intent on making changes."[42] Translation: Anyone who is anti-gun, most probably a Democrat. But Donna ended up being more albatross than delivering angel for the Democrats. One of Al Gore's top strategists later said that the vice president's biggest mistake was ever mentioning the word "guns." Gore's position on guns cost him the traditionally Democratic state of West Virginia and thus the presidency. Exactly the kind of hardheaded political truth that *West Wing*'s Josh Lyman would understand and would put his pal Amy into a pouty sulk.

It's during what political pros call the silly season campaign time that editors seem to drop any pretense of objectivity and let their liberal instincts run amok. But don't take my word for it. Just listen to what Media Watch, an ultraliberal feminist media-watchdog group, had to say about how women's magazines covered the last presidential campaign.

Focusing primarily on publications for young women, they concluded: "Overall the magazines support Al Gore, following his liberal sway on the issues and see him as the candidate who will best serve women."[43] So much for any pooh-poohing of conservative complaints about liberal bias. Here was a liberal watchdog group openly cheering on what they saw as the leftward tilt of women's magazines.

That was especially true of *Glamour*, which, they noted, ran a blockbuster combination of anti-Bush features[44] as well as pro-Gore articles, including one about Karenna Gore Schiff.[45] She, of course, would be the candidate's attractive blond daughter. After the election, Karenna, a lawyer, tried a part-time job as a first-year associate with a prestigious New York firm. Now she toils for the Association to Benefit Children—the perfect liberal Democratic perch from which to launch a political career, and *Glamour* is helping to pay the Gore Schiff rent. Not that they need to. Schiff's husband, a physician and biotech venture capitalist, is the scion of one of the wealthiest families in New York. Cindi Leive, *Glamour*'s editor-in-chief, threw a chic little bash for Schiff to celebrate the young author's contribution to the magazine's November 2002 issue—an article on child care and working mothers.[46] This was a bit of a stretch. She may have two children, but child care is not exactly a daily dilemma for people in the Gore Schiff family income bracket.

When a reporter from *The Hill* newspaper in Washington asked about Karenna's obvious political biases, Cindi spouted rather defensively, "I think speaks with great authority about what it is like to be a young mother and a politically concerned young woman today" and "that Gore Schiff would definitely write again."[47]

Karenna, a favorite of the Spin Sisters throughout the campaign, was recently rewarded by Miramax with a $200,000 advance for her first book on American heroines.[48] You remember Miramax? The Disney offshoot, headed by mega-Democrat Harvey Weinstein, who supported her father's presidential campaign and who also funded Tina Brown's magazine flop, *Talk*. Yes, the Girls' Club manages to keep it in the family. But then, Democrats have always liked "welfare" and when it's six figures, you can understand why.

In analyzing *Glamour*'s political reporting, Media Watch wrote:

"*Glamour* magazine actually gave the elections a lot of coverage. In September, they ran an editorial entitled, 'Election 2000: Time for a Supreme Decision—Are You One Robe Away from Losing a Century's Worth of Civil Rights?'"[49]

Scary, huh? The piece dramatically plays up the progression of women's rights over the years, and then gives scenarios of what could happen if rights are taken away by the appointment of new Supreme Court justices. One such scenario depicts a friend calling to say she needs an abortion . . . only she'll have to find $3,000 and take a trip to the Caribbean to get it. *Glamour* then ominously asserts, "These scenarios sound like throwback nightmares, but they're just a taste of what you might wake up to if the next president names additional conservative justices to the Supreme Court."[50]

The article also recounts recent appointments and adds that if a conservative justice were appointed, then job opportunities, advancements, and rights that women have taken for granted "could be ripped to pieces."[51] I'm surprised *Glamour* didn't sell the film rights to Miramax for a horror movie. I can see it now. "Coming soon to your local theater: George W. Bush in the *Texas Chainsaw Massacre of Women's Rights.*"

The editorial discusses how each presidential candidate would fill vacated Supreme Court seats. Sarah Weddington, the Texas lawyer who argued *Roe* v. *Wade* in 1973, is quoted as saying, "The price of freedom is voting in November."[52] Comments Media Watch, "*Glamour* obviously supports Gore in this editorial, but does not come out and say it."[53] Do they have to?

But just in case you weren't sure how *Glamour* really, *really* felt, the magazine did come out and endorse Gore in the November issue by declaring, under a picture of the vice president and his familiar daughter: "A vote for Gore is a vote for you."[54] Of course the catch is that *Glamour*'s editors are ignoring what many of their own readers want. In a poll the magazine conducted, 40 percent of the readers said they would vote for George W. Bush, which was exactly the same number who would vote for Al Gore.[55]

Marie Claire's get-out-the-vote article was written, surprisingly enough, by Democratic supporter movie producer Harvey Weinstein who is, according to the magazine, "a closet journalist." Well, Harvey stepped out of the closet to tell readers why he was going to vote for Gore, and you should too.[56] Not exactly impartial journalism.

Not to be outdone, *Cosmopolitan,* in its November 2000 issue, asked former model Christie Brinkley, an anti–nuclear power activist and delegate to the Democratic Convention, to encourage *Cosmo* girls to get up, get out, and vote. And though the piece told readers to vote for whoever they wanted, Christie just wanted to let us know which lever she was going to pull. She wrote that Al Gore "advocates stronger gun control and defends abortion rights so that women can choose what happens to their own bodies. His views on education and health care are also parallel to mine, and, well, I just happen to believe that he has the depth, character, and experience to stand up to the people and organizations that threaten our country's future."[57]

Now *that's* nonpartisan.

After the election, these magazines continued using the same tactics. *Glamour* once again turned to the now very bitter Karenna Gore Schiff for advice on "how to make George W.'s term a lot less scary."[58] Like that sophisticated, more informed friend I talked about earlier, Karenna lets you in on all the organizations you absolutely must depend on to get your unbiased political information, including such notably objective, nonpartisan groups as the Feminist Majority Foundation, the Children's Defense Fund, the Million Mom March, and the Public Interest Research Group.

Cosmo saved its post-election advice for the Bush twins. "Work your dad (please)" just the way Chelsea did. In the *Cosmo* story, we read, "According to Iris Martin, a psychology expert who spent three years as advisor to Bill Clinton, Chelsea was instrumental in her dad's decision to enact the NAFTA trade agreement." Martin says that Clinton told his cabinet that when he thought about what was most important, it was to give Chelsea the best future he could. (I guess maybe he wasn't thinking about that *all* the time.) It was Papa Clinton's concern about Chelsea, Martin insists, that cemented the NAFTA deal. Despite the absurdity of this claim, *Cosmo* coyly editorializes, "If Barbara and Jenna Bush have any such charge over their father, pro-choice women across America should hope they have a more liberal view on abortion than he does. Now does arch-conservative Attorney General John Ashcroft have any daughters?"[59]

Cute. Well, if he does, I'm sure they wouldn't be given 1,500 words to sound off the way Karenna was.

Marie Claire doesn't even try to be cute. How can it be? All these beauty and fashion magazines that use so many of their pages to tell readers to get gorgeous for him or to shop until you drop because you deserve nothing less, remain stridently feminist when it comes to politics. Since their version of feminism has now neatly morphed into narcissism and consumerism, they probably see no contradiction in such views. *Marie Claire,* for example, in a November 2002 column, entitled "What Women Want," came out swinging and endorsed an old-style feminist agenda that even most fire-breathing feminists gave up a quarter of a century ago. *Marie Claire* claimed that the Equal Rights Amendment now has "a better chance than ever" of being passed.[60] Perhaps in a parallel universe. And it offered the familiar statistics about the wage gap between men and women, making readers believe once again that women in general are paid less for exactly the same work as men.

It just isn't so. The "wage gap" *Marie Claire* loves to cite is a crude comparison, based on the average wages of men and women, without regard to important factors such as age, education, occupation, or experience. When those key variables are taken into account, women earn essentially as much as men. In fact, as *Marketing to Women* reports, some more recent statistics show that young unmarried professional women—target *Marie Claire* readers—now earn exactly as much as if not *more* than men in similar jobs.[61]

Nancy Pfotenhauer, the economist president of the Independent Women's Forum, has often countered the NOW-familiar claims of widespread wage discrimination. On Equal Pay Day, April 3, 2001, her group held a press conference on Capitol Hill just after Hillary Clinton and the National Committee on Pay Equity held theirs—the annual women-as-victims whine-a-thon on pay scales.

"Their study was done originally in the Clinton Administration but was so full of flaws, it was never released," Nancy recalled. "After they gave their report, I think we were able to very clearly and very effectively bust the wage-gap myth. But there was only one problem," she admitted. Part of the public relations campaign that the committee had concocted for Equal Pay Day that year was to ask women to wear red to show their concern about the alleged wage gap. "When I walked into the room and looked at the women reporters gathered there, I was facing a sea of red—red suits, red sweaters, red dresses."

Nancy says she has grown used to partisanship displayed by female journalists covering women's issues. "I remember the first time I was on a television talk show. I realized within a minute that I not only had to debate the person who had a different point of view from mine but that I was going to have to debate the host as well. That is usually the case. I must really know my stuff and have my facts and figures exactly because I am always challenged. My opponent can say something that is not true or cite some figures that I know are absolutely wrong, but she very rarely gets tough questions. I always do."[62]

Trash Talking the "Crazies"

Because of its increasing influence with the current administration, the Independent Women's Forum has become a prime target of one-sided women's media reporting. Comedian Janeane Garofalo, best known for her sputtering anti-war rages at the Bush administration, calls the forum a bunch of "crazy women," though its board is made up of academics, lawyers, and economists, most with Ph.D.s. Janeane apparently dreams of being the first stand-up comedian to be appointed Secretary of State.

A *Washington Post* article, written by Richard Morin and Claudia Deane, gave a more accurate picture of the group's beliefs and its aims: "The Independent Women's Forum champions a laissez-faire brand of conservatism that stresses limited government, free-market capitalism and personal responsibility, but with a gendered twist. It is one of the few women's groups willing to challenge the central beliefs of feminist organizations, arguing that contemporary feminism is too willing to cast women as victims."[63] Amen!

But six months later, another *Washington Post* staffer, Mary Remuzzi, did a "Lizzie Borden" on the group in a *Marie Claire* "What Women Want" column. The piece, titled "Are Your Rights in Jeopardy?" had a caption: "A group on Capitol Hill wants to throw out laws guaranteeing equal rights for women."[64] (Doesn't the hysterical hyperbole of many women's magazines when it comes to conservatives make trial lawyers and consumer groups seem almost tame in comparison?) In the piece, Kim Gandy, president of NOW, declared, "They are a very small elite group that holds extremists views by almost anyone's standards." This from the woman who heads an organization that has opposed all welfare reform, calling it a "death sentence for tens of thousands of women and children." Gandy herself once said, "I think promoting marriage as a goal in and of itself is misguided."[65] That certainly sounds mainstream.

Nancy Pfotenhauer counters, "I am not an extremist. I feel I am a real feminist. I believe in rights for women. I want what feminists want, to vote, to have my daughters educated. I want to be paid the same as a man if I am doing the same job. But I don't think women, because we are women, are victims and I believe in personal responsibility." Pretty extreme, all right.

Here's the real deal—the real reason Gandy and her friends are so consumed with attacking the IWF. Just follow the money—government money. The Independent Women's Forum does not get any funds from the federal government while the NOW Legal Defense Fund receives hundreds of thousands of dollars in aid each year. Your tax dollars at work. In just one grant, the U.S. Justice Department's Office of Violence Against Women forked over $455,000 to the NOW Legal Defense Fund. When Nancy Pfotenhauer was appointed to the office's National Advisory Committee, Gandy huffed, "I'm appalled."[66] Pfotenhauer, whose group has criticized the Violence Against Women Act for its one-size-fits-all framework, said she never had an intention of undoing the law but rather to give states more flexibility in how it is implemented. Exactly what such an organization doesn't want—more local control of funding, which might cut them out of the action.

Donna Dees-Thomases, Susan Sarandon, Ann Richards, Marian Wright Edelman, Hillary Clinton, Karenna Gore Schiff. Campaign season or not, the Spin Sisters promote and praise these same women and causes again and again. Of course, editors do realize that First Lady Laura Bush is popular, and she appears on an occasional cover and on an interview show. And there have been one or two features during the past couple of years on Lynne Cheney, and Condoleezza Rice, who often turns down requests for such interviews. But a constant array of liberal, feminist, or just garden variety Democrat second stringers are the regular recipients of puff pieces. In *Good Housekeeping*, for example, which is scrupulously nonpartisan when it gives its yearly awards for women in government, there were also pieces on Senator John Edwards, Senator Jean Carnahan, Geraldine Ferraro, and several on the former Texas governor Ann Richards—all Democrats.[67] In 2002, a historic election year when Republicans kept their control of the House and won back the Senate, the politician who was one of *Glamour*'s Women of the Year was Democratic Congresswoman Nancy Pelosi.[68] Shining the spotlight on Pelosi's role as the first woman to serve as Minority Leader in the Congress was perfectly justified, but couldn't a Republican senator or congresswoman have made the list as well? Congresswoman Deborah Pryce was elected to head the important Republican Conference that same year, the first woman to hold that leadership position, but *Glamour* just couldn't summon the wherewithal to actually honor a Republican. So much for balance.

Why don't such women appear as often in print or on television for that matter? Why aren't their impressive accomplishments celebrated? How come even those blond bombshells, Ann Coulter and Laura Ingraham, who certainly are successful and photogenic, are almost never written about or featured in women's magazines? In part, because, in Manhattan media circles, conservative women are the political and social equivalent of a Quaker in a Ferrari—they simply don't belong. Venture in with conservative credentials, and you'll be shunned with or without a book at the top of *The New York Times* best-seller list or your own radio program or think tank.

Here's an example of what I mean. One of the Independent Women's Forum's most interesting initiatives is the Infant Care Project, which was launched to enable new mothers widowed by the events of 9/11 to pay for in-home child care for their babies. Nancy, who has five children under fourteen, told me, "We wanted to help address a unique challenge that these young widows faced—taking care of their babies without the physical help and support of a spouse. When it comes to infant care, too often the dad's role is discounted. Most people tend to think first about the loss of a husband in terms of loss of income. For these mothers, it also means the loss of that extra pair of helping hands."

Ultimately, IWF gave $4,000 grants for child-care assistance to each of the 102 pregnant mothers who lost their husbands in the attacks. It also hosted a baby shower luncheon in New York for the mothers around the first anniversary of the attack. Almost sixty of the moms, many with babies in tow, attended the event. A *Wall Street Journal* editorial lauded the project: "No one is going to pretend that a few thousand dollars for baby care meets all the challenges that these families are facing or that there aren't other wonderful things being done. But the IWF effort strikes us as a particularly striking note of grace, one designed to give women so busy responding to the demands of their young ones the wherewithal for the simple but crucial things that other families take for granted."[69]

As the 9/11 event was being planned, a producer for ABC, who had also brought together some of the new mothers for a special *Primetime* with Diane Sawyer, told IWF that the program would do a story on the project and luncheon but only if they had a guaranteed exclusive. Charity or not, national tragedy or not, snagging the exclusive "get" supersedes all other causes.

"We agreed because we thought it would mention our Web site and increase fund-raising for the mothers," Pfotenhauer recalled. Just a few days before the luncheon, Sawyer and *Primetime* suddenly backed out.

A publicist working with IWF was astounded by their unexpected change of heart. Maybe Diane didn't want to share credit for her "get." Or maybe the *Primetime* producers were uncomfortable with IWF's politics and didn't want to be positive about a women's group that didn't talk the usual talk. Someone at ABC asked if Ann Coulter belonged to the group. She never has. But so what if she had? Was this producer unwilling, even for the best of causes, to highlight the efforts of a women's group without the usual agenda?

Ask Dr. Laura

The press's dissing of the Independent Women's Forum is mild compared to what has happened to other extremely well-known women whose opinions might be fairly typical of many women in this country but far different than those of the Spin Sisters. Remember the trashing that all the women—Kathleen Willey, Monica, Linda Tripp of Monicagate—got (except, of course, Hillary). Or the joke Katherine Harris became? But nobody was hit harder than Dr. Laura Schlessinger. When I even suggested to an agreeable, mild-mannered editor who was working on an issue of *Women's Faith & Spirit* magazine that maybe we should interview Dr. Laura for one of our stories, the editor, who considers herself both very spiritual and very tolerant, vehemently protested.

"That makes me very, very uncomfortable," she declared, raising her voice (and she never, never raises her voice). "Laura Schlessinger is so prejudiced. So intolerant. So full of hate. She hates gays, doesn't she?"

Had she ever listened to Laura Schlessinger, I asked? Schlessinger is *the* most listened-to woman ever on radio, with a weekly audience of 18 million.

"No," she said, "but my sister listens to her. As a matter of fact, my sister loves her." And is her sister full of hate?

"No, she's great. Of course, she's very religious. . . ." Her voice trailed off, and she thought a minute. "But if we wrote about Laura Schlessinger, wouldn't that be a problem? Wouldn't there be some kind of protests? Do you think we'd get in trouble? I don't think it's worth it."

And there you have it—the typical reaction to Laura Schlessinger by women, no matter how gentle or spiritual, in media. They won't go near a conservative woman and her views if it could lead to trouble with a relentless foe like GLAAD, the Gay and Lesbian Alliance Against Defamation, or NOW or other establishment liberal groups. Besides, GLAAD and NOW have great influence with celebrities, and we all know how much media depends on celebrities. There is the social aspect as well. Spin Sisters constantly attend fund-raisers or win awards from these groups. At a recent series of star-studded GLAAD galas held in New York, Los Angeles, and San Francisco that raised

$2.5 million for the organization, Diane Sawyer won the Excellence in Media Award. Other celeb honorees, entertainers, and presenters that evening included Rosie O'Donnell, Eric McCormack, Tony Bennett, k.d. lang, Cyndi Lauper, Nicole Kidman, Lauren Bacall, Phil Donahue, and Marlo Thomas. One hundred corporate sponsors footed the bill.

But when it came to Dr. Laura, GLAAD was determined to make her a commercial persona non grata. So editors and producers had two choices—beat up on her, too, or play it safe and ignore her completely. In the fashion of the worst censors of the McCarthyite '50s, these groups, by threatening economic retaliation against advertisers, scared off even the few brave editors out there willing to consider running an opposing viewpoint. And ironically, GLAAD and others like them are portrayed by the media as the defenders of tolerance in America. Go figure.

In 1999, Schlessinger inked a big deal with Paramount to launch a syndicated television show and a slew of sponsors immediately signed on. Dr. Laura is tough-minded, traditional, and judgmental, and her millions of listeners respect her for her views as well as for expressing them unequivocally. Although she was the first person on radio to take calls from openly gay callers and to discuss their problems, she has also called homosexuality "a terrible sadness" and "deviant sexual behavior."

Explaining her views, Laura says, "I never called homosexual human beings deviants. I have pointed out that homosexual behavior deviates from the norm of heterosexuality and is forbidden by Scriptures." Laura has also said, "People who are gay are not to be hated or attacked. I spent most of my career supporting groups like Parents and Friends of Lesbians and Gays because I didn't want families to throw out their children because they were gay or lesbian." Are Laura's views so outrageous? So absolutely out of the mainstream? Probably not. Still, she has been turned into a symbol of hate-mongering and intolerance.

Laura explained to me, "They didn't like me when I was on radio. But they thought that when I had a television show, I would have even more influence—too much influence. That was the trouble. I could influence people. I could influence voters. I supported [California's] Proposition 22. [It forbids homosexual marriage.] GLAAD hated that, and so they decided to get me. And they did."[70]

A carefully constructed campaign combined the forces of GLAAD with an Internet site called StopDrLaura.com and the Horizon Foundation, aided by the public relations skills of Fenton Communications. Dr. Laura's potential sponsors, as well as Paramount, which syndicated the TV show, were targeted. GLAAD and other gay groups viewed Schlessinger not as an adversary to be debated but as an enemy to be silenced. Many carefully planned and well-staged anti-Laura activities were aimed at making her a liability to her production company and sponsors. Among them was a rally held outside Paramount studios where Joan Garry, GLAAD's leader, declared that the company should realize that it didn't buy "controversy when they bought this show. They bought trouble." Garry also declared to the cheering crowd that if Schlessinger couldn't be "controlled" then "she must be stopped." Joseph McCarthy would have been proud.

While sponsors received anonymous bomb threats, Dr. Laura was subjected to death threats. Using the same kind of tactics some anti-abortion groups use against family planning clinics—which liberal groups rightly decry—Laura was hounded and harassed. Flyers were passed out in her neighborhood comparing her to Hitler and Milosevic and suggesting she be "confronted" personally about her "behavior and destructiveness" to the lives of gays.[71]

Now where was Glenda Bailey, the crusading editor for Princess Abankwah? Certainly not protesting the genuine injustice done to this woman wrongly accused and abused. Dr. Laura was a real victim of hate and intolerance for promulgating an opposing view, but women in media all but ignored her politically incorrect plight. Besides, Glenda and the rest of the Sisters, I'm sure, didn't want GLAAD harassing their advertisers, either.

Ultimately, Laura's television show was canceled and even her extremely popular radio show lost over $30 million in advertising. "I took the hits. I couldn't get a speaking engagement for two years," Laura said. "But the radio show was so strong they couldn't hurt it. Ultimately, my listeners were just too loyal."

It is interesting that a prominent woman in media who simply didn't share the views of Spin Sisters and the intolerant left was so successfully attacked and with such unrelenting viciousness. This has made it impossible for any of her achievements to be even noted in media for women. Laura is almost never featured, certainly never lauded, never even photographed—though she is slim and attractive and, by the way, a perfect example of a working mom able to balance career and family. Though talk radio is a particularly difficult beat for women, Laura was the first and only female ever to win the National Association of Broadcaster's Marconi Award for outstanding radio personality. Laura says, half jokingly, about receiving this award, "Did I get touted as a Woman of the Year?" Remember, more women listen to her each night than have seen all of the performances of Eve Ensler's *The Vagina Monologues* everywhere in the world. "Did I get a phone call from NOW for this breakthrough achievement for women? Get a congratulatory phone call from Gloria or Pat Ireland? Nope. But, then, maybe they didn't know about this breakthrough milestone for equality because our 'sisters' in media saw to it that not a word of the award made it into magazines or onto TV news."

Inside the Matrix

Though men in the media elite may have divergent opinions and can joke about it, women very rarely do. Toeing the party line in sandals or slingbacks is serious business, very serious. The best proof I can offer you is something called the Matrix Awards luncheon held every year by New York's Women in Communications. It is a sold-out spring event at the Waldorf Astoria Hotel paid for by magazine companies, networks, and the top advertisers of beauty and health products for women. Billed as a celebration of women's achievement, the presenters of the awards at the luncheon can be even glitzier than the award winners. Let me fess up before I go any further: I won a Matrix Award, but that was in the days when it was celebrated with a low-key, cozy little luncheon. And my boss at the time, similarly low-key, was the one who presented my award. Obviously, I peaked too soon.

Nowadays, the Matrix Award presentation is a superglossy production with full-page ads in *The New York Times,* and paparazzi in attendance while *Extra* and *Access Hollywood* show snippets of the event, cooing over the recipients as if they had just been handed an Oscar.

So who gets what from whom? Well, during the last few years, Hillary gave Katie Couric her Matrix Award. Barbara Walters gave Kati Marton, wife of Clintonista Richard Holbrooke, her award. Longtime feminist activist Marlo ("Free to be you and me") Thomas handed the prize to Carole Black of Lifetime. Susan Sarandon wannabe, actress, and AIDS activist Rosie Perez gave Eve Ensler—you knew she'd get one—her award. Sheryl Crow did the honors for Judy McGrath, the president of MTV. Democratic senator Mary Landrieu came up from Washington for Sally Minard, an advertising expert who was on the team that helped elect Hillary to the Senate.

The only way this luncheon could get any more incestuous is if it were held somewhere in the backwoods of West Virginia. It has become absolutely the biggest event celebrating and highlighting New York media women. Occasionally, even men are allowed to get into the act. But only certain PC guys. One year Robert Redford was the surprise presenter of the award to his longtime publicist Lois Smith. Director Mike Nichols, Diane's husband, gave an award to Meryl Streep. And Bill Clinton was the perfectly tailored "surprise presenter" for octogenarian reporter Helen Thomas. He flattered her—and she flattered him back—while 1,500 women swooned and applauded. At that lunch, Helen launched into her first news-making tirade against President Bush, which she continued at almost every White House press briefing she attended.

On one episode of *The West Wing*, even C.J. Cregg, President Josiah Bartlet's feminist press secretary, goes to New York to pick up her Matrix Award. Through the years, I have attended at least fifteen of these lunches and it is obvious that C.J. Cregg would certainly fit right in. No doubt snooty Amy is next in line, and she'll probably choose Katie Couric to present her Matrix.

Is this media back scratching a planned feminist conspiracy? Not really, though the absence of a cabal doesn't mean these women don't exert enormous influence. They do, but the media Girls' Club is more like a high school clique than a political action committee. In fact, somebody once compared Michael's to a high school cafeteria with a lot of money. Who sits with whom. Who waves at whom. Who air kisses whom is what's important. Many of these women are like the girls back at North Side High, desperate to belong to the in crowd. They want to be friends with the cool girls, the popular ones, the ones with the hottest clothes and a direct line to the hottest guys, and are willing to do just about anything to make it happen. They want to sit on the dais someday too and get or give the awards. And when it comes to echoing opinions of the girls like Katie and Diane and Hillary, who were Most Likely to Succeed, and did, the freshmen up-and-comers understand the rules of the game: never get on the bad side of a Spin Sister. Full membership in the Girls' Club goes only to those who stick to the party line and suck up. These younger women find it is a lot easier to get along by going along, to get ahead by agreeing. As any high schooler will tell you, taking on the most popular girls in the class is risky business that rarely pays off. In all the years of the Matrix Award, it is amazing that not one woman who is well known for having a right-of-center viewpoint has received an award. (I got mine before I'd morphed into the unashamedly outspoken Republican I am today.) Meanwhile, Eve Ensler, whose current anti-violence campaign sports the sweeping slogan "Afghanistan Is Everywhere," and draws parallels between women terrorized by the Taliban and unhappy American housewives, is a sure winner. Drat! And I've just packed my burka away for the summer.

The funny thing is that while the members of the Girls' Club may laughingly acknowledge that they suffer from at least a mild case of Manhattan provincialism, trust me, deep down they really don't think they are being provincial. How can they since they believe themselves to be the true voices in the cultural dialogue? These women really think they are always fair in the way they report news or edit stories or position a celebrity because they are not promoting a strident feminist agenda and don't even want to. Anna Quindlen is a feminist writer in *Newsweek* and proud of it, but she presents herself differently in *Family Circle*. Shrewd editors and writers know an old-style blatantly feminist message would not go over with their audiences. American women are positive about the gains women have made in the past decades, but they dislike a strident "feminist" label.

So it is a mix of Manhattan provincialism—hey, if we believe it here, they should believe it everywhere—combined with elitism, liberalism, and plain old ambition that keeps this sisterhood together. And keeps magazines and television aimed at women from fairly reflecting the rainbow of opinions that ordinary women embrace.

You aren't really a lot like them.

And they just don't get it.

CHAPTER 10

Not a Bit Like You

But what about you? I've been telling you how women's media think you think. Are they on target or way off-base? How do most women really feel about politics? What issues really matter to women when they enter a voting booth? Deep down are we liberal feminists pulling the lever based on issues like abortion, gun control, and gay rights? Or for most of us, isn't there a range of issues like health care, personal security, education, and the economy that really pushes our buttons? And don't we have as many different opinions about these issues as we do about everything else, from getting ahead at the office to getting a teenage son to do, well, anything?

Funny, isn't it, that women's magazines like *Marie Claire* and *Glamour* and *Redbook* and so many others give you lots of options when it comes to prices and styles in their fashion features, plus lots of different products to mull over on their beauty pages. But whether in their editorials or between the lines of their feature stories, they offer you only one opinion, about any and all social or political issues.

Remember that in *Marie Claire*, a magazine half-owned by a French company, its frequently over-the-top, far-left editorial column is called "What Women Want," not "What Some Women Want" or "What We Want Women to Want." But this arrogant one-view-fits-all approach doesn't work. In a *Ladies' Home Journal*–iVillage survey, we found at least six different kinds of women voters, including the SUV Mom, the True Believer, and the Young and Hip. Republican pollster Linda DiVall says that there are at least sixteen different subgroups of potential women voters. Our bodies are not all the same. Neither, thank God, are our minds.

Falling into the Gender Gap

The original suffragists envisioned that once women got the vote in 1920, we would vote as a cohesive bloc. Never happened. Except when we made a really big mistake and voted for Prohibition. What were we thinking? After that, up until 1980, women tended to vote the same way as the men in their lives. And, if anything, women tended to be a little more conservative than men. In a lot of families, Dad was the Democrat, and Mom was the Republican. But in 1980, Eleanor Smeal, a political scientist who became NOW's president, noticed one small bit of good news in what she considered the bad news of Ronald Reagan's victory over Jimmy Carter.

Though more women (46 percent) had voted for Reagan than for Carter (45 percent), a higher percentage of men (54 percent) had voted for the Republican candidate. According to Kathy Bonk, a public relations expert who has written the official history of how the gender gap was sold to the press, Smeal turned that statistical disparity into an effective long-term political game plan. While Reagan's pollsters were also trying to understand the meaning of his trailing numbers with women, NOW prepared for a meeting with the Democratic National Committee by putting together a chart highlighting what they labeled "Reagan's Female Problem." Both Reagan's pollster and a NOW official came up with the term "gender gap" almost simultaneously, though NOW has always claimed the phrase as its own. But far more important was the fact that NOW had effectively promoted yet another new difference between men and women at a time when feminism was still fashionable.

Bonk wrote, "Until the gender gap made front-page headlines in 1980, a woman's vote was not taken seriously."[1] But in elections throughout the next two decades, the notion that women and men voted differently and that despite class, education, and income, women all voted alike simply because they were women, became an accepted fact, endorsed by Democratic operatives and a sympathetic media. Democratic pollster Celinda Lake, just like Amy on *The West Wing*, gave support to this notion by proclaiming unequivocally, "Women are Democrats; men are Republicans."[2] Excuse me. What am I? Chopped liver?

Actually, she may be half right. In the recent 2000 and 2002 elections, some political analysts noticed that the real gender gap belongs to the Democrats, who have trouble getting men to vote for their candidates. As pollsters Morin and Deane wrote before the 2000 election, "A recent *USA Today* headline said: 'Women hold the key. In a close race female vote might deliver victory.' Oh please. 'Deliver victory?'" they scoffed. "Certainly, there are persistent differences between men and women at the ballot box, but they are typically smaller than people believe. More important, the changing nature and size of the gender gap is not about women and their growing attraction to the Democratic party. It's mostly about men and how guys disproportionately have dumped the Democrats and turned their attentions to the Republican party."[3]

Still, the gap between men and women, which, according to Morin and Deane, is more a crack than a chasm,[4] is important because women are a larger share of the population and a greater proportion of us tend to vote. In some recent elections, women have cast more than 55 percent of the votes. Pretty darn good for a group that can barely manage to get through the day, or so our Spin Sisters would have us believe. The gender gap was most apparent in the presidential election of 1996 and continued in 2000. It was less evident in 2002. Yet even in those elections, women did not vote as a unified bloc. Could it be that women don't actually think alike—at least outside the confines of Manhattan? Surprisingly, it is Harvard professor and Democrat Anna Greenberg, daughter of Clinton and Gore pollster Stan Greenberg, who deconstructed the gender gap, noting that every presidential election in the 1990s came with its own gender story, which was widely publicized but was, in fact, more myth than truth.

"In 1992, it was the 'Year of the Woman.' In 1994, apparently 'Angry White Men' elected a Republican Congress. And in 1996, it was the 'Soccer Moms' who, supposedly, enthusiastically endorsed Bill Clinton. These stories were not based on empirical reality," Greenberg wrote, "but rather are the construction of the media, political consultants, and interest groups. For instance, the Soccer Mom story . . . referred inconsistently to a variety of women and certainly did not tap a recognized identity group in American politics. The Soccer Mom story also obscured the fact that working-class women were more likely than middle-class suburban women to support Bill Clinton's re-election bid."[5]

In the *Journal*–iVillage study, our SUV moms, akin to Soccer Moms, were more likely to be Republicans, 44 percent to 30 percent. Earth to media: Not all Soccer Moms think alike, vote alike, or drive Volvo station wagons.[6]

So why the fascination with the gender gap? Because it continues to be a handy way to paper over differences between women, and to once again sell women the notion that "sisters" all think alike. Greenberg is even more blunt: "The term 'gender gap' was a deliberate creation of the leaders of the women's movement and forcefully sold in [an] intensive and continuous effort to give reporters information and documentation on the women's vote. [But] like other gender stories, the gender gap also conceals important political differences between women. I would argue that it is certain groups of women that drive the gender gap rather than 'women' as a group."[7]

Who are we talking about here? In general, Democrats tend to capture the vast majority of African-American women voters, single women, and economically vulnerable women. White married women—especially those with children—tend slightly to favor Republicans while more traditional homemakers and evangelical Christian women are in the Republican camp.

"A majority of white women supported neither the Democratic Party nor President Clinton in the 1990s," wrote Greenberg in her gender gap analysis. "The Democratic winning margin among women in national elections is . . . provided by women of color."[8] Pollster Karlyn Bowman of the American Enterprise Institute says, "The gender gap is not the largest gap in our politics. The differences between married and single voters for example are larger." While William Kristol, editor of the *Weekly Standard*, has said, "Bigger still is the religious gap."[9]

But whether the gender gap is significant or a statistical anomaly, women's media embraced it and the agenda that went with it. Over the past decade, as magazines aimed at women increasingly told us how stressed we are and how afraid we should be, women more than men looked to an activist government to help them cope with problems in their lives, especially the personal problems of raising their children. By the mid-'90s, it seemed no truly "caring" politician could make a speech, no legislator could propose a law, that was not somehow "kiddie-centric." It got so bad I felt like force-feeding strained carrots to any candidate, Republican or Democrat, who uttered the word "child."

You want evidence of the infantilizing of politics? In the 1996 Democratic platform, the words "child," "childhood," or "children" appeared ninety times, and almost every government program that the platform endorsed was somehow related to kids. Clinton won reelection by talking to us about "soft," child-centered issues like school uniforms and teenage smoking. Forget that the federal government could do little about either. Clinton's uncanny ability to empathize worked, and other politicians took note. In the 2000 election, some commentators complained that candidates increasingly behaved as if they were auditioning for the role of Santa Claus rather than running for public office.

The "Nanny State"

Women in media, so focused on the new and trendy, would be horrified to hear themselves called old-fashioned. But they are. Children of the late '60s and '70s, most of these women are the generational leftovers of a far more liberal time when government was becoming bigger and government programs more and more bountiful. They are averse to risk and uncomfortable with change or even the idea of change. But in their belief that the federal government should act like Mary Poppins, they are clinging to traditional liberal notions that they pass along to you in magazines, on talk shows, and on evening news magazines, often subtly.

Up until the election of 2000, women, to a greater degree, said they preferred a large government with more services to a smaller government with fewer services. That's not surprising. Doesn't nearly every fear factor or victim-virus report imply that our government must do something to alleviate or solve an individual's problem? Usually it is the only solution that is ever offered. Like the young, unemployed, and uninsured mother of two asthmatic children featured in an August 2000 *Dateline* about people without health care. The program opens with an ominous-sounding announcer telling us, "Health care . . . you'll never see it the same way after meeting this little girl. She almost died because her mother didn't have thirty dollars."[10]

Reporter John Hockenberry then tells a weepy tale of a young couple with no health insurance trying to keep up with thousands of dollars in medical bills. We hear the mother complain that she can't afford medicines, and how her children's health may be permanently damaged as a result. We hear the story of her daughter's asthma attack that was nearly fatal though the mother waited three days to take her to the free clinic because "I didn't want to ask anybody for the thirty dollars." Huh?

We also discover that Dad is a computer repairman who makes $2,200 a month and that they live with his parents. He has decided against enrolling in the company's optional health plan because of its cost, while racking up as much as $900 a month in emergency room visits.

"I don't want them to look back and think, 'Well, Mom . . . why didn't you get that medicine for us?'" the mother says of her kids. Good question. Here's another one that Hockenberry, apparently, wasn't interested in asking: Exactly why hadn't getting a job crossed the mind of this seemingly able-bodied woman? Wouldn't part-time at McDonald's have covered the health insurance premiums or at a minimum $30 for a clinic visit? As in most of these sob stories in magazines and particularly on television, however, the obvious—especially if it entails personal responsibility—rarely enters into the discussion.

Instead, we saw only a weepy mom defeated by "the system," sick children, and the kind of heart-wrenching story that all but demands "Hillary care" as a national moral imperative.

In fact, we have been told so often that we should rely on government that the conservative alternative of smaller government and increased reliance on personal responsibility to solve problems can seem uncomfortably extreme and hard-hearted to many women.

Even more, there is the compassion factor. Women are nurturers. We like to think of ourselves as caring and giving, and are sympathetic to those we believe need our help. Stories in the media are masterfully spun for a women's audience to tug fiercely at our emotions, to make us feel as "stunned" as the sympathetic-seeming Spin Sister recounts yet another tragic tale. These stories often have political implications, but don't on the surface seem overtly partisan. So we are not even aware that our emotions are being manipulated for what could be a very specific political end.

This happens seamlessly all the time. Like the *Dateline* mother with the asthmatic children. Or Rosie O'Donnell's "For the Sake of the Children" prime-time special. Or the *Redbook* story about the mom with lead paint in her house. We are made to feel that if we even questioned the actions or motives of the victims, or just wanted more information about their plight, it implies we are harsh and uncaring. And women, especially, don't want to feel that way. Besides, there is this emotional double whammy: If we are so often made to believe we are victims ourselves, shouldn't we be unquestioningly sympathetic to victims who have even greater needs?

Gotcha and gotcha again.

As for Rosie and her slickly produced coming out? Look, if you are gay, I figure that's your business. You want to go on television and talk about issues that you care about? That's fine, too. My problem, as I said earlier, isn't hearing what Rosie had to say. It's the one-sided portrayal of issues like Rosie's adoption-law crusade by influential journalists like Diane Sawyer. Fairness simply demands more balance than we are currently getting. When it comes to politics, women are encouraged to be boundlessly sympathetic to one point of view. Not thoughtful. Not questioning. Often not even logical. Enough already!

A couple of years ago, I took part in a Washington forum on sex discrimination in which Democratic congresswoman Eleanor Holmes Norton was also speaking. I mentioned that in the magazine business, women and men who sell advertising space receive incentive payments based on a mathematical formula. If they produce revenue, they get well compensated. A magazine company didn't care if it was a man or woman who was bringing in the advertising page. In fact, today many ad sellers for magazines of any kind, not just for women's or fashion magazines, are women. I also said that women who made money for their companies found it a lot easier to negotiate for flex time and job sharing. Afterward, I was pointedly told that I was talking about very "special women," which missed the point of the conference, and that I had appeared "unfeeling" and "uncaring" about the plight of most women. I had rained on their parade. If what I had said was true—that successful, competent women had more control— well, then, all women aren't victims, are they? Like the veritable skunk at the garden party, I had spoiled the knee-jerk reaction that women are in need of special help. They didn't want to hear it. And I thought it was *good* news. So much for reality.

In a recent conversation I had with Kathy Bonk, the original gender gap historian, she admitted that the gap had grown considerably smaller in the congressional election of 2002.[11] And that women are, once again, becoming "swing" voters. The truth is, women have been swing voters to a greater degree than the media has let on for most of the last twenty years. *Vive la différence!*

So are men from Mars and women from Venus, politically speaking, or not? Well, kind of. Women, no matter their point of view, do look at political issues differently from men. Traditionally, guys think in more abstract terms. Women are more practical in how we view the world, which, I think, is a good thing. We want straightforward solutions to problems, and we vote for the candidates we think have the best specific ideas to solve those problems. We also see issues as values. What do I mean by that? Well, values reflect our hopes and dreams in a broad sense. Issues reflect specific policies that can help fulfill those dreams. For example, the safety and security of our families is a value. Gun control or arming pilots is an issue.

Often, conservatives haven't been very good at understanding that difference. Women are focused on outcomes while men are usually focused on process. In that context, the liberal message of more government offers concrete solutions—often wrong-headed ones, I believe—but specific actions to fix a problem.

To illustrate the political difference between men and women Republican pollster David Winston, head of the Winston Group, likes to talk about an AT&T commercial aimed at potential women cell phone users. In the ad, a young working mother is torn between taking her daughters to the beach or meeting with a client.

When the littlest girl asks, "Mommy, when can I be a client?" the working mom decides to take her phone and her kids to the beach and talk to the client from there. As Winston says, "AT&T isn't selling phones to working mothers in this ad. It is selling phones as a way to be a better mom and being a good mother is a value. Politicians who develop solutions to problems and respond to women's values are successful."

This has been especially apparent since 9/11. Women have always been more concerned than men are with personal security and safety. For the past couple of decades, the notion of security has been centered around the family and issues like health care, the economy, and domestic crime. But the direct attack on New York and Washington and the loss of three thousand lives changed our definition of security in one horrible morning. What 9/11 did was add terrorism to the value of personal security and safety; and in doing so, changed how many women viewed this key value. It has changed many Soccer Moms into Security Moms.

Pollster Kellyanne Conway conducted a national survey across the country in the months after the attack. She found that women, who are traditionally more opposed to military action, were just as supportive as men of America's campaign in Afghanistan. A month later, she found that when asked how America should pay for military action, slightly more women than men said that social programs should be curtailed.[12]

Winston, in his research, discovered that married women with children were the biggest supporters of arming airline pilots.[13] Upon this news, Donna Dees-Thomases and her pal, Rosie, must have plunged into a state of shock along with the many magazine editors who had put such faith in the notion that women were, with the exception of the NRA's gun-toting Ma Barkers, all passionately anti-gun. Apparently not when their lives and, more important, the lives of their families, are at stake.

This new focus on security continues. President Bush's top political adviser Karl Rove believes a shift among moms with children under eighteen was a major factor in the GOP's historic gain in the 2002 midterm elections. Says a Bush advisor, "Nine-eleven changed everything. Everybody's more concerned. But what's driving the movement is women, especially women with children."[14] Yes, we are a practical bunch, we women.

Heading Right

Over the past twenty years, we all know America has become a more conservative country both philosophically and politically, and women are part of the shift. Pollster Madelyn Hochstein, in her study

"Gender-ations," says that baby-boomer women especially have grown more conservative about social issues. Only 28 percent of women overall and only 20 percent of college-educated women agreed with this statement: "It is a very good thing that our society has become more open-minded about sex."[15] Yet you'd never know that from listening to the chirpy little sex debates on *The View*, whose viewers are primarily these same baby boomers.

On one program, Meredith, Star, Joy, and Barbara giggled like schoolgirls on the touchy-to-some but apparently rib-tickling to them topic of "lesbian chic." In this case they were discussing what to do if you found your teenage daughter in bed with another girl. "Well, she couldn't get pregnant," one joked. Another asked, "Would you send the girl home?" The panel erupted into indecision. Excuse me, you find your fifteen-year-old daughter in bed with a Britney wannabe, and you have to think about sending the pop tart packing? Gimme a break.

That *View* discussion sent the mother of a teenage boy I know practically over the edge. She told me how outraged she was by the gals' jokey, smug chitchat over what she saw as a serious situation. "If I found my fifteen-year-old in bed with another boy, or a girl for that matter, this wouldn't be a laughing matter at our house." She wondered if many viewers of the program would have the same attitude as the hosts of *The View*. Probably not.

In fact, Hochstein also says that one of today's most significant trends is that families are moving away "from the once-fashionable notion that each person develops his own sense of right or wrong." Rather, we are finally "coming back to the belief that there is a place for some set standards of behavior and conduct. This means families now take the responsibility for deciding, practicing, and teaching their children what is right and wrong behavior."[16]

The truth is that our political opinions and attitudes about social issues are far more diverse than the media portrays. For example, we rarely hear that the majority of women in this country support the death penalty.[17] I've seen women editors shake their head in disbelief over that. Or that one in four women owns a gun.[18] Again, that fact just doesn't fit the anti-gun picture of women painted by media for women. Even our opinions about the environment are far more complex than we are usually told. Haven't we all read in magazines that the environment is one of those "hot button" concerns for all women? Right. That's why half of us drive minivans and the other half SUVs! But it is the media's belief that all women are screaming greenies that is at least part of the reason we read and hear so many stories about toxic mold, lethal paint, and leeching baby bottles. But are we buying? Not all of us. A significant portion of women don't totally believe all those scary claims about environmental threats.[19] I love that older women, more liberal about most things, appear to be the ones most likely to discount those typical terror tales like the attack of the killer cheese.[20] If they're like me, they look around and realize it can't really be all that toxic out there if so many of us women are still here, staying fit, looking young, and living longer than ever before.

The No-Compromise Issue

For the Spin Sisters, however, one issue—abortion—is *the* binding pledge of their sorority. The issue on which there can never be any equivocation or discussion. Listening to them chatter at an editorial meeting or over cocktails, one learns that, according to these experienced politicians, abortion is unquestionably the most important issue for all women in America. Certainly, that is how the many women's magazines play it. Reproductive rights is the issue that all women must care and agree about. To keep the support of the Spin Sisters, politicians may not stray even a hair from the Planned Parenthood position, and probably neither can the writer in the cubicle next door or the producer at a party for Connie or Katie.

When writing about abortion, the women's magazines call in their big guns—"political pundits"—to write impassioned pro-choice editorials. Policy experts like Oscar nominee Julianne Moore[21] and *Ally McBeal*'s Lucy Liu,[22] who admits she isn't a lawyer but just played one on television. But, hey, isn't that just as good?

Yet political strategists will tell you that one of the dumbest things a candidate can do when he is in pursuit of women's votes is to run on so-called women's issues.

"Candidates who focus on abortion, breast cancer, and spousal abuse, as though women cannot get beyond their own bodies, have missed the point," Jody Newman and Richard Seltzer wrote in their book *Sex as a Political Variable*. And Kellyanne Conway has often said, "Abortion is conspicuously absent among women as an important issue." No matter what Jennifer or Julia or Susan or Jane thinks. "When you ask women what is really important to them," Kellyanne says, "abortion is always far down on the list." Say that to a Spin Sister, and she'll fall into a state of total denial not seen since Hillary's performance in the early going of L'affaire Lewinsky. They simply don't believe it because it is such a core issue to them. It is how they define themselves and each other. No one they know is pro-life, and they like it that way.

Let me tell you that I am pro-choice, but pro-choice in the same conflicted way many women are. We don't want *Roe* v. *Wade* to be overturned.[23] At the same time, we are uncomfortable with a law that allows abortion for just any reason at all. That seems too selfish. The debate about abortion may be partly about a woman's right to choose, but few of us who have had a sonogram and heard a fetal heartbeat can pretend that this issue is not a more profound life-and-death decision than the gang at NOW would like you to believe. Interestingly enough, the original suffragists, including Susan B. Anthony, Victoria Woodhull, and Elizabeth Cady Stanton (after whom NOW president Kim Gandy named her daughter) were vehemently anti-abortion.

They felt that being a mother was one of the few unique and innate powers that women had.

In general, media has been pro-abortion from the start of the modern women's movement, and I don't mean media only aimed directly at women. While television news reports in the early 1970s were still making fun of "bra-burning hairy-legged feminists," these same programs were respectful of feminism's three original political goals: equal pay for equal work, reproductive rights, and improved child care. As journalist William McGowan says in his recent award-winning book *Coloring the News,* "for most journalists"—male as well as female—"opposition to abortion is not a civilized position."[24]

In 1990, writer David Shaw studied reams of reporting and hours of videotape, and interviewed dozens of reporters and editors for a famous three-part series on bias in the media's coverage of the abortion issue. Lisa Meyers of NBC News, one of the many reporters he interviewed, agreed, "Some of the stories I have read or seen have almost seemed like cheerleading for the pro-choice side."[25]

In his report, Shaw also noted that Faye Wattleton, the extremely beautiful and elegant African American woman who for years headed Planned Parenthood, has always been extolled in the press as "relentlessly high-minded" and "a stunning refutation of the clichéd 'dowdy feminist.' "[26] Faye, a great favorite of women's magazines, has been featured and photographed many times as both a model and role model.

During the recent debate about partial-birth abortion, McGowan concludes that the bias Shaw described is still at work. "Journalists who should have been trying to help the public sort through a complex and deeply felt issue struck poses and insulted those they deemed to be on the wrong side."[27]

When bills to outlaw federal funding for partial-birth abortions were before Congress, Bill Clinton, a staunch defender of the procedure, trotted out teary women who told stories of choosing this method only because their fetus was so deformed or their own life was so endangered, they had little choice. Individually, these were terribly sad stories, but they left a misleading impression. Unfortunately, most of the media bought the line that the White House and feminist organizations were spinning that only five hundred of such abortions were performed each year and mainly for health reasons. For example, *60 Minutes* interviewed a woman whose fetus was developing with its brain outside its skull, a horrifying and extremely rare birth defect.[28] When Bill Clinton vetoed the bills to ban partial-birth abortion bills, he was applauded each time as a friend of women, one who was able to understand their greatest concerns and especially, in this instance, to "feel their pain" at a most vulnerable moment.

Only afterward was some hard-nosed, unemotional reporting done on the subject by reporter Ruth Padawer of *The Record* (Bergen) and by David Brown of *The Washington Post*. Padawer simply picked up the phone and called doctors around New Jersey. She found that, contrary to what had been conjured up by the rest of the media, there had been more than 1,500 abortions in New Jersey alone using this method, which is also called dilation and extraction or D&X, and the vast majority were not for health reasons.[29] Brown also found most of the fetuses aborted with this method were not deformed but healthy.[30]

After the 2000 election, passing a law to ban this procedure continued to be a highly emotional battle. To counteract the growing support for a ban, pro-choice advocates continued to supply the media with stories of women who had used this method only as a last alternative and when the fetus was fatally malformed. In *Glamour*'s October 2001 issue, "I Had an Abortion When I Was Six Months Pregnant" told the story of a woman who was carrying twins, one suffering from "fetal hydrops and pleural effusion" and the other with "a malformed umbilical cord and smaller vital organs."[31]

In the as-told-to piece, the woman says, "If I continued the pregnancy I could put my own health at risk" and so had opted for the procedure. She concludes, "The most humane and safest option John and I had available to us is being threatened by lawmakers who do not understand our heartache. I used to vote straight ticket Republican, but I couldn't bring myself to vote for George W. Bush, who used his acceptance speech at the GOP convention to promise to sign a law against partial-birth abortion."

In the fall of 2003 Congress voted overwhelmingly in favor of legislation to ban this procedure. The president signed it into law, although it will face a challenge that will inevitably go to the Supreme Court. I'm sure some of the Spin Sisters hoped women would march in the streets against the "assault on women's rights." But it didn't happen. Maybe because a majority of women support the legislation.

So, how do women, in general, feel about abortion? Here's one statistical breakdown: According to the National Opinion Research Center of the University of Chicago over 83 percent believe a woman should be allowed to obtain a legal abortion if her health is seriously endangered; 73 percent if she becomes pregnant as a result of rape or if there is a serious defect in the baby. But only 36 percent believe a woman should be able to obtain an abortion if she is married and does not want to have any more children, and only 34 percent agree if she is unmarried and does not want to marry the father.[32] The majority of women do not object to some modifications of the law. If parents have to give permission for their fifteen-year-old to have her ears pierced, why shouldn't they be notified if that same daughter is going to have an abortion?

Surprisingly, one of the most interesting and balanced features about abortion ever done in a women's magazine was a report in *Marie Claire* that included personal stories from a variety of women with differing views.[33] There was a memoir from a young singer who has spent years regretting the abortion she had as a teenager. She writes, "I know now that abortion is the destruction of human life, and it's never justified. I'll always regret my decision." That feature was coupled with a piece by a lawyer who said, "Mine was not terrible at all—physically or morally. I'm not pro-abortion, but I am pro-choice."

Another story was written by a doctor who performs abortions and says her life has been threatened and she is now forced to go to work in a bulletproof vest. That was contrasted with a memoir by a young woman, adopted as an infant, who learned that she was the child of a rape and that her mother had wanted to abort her but was unable to have an abortion. She is now a pro-life activist. The final pieces were about two women who had learned they were pregnant with children who would have serious disabilities. One chose to have the child, and the other, Maureen Britell, who heads Voters for Choice and was lauded as a *Redbook* "Mother and Shaker," did not.

The pieces were all interesting and effective, and the entire report confirmed how divided women are on this issue. In 2001 *Marie Claire* surveyed its own readers who, if you believe the magazine's usual stories, like to talk about how many lovers they've had and how long it usually takes them to hop into bed. You'd assume they would also have fairly casual attitudes about sex and, subsequently, about abortion. They don't. Forty-three percent of their readers, whether they are pro-life or pro-choice, consider abortion murder. Forty-eight percent of those who have had an abortion consider it murder. Sixty-two percent think that if a woman has *had* two abortions, she should not be allowed to have a third. Fifty-seven percent say abortion shouldn't be allowed if the father objects. Fifty-nine percent think it should be permitted if the baby is severely handicapped, a considerably smaller percentage than the national average. Only 40 percent said they would ever have an abortion. One assumes 60 percent would not. That, dare I say it, is pretty conservative for the magazine that promotes sexual liberation the way Madonna promotes, well, Madonna.

In early 2002, Spin Sisters all over Manhattan, no doubt, choked over their morning lattes—skim milk, please—reading a front-page story in the Style Section of *The New York Times* about the changing attitudes of young women toward abortion. The feature, called "Surprise: Mom, I'm Against Abortion," contrasted differences between mothers and daughters. The writer maintained that people who equate youth with liberal opinions are, nowadays, in for a surprise. A study of college freshmen shows that support for abortion rights has been dropping steadily since the early 1990s. Fifty-four percent of more than a quarter of a million students polled at 437 schools by UCLA in 2002 agreed that abortion should be legal. That was down from 67 percent a decade earlier.[34]

"Abortion isn't a rights issue—it's become for increasing numbers of young people a moral, ethical issue," explained Henry Brady, a professor of political science and public policy at U. C. Berkeley, who has also taken surveys about this question.[35] Seems to me it might also be called a values issue.

Obviously, young women are struggling with this. Yet *Marie Claire,* which accurately reported their differing attitudes, made the magazine's own position crystal clear with an editorial, "Your Abortion Rights: Going, Going, Gone." The magazine then invited readers to sign their Web site petition, "Stars for Choice," pledging to send it on to the White House. Already on board were thirty-two of the usual suspects, including Eve Ensler, Jane Fonda, Sharon Stone, and Meryl Streep. Ignoring the surprises in its own readers' poll, the magazine did not encourage any type of activism except the activism it endorsed as appropriate. Sign on the digital line; join "the club."

Promoting activism on both sides of any issue in women's magazines is as rare as a Frenchman on the front lines. Theoretically, it's possible but not probable. To editors, this lack of objectivity is okay because they keep assuming you all think just like them.

But you don't.

Here are some facts:

If you're like the majority of American women, you are for the death penalty. According to the National Opinion Research Center at the University of Chicago, 59 percent of women support the death penalty while 32 percent oppose it.

You favor abortion with restrictions and with reservations rather than the "anything goes" position of the Spin Sisters. Though poll figures vary slightly, in an ABC News/*Washington Post* poll taken at the thirtieth anniversary of *Roe* v. *Wade* in January 2003, 88 percent of women favored abortion to save a woman's life. But 57 percent opposed it simply to end an unwanted pregnancy. And you oppose partial-birth abortions. In fact, 69 percent of women are against this procedure.

You probably oppose gay marriage but don't want gays discriminated against. A Gallup Poll reported in May 2003 that Americans, both men and women, overwhelmingly agreed that homosexuals should have equal rights in terms of job opportunities. However, 58 percent of women did not believe that homosexual marriages should be recognized.

You favored the war against Iraq. An April 2003 ABC News/*Washington Post* poll found that 72 percent of women supported the war.

You want pilots armed. According to a poll taken by the Winston Group 76 percent of women favored arming pilots.

If you're a boomer, you probably believe sexual freedoms have gone too far. Researcher Madelyn Hochstein, president of the DYG polling company, found that a surprising 43 percent of baby-boomer women now think "It's wrong for people to have sex if they're not married," up from 35 percent a decade ago.

Ninety percent of you believe in God and two thirds of you pray at least once a day, according to figures compiled by the National Opinion Research Center at the University of Chicago. Many other surveys confirm these findings.

Thirty percent of you call yourselves conservative politically, more than call yourselves liberal. That's the conclusion based on figures from the University of Chicago's National Opinion Research Center.

But perhaps here's the most surprising fact of all. Most of these issues don't even make the first cut when it comes to what women really care about most. While issues like reproductive rights and gay rights, the environment, and gun control are the focus of endless stories in women's magazines and on television aimed at women, and while the female media elite believe these are the issues that must be most important to women, any pollster will tell you that none of these are what drive most women's vote.[36]

What women are really interested in is whether Johnny and Susie can actually read Mom's list of chores, not NOW's latest pitch letter. They fear the HMO will jack up their co-payment, not the next trip to the nail salon. And they don't spend their time wondering if the groceries are laced with pesticides or the family home has toxic mold. They're more worried about paying for them. And in this post-9/11 world, they're worried, as well, about the safety and security of themselves and their families. Not sexy issues, most of these. Not issues that the top women in media worry much about because they can afford not to. Certainly not the issues that celebrities want to pen editorials and parade around Washington or Baghdad about. Or persuade advertisers to champion as their latest cause. But who said life was going to be a walk in the park—especially Central Park? It's not, and neither is governing. It's hard, complex work trying to solve complicated economic and cultural problems, but women in media have synthesized what are supersized problems down to a standard formula. It's always victims, defined through a liberal prism, versus villains, who can only be defeated by liberal, usually big government solutions.

Too simplistic? Absolutely. But that is how most of the Spin Sisters view the world and the women in it. How sad to see these bright and talented women squander the opportunity they've been given to help you and millions of women like you to better understand our country's problems and the pros and cons of solutions on all sides.

But getting a balanced view from big-time media is about as likely as Dr. Laura winning next year's Matrix Award.

But what about me? Where do I fit in? Awkwardly, these days. I've changed more than my hair color over the years. More and more, with every editorial meeting, every lunch at Michael's, and every awards ceremony, I realized that my own views were no longer simpatico with those of my colleagues. Do I begrudge them those views? Certainly not. Would they give my views the same respect? Not likely.

The late Pauline Kael, the acerbic longtime film critic for *The New Yorker* and a Media Queen in her day, supposedly reacted this way to Nixon's landslide victory over George McGovern in 1972. "How can that be?" she wondered. "No one *I* know voted for Nixon." And she was telling the truth. Over thirty years later, riding up in the elevator of my West Side apartment building, where Al Franken also happens to live, a writer I know commented, "I read that more than seventy percent of people support the president about the war in Iraq. I don't know anyone who does. Do you?"

Uh, yes.

But then I've gotten used to feeling a little like Richard Simmons at a bikers' bar, and I usually don't mind. And the truth is that my politics were once a lot like that of the Spin Sisters.

How did I get from their views to mine? Let me explain.

CHAPTER 11

Never Underestimate the Power

There's an old adage that goes: "If you're not a liberal when you're in your twenties, you haven't got a heart; if you're not a conservative in your forties, you haven't got a brain." Like many other Americans of my generation, I went through that political transformation. It's been a very typical experience for many men of my generation, and for many women, too. But it's not one that the vast majority of women in media ever undergo. Young or old, they seem stuck in a late '60s, early '70s time warp. The only things missing are the love beads.

Back in the first wave of the women's movement, I thought of myself as a feminist, too. Before that, in high school and in college, I supported the civil rights movement, though I never could bring myself to demonstrate against Vietnam. Like so many others, I felt confused and

283

conflicted about that painful war. Those were the years I was pushing a baby carriage or a stroller for a couple of little boy babies. Somehow, I just felt it wasn't right to demonstrate when somebody else's little boy was an American soldier in danger half a world away.

During the ensuing years, my ideas began to change, mainly because of my two sons and the way I wanted to raise them. I think I was a very involved, very loving, but pretty strict mother. That's the way I saw it, and the Mommie Dearest jokes notwithstanding, I hope my kids see it the same way. Although my sons were raised in New York City, in some ways they may have had more of a home-centered life than kids raised in a suburb or a small town. We ate dinner together every night. We spent every weekend together involved in family activities. I drilled multiplication tables, checked homework—all the standard stuff. Because the city was full of danger—the crime rate was much higher then—they could never roam free. They were always supervised until they were teenagers and even in their teen years were never out at night cruising in cars. You can't just cruise around Manhattan. They always had to let us know where they were and exactly when they would be home.

When I was growing up, most parents didn't have to reinforce high standards of behavior and morality because they were simply understood. Unmarried and pregnant didn't get you a baby shower and a pat on the back. It got you a fast ticket out of town while your parents concocted a lame story explaining your sudden absence. Like, "Gee, we hated to see Susie go, but she just insisted on taking care of Aunt Martha who's down, darn it, with a bad case of leprosy. She's a saint, that girl."

But during the 1970s and early 1980s, my husband and I found we had to make it clear to our kids what we thought was right and wrong, and what we expected from them. My sons were in schools with an affluent and sophisticated student body, and so we spent a lot of time teaching them to just say no, the mantra of the day to the current teenage drug of choice. We were fairly demanding, too. As parents, I guess you learn you really do have to decide what you believe about behavior and morality and make choices. And I found that the choices we made and the standards we communicated were always fairly conservative.

There was also my older son who sometimes made me wonder: Can someone simply be born a patriot? He didn't arrive in the world waving a flag, but even when he was quite young Jonathan always seemed to want to talk and think about what it meant to be an American. He was always very interested in American history, too; the kind of kid who runs for class president with a full-blown campaign. One year, he insisted we make a special trip to Washington. He wanted a picture of himself standing in front of the White House for his eighth-grade class yearbook. Just in case.

He told me recently that he really started thinking about America when he was in the fifth or sixth grade, when Jimmy Carter was president. "I hated it when we had the hostage crisis," he says. "I remember I used to watch the news, and they would count how many days they had held Americans hostage." He also said, "I really got excited when we won the hockey games during the Olympics in 1980. I remember everyone started cheering 'U.S.A.! U.S.A.!' and I thought that was great. Hey, we can do things; we can be winners. We are winners."

Like the character Michael J. Fox played in *Family Ties*, as a young teenager, Jonathan became one of "Reagan's children," inspired by the president's deeply felt view of America as "a shining city on the hill," a special place with a unique destiny. It's amazing that he stuck to his guns as his mother, like the good liberal I was then, complained about what was wrong with America, the way liberals still do. Still, my son instinctively focused on what was right about this country and how to build on its strengths. Through the years, we used to read the papers together and watch the news, argue, debate, discuss, and finally agree.

Here's a story I like telling. In New York, you have to be a registered party member to vote in a primary. One primary day, I went to the polling place with Jonathan, who was a young teenager at the time. I intended to vote in the Democratic primary. But the woman at the voting booth checked the records and told me I wasn't a registered Democrat. I was a registered Liberal!!!! It was a perfect *Family Ties* moment. My son shook his head wearily.

"Mom," he said, "this is the most mortifying moment of my entire life." Poor baby.

A Visit to Beijing

In 1995, I was an official United States delegate to the U.N. World Conference on Women in Beijing. I told that story about trying to vote in the primary a couple of nights before the group left for China. Former Democratic congresswoman Marjorie Margolies-Mezvinsky, the head of the delegation, grew pale, and exclaimed, "But Myrna, we thought you were a Republican! You're the only one in the delegation." I told her to cheer up. Jonathan had done his work. By that time, I was a registered Republican, so their "token" delegate was safe.

A lot of people criticized the Women's Conference and all those who attended it as "liberal activists." Excuse me, I had to assure the White House I was exactly the opposite in order to get there. My old friend, the writer and erstwhile candidate for governor of California, Arianna Huffington, was one of the conference critics and wrote a stinging column against the women attending it. A British reporter once called Arianna "the most upwardly mobile Greek since Icarus." In those days, she was an admirer of Newt Gingrich and all policies conservative. We must have passed each other on our mutual political journeys as I headed right, and she sped off, stopping somewhere to the left of Michael Moore. I evolved; Arianna whiplashed.

Actually, the conference was a fascinating experience. Within a few hours of being in Beijing, we had already gotten an unvarnished picture of the Chinese Communist regime. These were not Mr. Nice Guys, and they didn't care one little bit whether you thought they were Mr. Nice Guys. In a way, it was instructive to see figures in authority so absolutely uninterested in what the media or anyone else thought. The Chinese security guards, who were everywhere, not to help or protect us but to control and hinder the women at the conference, were utterly unconcerned with outward appearances.

To keep her from attending a meeting, I watched as Donna Shalala, a cabinet secretary and an official delegate, was simply shoved aside by the guards. And Jane Fonda, who wasn't part of the delegation but was, of course, there anyway, got shoved aside, too, in a downpour. It was always raining at the conference. Jane wore Ultrasuede, head to boot, and looked okay. Donna, I, and everyone else wore tattered, dripping plastic rain ponchos the entire time and looked like hell.

At the tent city where representatives from different women's organizations were housed, a bumpy hour's drive from Beijing, protests—not exactly a familiar sight there in Tyranny land—erupted as women demonstrated against governments that oppressed women, against men, and against each other. Barnum and Bailey couldn't have put on a better show as progressive Muslims without head scarves were hissed at and taunted by their more devout, heavily veiled sisters. Exiled Tibetans were called "traitors and scum" by "official" Tibetans. And Catholic activists on both sides of the pro-choice, pro-life debate accused each other of un-Christian behavior.

What many considered the conference highlight was Hillary's appearance. There had been much controversy about whether she should even attend. Dressed in her most girlish gear—her favorite pretty-in-pink suit with her hair long and flowing—she gave a strong, forceful speech that had the delegates cheering. Without naming names, she managed to criticize China's policy of forced sterilization, female infanticide, and abortions. She also criticized as "indefensible" the Chinese government's refusal to grant visas to many who had hoped to attend the forum.

"Freedom means the rights of people to assemble, organize, and debate openly. It means respecting the views of those who may disagree with the views of their government." She also declared, to much applause, that, "Human's rights are women's rights and women's rights are human's rights." Editorial writers and yours truly gave the First Lady a thumbs-up for "more courage, confidence, and candor than most expected . . . in this controversial setting."[1]

But I have one other little story about that Beijing conference and Hillary. Not the Hillary who spoke so effectively about human rights but the Whitewater, Travelgate Hillary with that strange Clintonian talent for finding funny money in the most unexpected places.

Just a couple of days before the conference, I was introduced to a woman called Nina Wang by her public relations person, an Englishman who was an old pal of my husband. Nina, an odd little woman in her late fifties, wore a miniskirt and her hair in two stiff pigtails reminiscent of the last dowager empress of China. According to that PR guy, this unusual character was "the richest woman in Asia." She's still on *Forbes*'s billionaires' list with a fortune estimated at $2.8 billion.

When Nina heard I was going to the conference, she became very excited. Although she lived in Hong Kong and had vast real estate interests, she seemed able to travel freely to both the People's Republic and Taiwan. She told me she would be in Beijing too, and wanted to give a dinner for the American delegation. Afterward, her public relations man sidled up and told me that Nina had one burning ambition in life—to meet Hillary Clinton. I assured him I absolutely could *not* arrange that.

During the conference, Nina did hold a small dinner party at the official guesthouse where Nixon had stayed when he was in China. I managed to convince a few members of the delegation from the State and Commerce Departments to come with me. The women from the government, several of whom spoke both Mandarin and Cantonese, thought Nina, with her miniskirt and her pigtails, was a joke. When I told them about her desire to meet Hillary, they laughed. She was too "weird and creepy," they said. It would never happen.

Quite a while later, back in New York, I ran into my friend, the PR guy. "I guess Nina never got to meet Hillary," I said.

He laughed. "Of course she did." He didn't explain how.

Only afterward, I learned that Nina met the president and had breakfast with Hillary in the White House in December 1995, just a few months after Beijing. Soon after that, Nina flew eight thousand miles from Hong Kong to Hope, Arkansas, to donate $50,000 to refurbish the two-story house that was Clinton's home for the first seven years of his life, boosting efforts to turn it into a museum.[2] Obviously when Hillary's good, she's very, very good, and when she's bad . . .

Still, the very best moment for me in Beijing was personal. During each of the conference's sessions, at least one delegate had to be present in the main hall while speeches were being made. We agreed we would share this duty. In turn, each of us would be the official United States representative sitting in the chair directly behind the U.S. delegation's sign. In the hall, the "United States" was seated between the "United Kingdom" and "Uruguay." During my turn, I found myself sitting with a titled Englishwoman on one side and, on the other, the Uruguayan delegate who told me she was there because her husband was in the government. While I sat, half listening to the speeches, I kept thinking about my family. My two sets of immigrant grandparents, my father who never went to college, never even finished high school but instead went to work when he was a teenager. It was so amazing. I felt sure that nowhere else in the world was there a society quite so decent and wonderful that no matter one's background, a woman could enjoy such a moment not because of birth or privilege but through her own hard work. That nowhere else would I have had the opportunities that would lead me to be the representative of my country, even briefly, at an international conference. It made me feel fortunate, grateful, and so very proud of being an American. I guess Jonathan raised me right.

Maybe that's part of the reason why it has come to concern me so much that media for women and the women who decide what's covered and how are so one-sided about using their megaphones to spout their liberal political opinions and shine their activist bent. So quick to criticize and decry so much about our country, especially when the party with which they don't agree has any degree of power. So happy to tell their readers how unhappy they must be and what a raw deal they have if they are women.

Those who don't know any better would probably say, "Heck, they're just women's magazines, not political journals or newsmagazines. What's the big deal?" In a word—fairness. Sandwiched between diet tips and fashion layouts, magazines are selling a political point of view and every month at least 50 million women are buying or sharing with their friends—the magazines if not always the political message. It should matter to all of us who believe women deserve to hear both sides of issues at least some of the time.

Fair and Balanced

At the *Journal* and at *MORE*, I tried to be fair. Long before I knew about the Media Research Center, that press watchdog, it reported that *Ladies' Home Journal* was the most "politically balanced" of the women's magazines.[3] In both 1996 and 2000, the *Journal* gave considerable coverage to the presidential election and the issues that were most important to women at the time. For the November 1996 election-month issue, I interviewed Bill and Hill (he talked; she didn't) and then flew with Elizabeth and Bob Dole to Abilene, where they opened their campaign. During the Clintons' photo shoot, the president appeared to impulsively kiss Hillary. The photographer missed the shot. "Do it again, Mr. President," we begged. He demurred coyly, "No. No, it won't look presidential." Kind of funny to think that Clinton acted as if kissing his wife might sully his dignified image. Finally, he gave in and pecked her demurely on the cheek while she giggled. On the plane during a similar photo shoot, I told the Doles the president had kissed Mrs. Clinton. I asked, "Now, Senator, will you do that?"

"Kiss Mrs. Clinton?" Dole shot back. "Nah," and then kissed his wife on the lips. Typically, his comeback was snappier than his answers to my questions.

In 2000, we worked with the women's Web site, iVillage, and again wrote about issues that mattered to women. I also had the chance to see some old-style politicking that election year. Nancy Evans, the editor-in-chief of iVillage, and I talked with George and Laura Bush on a campaign train crossing California's agricultural valley from Monterey to Sacramento. We both found the Bushes low-key, relaxed, and affable. I also spent a late summer afternoon with Tipper and Al Gore on a riverboat, making stops in small Iowa towns along the Mississippi. The Gores were enjoying a post-convention bounce in the polls and the vice president was in high spirits.

As we talked, he began to remind me of a misplaced Victorian actor. He spoke loudly, tossed his hair, laughed theatrically. Naomi Wolf's perfect "alpha male" in his natural habitat. He was so buoyant that at one point I thought he might jump in the air and click his heels or at least be capable of floating on the big river rolling past us. His very audible sighs during his first debate struck many as peculiar. To me, it was just part of his flamboyant, overly dramatic style.

In both the *Journal* and *MORE,* I did make it a point to feature women who were Republicans or conservatives more than my competitors did. The *Journal,* of course, always covered the First Ladies, Nancy Reagan, Barbara Bush, Hillary, and now Laura Bush. But through the years, I also sent reporters to India to work alongside Mother Teresa and to interview Margaret Thatcher at 10 Downing Street. Truly an Iron Lady, Thatcher said she did the washing up and hung wallpaper to relax. Even prime ministers need a "Martha moment" now and again.

We also profiled Republicans such as senators Kay Bailey Hutchison, Susan Collins, Olympia Snowe, and Congresswoman Deborah Pryce. And in *MORE,* we did features on what I like to call Alpha women, those women in their forties, fifties, and sixties who are on top of their game, including Lynne Cheney and Karen Hughes.

But, I confess, I didn't do enough. While some of my colleagues were propagandists for a liberal agenda, I tried to be balanced and nonpartisan even as my own views changed. What I regret is that as an editor I didn't use that bully pulpit as much as I probably should have. One of the things I did do, however, was write an editorial, which was clearly labeled as an editorial, in the mid-1990s when I became enraged by the rising tide of sleaze that was not merely coarsening our culture but overwhelming it. It was at the very height of O.J., Lorena Bobbitt, and talk show trash on TV, of Howard Stern, and violent, misogynistic rap lyrics on the radio.

I knew how nearly impossible it had become to protect kids from the media's embrace of the violent and the vulgar. Oh, sure, media execs tell mothers that it is our responsibility to protect our kids, to just turn it off if we don't approve of what they see or hear. But that's like telling a mother to make sure nobody with the flu ever sneezes in her child's direction. It simply can't be done.

I felt, for once, that I just had to share my sense of outrage with the readers. In my piece, I complained about the "wise-assing" of America where everything had turned into fodder for a David Letterman Top Ten List.

I went on to say, "America has become a land where its citizens demand rights but forgo responsibilities." And I quoted sociologist Amitai Etzioni, "We must be ready to express our moral sense, raise our voice a decibel or two about what we really believe. In the silence that prevails, it may seem as if we were shouting; actually we are merely speaking up."

I asked the readers to let me know what they thought. Within a few days, my office was flooded with thousands of letters. Ultimately 150,000 women told me they agreed. In turn, I wrote to some lawmakers and media executives who I assumed would be interested, sending along the editorial and describing the tremendous reaction. When I got responses—and I didn't get many—they were polite, noncommittal, uninterested. I was a women's magazine editor, after all, not at *Newsweek* or *Time*; and these were merely the opinions of ordinary, mainstream women. Not much buzz there. Only briefly did I have a hope that I and 150,000 readers could, maybe, make a bit of a difference.

But maybe, in this case, *I* just didn't get it. While I was hoping for change, women in this country were already changing. What made me think I was ahead of the curve? Imagine how shocked I was to discover in myopic Manhattan, I was already behind it.

Pollster Daniel Yankelovich maintains that in this country, over the past decades, we have tended to "lurch and learn," go to an extreme and then work our way back. Our whole culture "lurched" to the left during the late 1960s and 1970s, becoming far more liberal socially, morally, and politically. In the last couple of decades, we have slowly worked our way back. DYG's president, Madelyn Hochstein, says all their latest research indicates, "We have become a much more conservative country, much more interested in returning to and promoting traditional values. You know, in the early 1960s when the times were changing, and we were becoming freer in every way, the leaders of business and the leaders of media didn't believe it. The changes that were happening made them very, very uncomfortable. Sometimes, when we lurch in another direction, it is the leaders, even the leaders in media, who are the last to know. They are the most skeptical and have the most invested in keeping things the way they were."[4]

And why shouldn't they? Why should they feel they have to change?

You still buy magazines and watch television, don't you? Take what you are given, and, usually, without complaint. Magazine readers can stay loyal for years and years, and magazines, at least, are so cheap. Publishers have taught women to pay almost nothing for our publications. Nowadays, because of new circulation rules, publishers can almost give them away for a few pennies a copy, and some do. Of course, that makes advertisers even more important to the economic mix and even more necessary for publishers and editors to coddle and please.

And sometimes you watch because it *is* mindless entertainment. We all need that, too, and that's okay. But we also use the magazines we read and the shows we watch as guideposts for our own lives. We just can't help that either. For decades, since those images of Happy Homemakers were imprinted on our psyches, we have been conditioned and influenced by the politically correct portraits, painted by media, of how women should live and work. And that, today, has become a problem. When we grab a copy of *Marie Claire* or *Redbook* or flip on *20/20* or *Dateline*, we see less and less depiction of our true selves and more and more of a frumpy, frazzled, and fearful victim class. We can stand up against this onslaught—but it *is* an onslaught. We deserve a far fairer, multifaceted picture.

So how should you handle it? Tune out and turn off? Don't watch or read unless you're in the doctor's office, and she's running, as usual, an hour behind? Cancel the subscriptions and hand him the remote? Won't happen. Can't happen. Shouldn't happen. This is a media-mad world, and it is only going to continue that way. A lot of smart magazine editors will keep trying to write those snappy cover lines to get your attention. Though that's getting harder and harder to do. Newsstand sales for most women's magazines are falling, and falling dramatically.[5] Dozens of producers will also try to make you sit down and watch—though that's become very challenging as well—especially if you are in the demographic group advertisers regard as particularly desirable. Still, I am sure you will find a feature in a magazine that interests you, maybe a few features in several magazines. I admit it. I am still a magazine junkie, though I read them less competitively and more critically than I once did.

I'm also sure you will want to zonk out in front of the tube, laugh at a sitcom, get hooked on a reality series, or watch Diane or Katie or Barbara's latest "get." And so will I. Media is part of the culture we share with other women. It informs, entertains, inspires, and sometimes infuriates. But now, whether you're laughing or reaching for the tissue box or ready to toss the magazine or turn off the tube, I want you to realize how often you are being manipulated, how frequently you are fed the story that all women feel and think and behave the same way. And note how much about your life and what is really important to you is left out because it is too complex for a dumbed-down media to handle. Or, worse, simply because many editors and producers don't respect what you respect or believe what you believe. If what I have said makes sense to you, there is one thing I really hope you will stop buying—and that's the spoiled goods of unhappiness.

I have tried to deconstruct some messages you get all the time, and to explain why these messages come from fairly biased sources. I can't end "this issue" without behaving exactly like the women's magazine editor I have been for so many years, get into gear, and compile a little sidebar of advice for you to take away.

Six Secrets the Spin Sisters Won't Tell You!

SECRET # 1
Stress—Fuhgettaboutit!

Yes, yes, yes. We all have stress. Sometimes. But not all day, not every day. Stress has become a knee-jerk, all-purpose gimmick for lazy marketers. Marketing executive Mary Lou Quinlan, in her book *Just Ask a Woman*, advises all her clients, "Think women. Think stress."[6] Think again. From the point of view of many women's magazines and television shows aimed at women, the best way to define us and to attract our attention is by emphasizing our inability to get through an ordinary day. But is that the way you really want to be defined? Isn't it downright insulting to keep telling women that we cannot keep it together when we are merely living our often good, often comfortable, if frequently complicated, lives?

And here's another flash: The newest research says the best way to handle stress is not by checking into a day spa or by indulging in any other activity that has stress reduction as its only goal. That binge-and-purge approach may make marketers big bucks, but it does very little to keep you relaxed.[7] Instead, researchers now advise that you simply acknowledge that life is full of little tensions because, hey, that's life. Handle it moment by moment the way women have always done, by taking a deep breath and getting some perspective. Condoleezza Rice, who must have her share of tensions—if you call conducting a war on terrorism stressful—has said, "I don't do life crises. Life's too short. Get over it. Move on to the next thing."[8]

SECRET # 2
Elephants Can't Stand on Basketballs

Neither can you. Stop worrying about trying to find balance in your life, especially when you have kids around. Kids take up all available time. It's the basic Murphy's Law of motherhood. No matter how much time you devote to them, whether you work from eight to eight or have a mild case of agoraphobia and are around the house all the time, you will still feel you have not been there enough for them.

That's because every American child born since 1970 seems to have the innate capacity to make his or her mother feel guilty. When I was growing up it was the other way around. Mothers were great at making their children, especially their daughters, feel guilty. Somehow, we have lost the knack. Nowadays, we just cannot give our kids enough and, too often, don't even expect them to be particularly grateful for what we do manage, because we feel guilty that we haven't given them even more.

That little conundrum would be difficult enough to sort out if women's media hadn't given us another time-consuming chore: babying ourselves while we are taking care of the small fry. *O, The Oprah Magazine* once urged its reader to "Declare today 'sacred time'— off-limits to everyone, unless invited by you. Take care of your personal wants and needs. Say no, graciously but firmly, to others' demands."[9]

Get real. Be gracious and firm while ignoring the crying baby, the shrieking toddler, the teenager who keeps hassling you about driving at night with only a learner's permit. It doesn't happen that way.

Oddly enough, in that very same issue of *O*, Dr. Martha Beck just throws in the towel and agrees it can't be done. Martha chirps brightly, "I don't have a job. My children are not young . . . I'm a life coach. You'd think I could live a balanced life . . . Ha. In fact . . . I can tell you with absolute assurance that it is impossible for women to achieve the kind of balance recommended by so many well-meaning self-help counselors. I didn't say such balance is difficult to attain. I didn't say it is rare. I said it's impossible."[10] At last, the truth.

Most of us, if we have kids and work, but even if we don't have jobs outside our homes, find we just can't pencil in one whole day for our "personal wants and needs." So why does media aimed at women constantly tell us we should? And make us feel we are failing ourselves once again if we don't?

In her happy little piece, Martha also tells us she has been up "for about 23 hours straight" because yesterday was filled with such daunting tasks as getting the car fixed and answering e-mails. And that she is going to "set a historic precedent by preparing breakfast" for the kids who "are not young."[11] Now, you could be wondering, legitimately, why you are supposed to take any advice from someone like Martha who, apparently, manages time the way Willie Nelson manages money? A friend once told me she stopped listening to Gloria Steinem's views on women's independence when she found out Gloria couldn't drive. But, Martha, I'll forgive you this once since you are trying to send the right message.

Here's the deal: When your children are around you will not have time to put your life in perfect balance any more than an elephant can stand on a basketball. And that is really not so terrible. You are *supposed* to think more about your children than about yourself. You had time for "you, you, you" (the title of a past *Glamour* column) before the kids were around; and, trust me, you will have time after they've left home. Here's a thought: Maybe you'll even have time for him, him, him, too.

SECRET #3
Get a Grip! Life's Not the Blair Witch Project

Okay, so media for women does its darnedest to try to scare you to death a lot of the time. When it wants to make a really big impression, media isn't shy about scaring all of us out of our knickers, as the British say. While we were still reeling from Iraq war coverage, PBS put on an eight-hour, angst-provoking documentary produced by Ted Turner. Called *Avoiding Armageddon*, it was narrated by Walter Cronkite, looking like the anguished patriarch straight out of Revelations. In one segment, Walter intoned, "Anybody, anyplace could become a victim," which is, of course, the basic thesis behind every fear-factor story, large or small, from killer celery to weapons of mass destruction.

That's because reporting and pessimism have become totally intertwined in so many areas, but especially in stories about health and the environment. Repent, the end is near! Michael Fumento, scaremonger defeater and junk-science debunker, says, "There is this tendency on the part of the media to believe that if you're pessimistic, you're probably telling the truth. This, being America, these scared people call their lawyers . . . the lawyer calls the media, [and] the media puts it on page one. Suddenly, there's a new bogeyman to terrify the uninformed."[12]

How to protect yourself from the effects of these constant guerrilla terror tactics? Dr. Kimberly Thompson of Harvard's School of Public Health always offers good advice about keeping risks in perspective. Here are several ways:

Remember that how we perceive and process information depends upon how it is presented. Positively (half full) or negatively (half empty).

If you hear about a small number of people stricken by a rare illness, it follows, doesn't it, that a large number of people, you included, are perfectly fine.[13] Don't forget, almost all media scare stories are about something dastardly that happened to a very small group of people like the unlucky women who shared the same infected foot basin in just one nail salon in California.

Dr. Thompson suggests that you should make sure that the source of the information is reliable. Al's Research Barn may not be your best bet. She also points out, "All sources have a motivation for providing information." Though we have been conditioned to think that information providers are always the good guys who have no agenda, this is rarely the case. It's worth saying again: "nonprofit" doesn't necessarily mean "nonpolitical" or "nonpartisan."

Other experts to be a bit suspicious of? Celebrities, especially when they are center stage for an environmental cause. They tend to express a generalized liberal environmental message wrapped in an emotional presentation when marching for the caribou or testifying against apples, not real scientific expertise. They are actors, after all.

Here is a quick checklist for you to use to fight against fear:

- Compare the hype to the facts.

When your sixteen-year-old has the family car out past curfew and blames temporary amnesia, a little healthy skepticism might be in order. The same goes for what you get from women's media.

- On TV, don't be taken in by the pictures.

Tears don't necessarily prove someone is telling the truth.

- In print, don't be overwhelmed by impressive-sounding scientific jargon.

An unfamiliar chemical like "dihydrogen oxygen" sounds as if could be dangerous, right? Wrong. It's another name for water.

- Remember that you can always find statistics to support any argument.

And realize the statistics you are given almost always accentuate the negative.

- If there's a victim, there must be a villain.

You must always ask: "Is there a specific agenda at work in this story?"

- Check out the disclaimers at the beginning and at the end.

"Might" or "could" doesn't mean that you, your family—or anyone else—are really in danger.

SECRET # 4
Nobody's Perfect

Here's what beauty and fashion magazines want you to believe: One day, we will get everything about our appearance exactly right. Starting at the top, we'll finally get that great haircut. Our roots will stop showing. Our eyes will be clear and bright. We'll use the right shade of eye shadow, the right type of mascara, the right finish of foundation, and our lipstick will stay on even after shoveling our way through a Caesar salad.

And just as if we were prepping for a glitzy stroll down a red carpet, we'll be dressed in the perfect outfit three sizes smaller than we are now, with the perfect accessories, and, of course, great shoes. Then it will be like putting the right key into the right lock. Click! The limo door will swing open. We will look so good we will have made over not merely our looks but our lives.

That's really what these magazines promise you every issue—their formula for looking great. It's a very seductive siren call. Of course, the ingredients change month by month, so you cannot possibly get it right after just one read. And you are always made to feel that there is something about you that isn't right. Quite a few things, actually. Otherwise, why would you ever buy another magazine?

But beauty and fashion mags claim they are really aspirational dream books and do their job when they encourage women to aim high and spend more. That's what advertisers like as well. But what do *you* like? Recent advertising studies confirm that women prefer images of themselves that reflect reality.[14] Nowadays we are turned off rather than prodded on by the unattainable. In these more serious times, we have stopped trying to live the fantasy splashed across fashion pages month after month. Besides, some of us have become shrewd enough to know that the fantasy usually is anorexic, liposuctioned, implanted, lifted, tightened, Botoxed, digitally altered, and probably not the brightest bulb popping on the runway.

Even the editors of some of the big women's magazines are getting a little nervous, sensing rebellion in the ranks. *Glamour* editor-in-chief Cindi Leive wrote in her May 2003 editor's letter, "In politics there's a pattern that goes like this, 'The more tyrannical the ruling party, the healthier the opposition; brutal dictators breed revolutionaries that want to overthrow them.' Maybe that's what we have in America circa 2003: *dictatorial ideas of what we should look like and a revolutionary movement that refuses to fall in line.*"[15] The emphasis is all hers. But she's describing what's really happening. A lot of women have already figured it out. I hope you have, too. Of course, we all want to look good, but without going to extremes or over budget.

We also learn along the way that you can shop until you drop, but you cannot buy sex appeal. A lot of the self-absorbed narcissism that is now the basis of so much beauty and fashion advice is really a big turnoff to the men in our lives. Guys are more frightened by women who are too obsessed with looking perfect than put off by those who are relaxed about their standard-issue bumps and lumps and blemishes. Though Cindi thinks it "takes strength and supreme self-respect to thumb your nose at a cultural obsession—to drop the towel and walk, not sucking your stomach in toward the water."[16] I disagree. I'd say it only takes the comforting realization that not everyone on the beach is looking at you. And the ones who are important to you already like the way you look.

SECRET # 5
Susan Sarandon Is Not Like You!

In Britain, they have just discovered a new mental condition ominously called CWS or celebrity worship syndrome. Seriously. According to a report in their *Journal of Nervous and Mental Disease,* almost a third of Britons suffer from a mild case.[17] How do you know if you've got the bug? You chat up friends about celebrities you like, buy magazines with their pictures on the cover, and if one of your faves is on the telly, you make sure you watch. Sounds pretty normal to me. But maybe that's because American media sugarcoats celebrities to a far greater degree than the Brits. Because of their still-ingrained class system across the pond, the English tend to envy rather than admire, tear down rather than suck up. Not like us.

John Carlin of the British newspaper *The Independent* noticed the difference when he reported, "Celebrities in America have a capacity to control things that are said about them on air and in print to a degree that Washington's crushingly vulnerable politicians can only envy. . . . Interviews with celebrities in otherwise intelligent magazines . . . or on talk shows invariably amount to no more than exercises in propaganda. Intimidated by the stars' agents and the vast companies that employ them, the media meekly acquiesces."[18]

He's got it absolutely right. This celebrity obsession is nothing new; but these days, it seems to be only getting worse. Publicists, as you now know, are most often the ones who decide what celebrity will appear on which cover or which Media Queen will get a ratings boost. And the story they prefer is as bland as possible. One publicist explains that you want Middle America to feel comfortable, so Courteney or Michelle act as ordinary as possible. They have to pretend they don't have three assistants and a chef, a limo. And they don't let their interviewer get anywhere near their multimillion-dollar homes.[19]

Typically, for a story in the launch issue of *Lifetime Magazine,* Faith Hill met the writer not at her six-bedroom mansion or at her sprawling eight-hundred-acre farm but only for a venti mocha at "her favorite Nashville Starbucks."[20] She's just like you. While in *Harper's Bazaar,* Michelle Pfeiffer's interviewer wrote: " 'My day-to-day life is really mundane,' says Michelle over steamed vegetables and whitefish in a Los Angeles restaurant." Michelle says she drives the kids around, climbs on the monkey bars with them. "You can't believe how hard the monkey bars are today." That her favorite feature is "her hands." And she wouldn't mind having "bigger breasts."[21] Gorgeous, talented, rich, and married to David E. Kelley, the super-successful writer and producer of *Ally McBeal* and *The Practice,* Michelle manages to sound just like your sister-in-law, the one who bores you stiff.

And that is exactly how she wants to sound. Stars now even play dumb, very dumb. Or maybe they really are that dumb, which might be worth mentioning. Faith Hill tells her interviewer that her daughters are "homebodies who like to stay in." Faith, they are five, four, and one. Where exactly should they go—clubbing on Sunset Boulevard?

But media, which is skeptical about so much and is so quick to take potshots at politicians and others they see as "villains," lets celebrities off easy. It's media, of course, that really has the most serious case of CWS. And that's part of the reason some of these stars have grown so comfortable and self-righteous about sharing uninformed political opinions because they have always been so very, very indulged. Some even like to think they're the voice of the people.

Of course, that changed when the semifamous Janeane Garofalo, along with Susan Sarandon, the Dixie Chicks, and several other entertainers, discovered that much of the public didn't agree with their anti-Bush opinions before the war in Iraq. Lori Bardsley, a thirty-eight-year-old North Carolina homemaker, grew so annoyed at celebrities mouthing off that she started a petition, "Citizens Against Celebrity Pundits," on the Web site called ipetitions.com that ultimately garnered thousands of signatures. Lori said, "These celebrities, they choose to enter a profession where they entertain the American public as a whole. If they open their mouths on political issues, religious issues and moral issues, they should expect a backlash because we all have differing opinions."[22]

Celebrities seemed kind of dumbstruck that, for once, they weren't getting their usual free ride. Natalie Maines, the lead singer of Texas's Dixie Chicks, told a London concert audience, in what might have seemed an easy applause line, "Just so you know, we're ashamed the president of the United States is from Texas." Suddenly, the Chicks' album sales dropped, radio stations stopped playing their music, and the gals were left with, dare I say it, egg on their faces. But the Chicks felt very victimized by the reaction. To try to make it better, and guided by PMK's Cindi Berger, who had guided Rosie's coming-out party, they wept and wailed and waffled for a full hour to Diane

Sawyer. It got both the Chicks and Diane big ratings. Déjà vu all over again.

SECRET # 6
Lisa Beamer and the Other Widows of 9/11 Are Victims— Not You and Me

When celebrities like the Dixie Chicks, the most coddled and cosseted of all, start playing the victim card, anyone can see that it has just gone too far. No, the Chicks are not victims. Nor are most of us.

In fact, this is truly a great time for women. Twenty years ago I thought I was cheerleader-in-chief for women. Well, nowadays I—and you—have a lot *more* to cheer about. It's really peculiar to me that some celebs and Spin Sisters are always so quick to criticize our country. It would be a lot more on target these days for them to be gratefully patriotic. Because the most significant story they can tell is about the constant and remarkable improvement in the lives of American women. No "could" or "may" or "might" about it. Now, that's a *really* big story.

And though it is no contest, in some instances we are doing better than the men. Certainly that's true when it comes to education. Currently there are more women in college than men (56 percent to 44 percent).[23] Today it's women who earn the majority of degrees awarded by institutes of higher education (57 percent), including master's degrees and doctorates.[24] (Among African Americans, women earn 66 percent of all degrees awarded.)[25] In fact, some colleges are out there right now recruiting an endangered species, male students.

When it comes to work, even in a tough economy women continue to move up. In 2002 more than 21 million women worked in managerial or professional positions, according to the Department of Labor. That's up from 14.7 million in 1992 and accounts for about 50 percent of employees in these higher level jobs.[26]

Women entrepreneurs may be doing even better. In nearly half of all privately owned firms in the United States, women have a majority or a 50 percent stake. These 10 million firms employ one out of every seven U.S. workers and generate $2.3 trillion in sales. And these companies with women at the helm are growing at a faster rate than the economy.[27]

Our increased educational and employment achievements have paid off. Overall, women's median incomes, adjusted for inflation, were up 25 percent between 1990 and 2000. Among couples where both husbands and wives work full-time, the median income stood at $78,604.[28] Nearly one third of these couples had lofty incomes of over $100,000.[29]

At the same time, some women were choosing to stay home with their young children. In 2000, 45 percent of moms with babies under one year old did not work outside the home. That's up 4 percentage points in two years, and the increase came primarily among married, college-educated women over thirty.[30] Isn't this proof that making the most of our opportunities can also mean making different choices at different times in our lives?

And with all those fear-factor stories about our health, life expectancy for women has never been longer. A female born today can expect to celebrate her eightieth birthday.[31] Women at every age overwhelmingly characterize their health as "good" or "excellent." Older women, because of the better management of chronic conditions, rate their health more highly today than in the past.[32] Just look around: Aren't women staying active and looking and feeling vital for years longer than ever before?

Can't we all cite personal examples that bring these positive statistics to life? A friend who has become a breast cancer survivor. (Breast cancer mortality rates have dropped 20 percent in the last ten years.)[33] Another who has started a successful business in a field where few women once ventured. (Construction, manufacturing, and transportation have seen the largest recent increases in the number of women-owned firms.)[34] One woman I know has just become the highest-paid woman in the world in her field. Yes, she's capable, hard driving, and wildly ambitious, but she also has been married for over twenty years and has four children. Another of my friends worked for years in top corporate jobs, married at forty-five, and had a baby at fifty! She looked and felt great during her pregnancy. Amazing? Yes. Could it ever have happened before? No. She's staying home for a while, enjoying her beautiful daughter, and why shouldn't she? She's very lucky, and so are many of us.

And we all should know it. Even Cathi Hanauer, the editor of *The Bitch in the House*, that compilation of whiny essays, who admits that like most of her friends in the media she is a perpetual "malcontent," can see the bright side once in a while. She confessed that she agreed with the motto on a T-shirt she'd seen touting a whitewater river known for its fierce currents. It read "This place sucks. Let's stay."[35]

Personally, I know—and I hope you do—that it's a lot better than that. Even after the darkest day in our recent past, I saw a photograph that confirmed just how extraordinary the changes in the lives of women have been. The photo, taken on September 11, was of Vice President Dick Cheney in the bunker beneath the White House talking on the phone to the president on *Air Force One*. The vice president was surrounded by three women: Condoleezza Rice, Mary Matalin, and Karen Hughes. On such a day, where else in the world and at what other time in history, would we see three shrewd, capable women giving their advice and counsel?

With their own lives, these extraordinary women tell the remarkable story of the genuine opportunities American women now have. Condoleezza Rice, who was raised in segregated Birmingham. Mary Matalin, who worked in a steel mill and once considered getting a beautician's license. Karen Hughes, an army brat, who became a TV reporter because she was the only one around willing to work on weekends. All three of them, through very different routes, and through their own hard work, ended up at the epicenter of power in the United States.

Since that photograph was taken, two of the women—Hughes and Matalin—have left their high-profile jobs. Does it mean that when women break through the glass ceiling, they find it is not all it's cracked up to be? I don't think so. Karen Hughes said her husband and teenage son were homesick for Texas and so was she. Mary Matalin has two small daughters and she wanted to earn more money and spend more time with them. Nowadays, what may be most amazing is not that women can get to the top and make it work but that they can quit at the top and make that work, too. Women can have different priorities at different times of life. And that can be an advantage, not a disadvantage, in creating a full, multifaceted life for ourselves and for those we love. Oh, yes, some of us may moan and groan about the tough choices we have to make, and put down the women who make different choices than we do. Media for women feeds on the moaning and the groaning and the catfights too. I wish it would stop.

Just as there are things that I hope you have learned from this book, there are a few that, I hope, my Spin Sisters will learn or at least acknowledge, as well. That maybe it is time to stop exaggerating the negative and ignoring the positive in women's lives. To stop treating every women under thirty as if she were equipped only with raging hormones and a credit card. And to stop picturing every woman over thirty as if she had no grit, as a perpetually whining, overwhelmed, and exhausted disaster. To acknowledge that personal responsibility is never unfashionable and ought to be a part of every woman's emotional wardrobe. And, most of all, to please stop insisting that all women should have the same cultural and political views as the Manhattan media elite. Just stopping that spin would be the biggest breakthrough of all.

Back in the 1940s an advertising agency created for *Ladies' Home Journal* the slogan "Never underestimate the power of a woman." It was a time when women had little power and the slogan was there to remind advertisers that women were more important than they might assume. That slogan still strikes a chord. But today I believe it is the media that too often underestimates you. Underestimates how practically you handle your problems. How sensible you can be about judging the best ways to solve problems, personally and politically.

I know you will still watch and read. But remember that you have *real* power when you think for yourselves.

NOTES

Introduction

1. Howard Fineman, "A Long Shadow," *Newsweek*, May 12, 2003.
2. Interview with Professor Robert Kubey, September 2002.
3. Women's television viewing, on average: 4.7 hours daily, *TV Dimensions*, 2003.
4. Survey of American Women, The Polling Company, November 2002.
5. *Marketing to Women*, EPM Communications, "Women in Advertisements are Getting Younger, Thinner and More Racially Diverse," June 1, 2002.
6. Women's purchasing power: Bureau of Economic Analysis statistic cited in "Marketing Messages for Women Fall Short," Hillary Chura, *Advertising Age*, September 23, 2002.
7. "Media Bias Basics," Media Research Center, mediaresearchcenter.org. An analysis of political leanings of the press including surveys by the *Los Angeles Times*, Pew Research Center for the People and the Press, Center for Media and Public Affairs, *Editor and Publisher*, American Society of Newspaper Editors, etc.

Chapter 1 — Spin, Sisters, Spin

1. "Rosie's Story: For the Sake of the Children," *Primetime Thursday*, March 14, 2002.
2. Ann Oldenburg, "War of the Rosie: The Comedian vs. the Publishers," *USA Today*, August 22, 2002.

3. References to influence of women's magazines in Naomi Wolf, *The Beauty Myth* (William Morrow & Co., 1991), pp. 61–84 and throughout text; Betty Friedan, *The Feminine Mystique* (W. W. Norton & Co., 1963), pp. 33–68 and throughout text; Susan Faludi, *Backlash* (Crown Publishers, 1991), pp. 92–94, 103–104, 109–111, and throughout text; Christina Hoff Sommers, *Who Stole Feminism?* (Simon & Schuster, 1994), pp. 200, 210–215; Danielle Crittenden, *What Our Mothers Didn't Tell Us* (Touchstone, 1999), pp. 43–44; Michelle Malkin in various columns including "Hillary and the Clitoridectomy Hoax," 9/18/02, townhall.com.

4. Sherrie A. Inness, *Tough Girls: Women Warriors and Wonder Women in Popular Culture* (University of Pennsylvania Press, 1999), pp. 52–53.

5. Valerie Bryson, *Feminist Debates: Issues of Theory and Political Practice* (New York University Press, 1999), p. 94.

CHAPTER 2—HOW WE GOT FROM THERE TO HERE

1. Margaret Carlson, "The Mummy Diaries," *Time Magazine*, October 7, 2002.

2. Cathi Hanauer, ed., *The Bitch in the House* (HarperCollins, 2002), pp. 160–161.

3. Ibid., p. xii.

4. Ibid., p. xiii.

5. Rosalind Rosenberg, *Divided Lives: American Women in the Twentieth Century* (Hill and Wang, 1992), p. 221.

6. Stephanie Dolgoff, "Could Acupuncture Prick Up Your Sex Drive?" *Glamour*, March 2000; Sharon Boone, "Are You Going to Hell?" *Glamour*, December 1999.

7. Betty Friedan, *The Feminine Mystique* (W. W. Norton & Co., 1963), pp. 15–32.

8. Ibid., pp. 305–308.

9. "The New Feminism. A Special Section Prepared for the *Ladies' Home Journal* by the Women's Liberation Movement," *Ladies' Home Journal*, August 1970.

10. Joanne Felder, "Exploring the Body Politic," *Sunday Times* (London), January 2, 2000.

11. S. Robert Lichter, Linda S. Lichter, and Stanley Rothman, *Prime Time: How TV Portrays American Culture* (Regnery 1994), a discussion of the evolving portrayal of women on television, pp. 137–144.

12. Rosalind Rosenberg, *Divided Lives* (Hill and Wang, 1992), pp. 224–227.

13. Interview with Betty Friedan, September 2002.

14. Interview with Phyllis Schlafly, October 2002.

15. Susan J. Douglas, *Where the Girls Are: Growing Up Female with the Mass Media* (Three Rivers Press, 1994), p. 232.

16. Interview with Carol Story, June 2002.

17. "Portrait of the American Woman Today," *Ladies' Home Journal*, January 1984.

18. Nancy Rubin, "Do I Have It All, but No Time to Enjoy It?" *Ladies' Home Journal*, February 1982.

19. Barbara Wagner and Roberta Grant, "The New One-Paycheck Family," *Ladies' Home Journal*, September 1984.

20. Sondra Forsyth Enos, "Work Plus Baby = The New Reality," *Ladies' Home Journal*, March 1984.

21. Rosalind Rosenberg, *Divided Lives* (Hill and Wang, 1992), pp. 157–161.

22. Amy Sohn, "A Mother's Love," *New York Magazine*, September 30, 2002.

23. Jim Karas, "Yes, You *Can* Lose Weight Over 40," *Good Housekeeping*, August 2002.

24. "Women's Magazines: A Liberal Pipeline to Soccer Moms," November 21, 1996, Media Research Center, mediaresearchcenter.org.

25. Interview with Av Westin, October 3, 2002.

CHAPTER 3—GOT STRESS?

1. Interview with Dr. Judith Reichman, *Today*, December 27, 2001.

2. Susan J. Douglas, *Where the Girls Are* (Three Rivers Press, 1994), p. 260.

3. Paul J. Rosch. "Hans Selye and 'They Just Looked Sick,'" from the September 2001 issue of *The Newsletter of the American Institute of Stress on Easy Diagnosis Health Controversies*, easydiagnosis.com.

4. Kate Walsh, "Chill Pills," *O, The Oprah Magazine*, October 2002.

5. John P. Robinson and Geoffrey Godbey, *Time for Life* (Pennsylvania State University Press, 1997), Introduction, p. iii.

6. Robert Kubey and Mihaly Csikszentmihalyi, "Television Addiction Is No Mere Metaphor," Scientific American.com, February 23, 2002.

7. Lifetime Television schedule, weekend of October 12, 2002.

8. Tunku Varadarajan, "Review/TV," *The Wall Street Journal*, October 18, 2002.

9. Robert Kubey and Mihaly Csikszentmihalyi, "Television Addiction Is No Mere Metaphor," ScientificAmerican.com, February 23, 2002.

10. Lisa Kogan, "Just Relax Now . . . Damn It," *O, The Oprah Magazine*, October 2002.

11. Sandi Kahn Shelton, "For a Happier Life, Say This Word," *Redbook*, May 2002.

12. Kathleen Beckett, "Unwinderies: A Guide to Stress Free Zones," *O, The Oprah Magazine*, October 2002.

13. The ISPA 2002 Spa Industry Survey, a PriceWaterhouseCoopers study commissioned by the International SPA Association.

14. Ibid.

15. Erlina Hendarwan, "U.S.: Aromatherapy's Evolution," *Global Cosmetic Industry*, November 1, 2002, citing data from Data Monitor.

16. Pankaj Kumar and Ana Maria Zaugg, "2002 IMS Review: Steady but Not Stellar," *Medical Marketing & Media*, May 1, 2003.

17. Todd Gitlin, *Media Unlimited* (Henry Holt & Company, 2001). Gitlin discusses the effect of speed and the media throughout his book, primarily in "Speed and Sensibilities," pp. 71–118.

18. Alan Macdermid and David Montgomery, "Relax, Stress Will Not Make You Have a Heart Attack," *Glasgow Herald*, May 24, 2002.

19. "Stress," *Yankelovich Monitor Magazine*, April 2001.

20. *The Early Show*, May 27, 2002.

21. Alice D. Domar, Ph.D., and Henry Dreher, "Secrets to Serenity: How to Manage Stress, Worry Less, Relax More," *Family Circle*, January 4, 2000.

22. "There's No Place Like the Office," *20/20*, September 5, 2001.

23. Marilyn Elias, "Ask 'Dr. Happiness,'" *USA Today*, December 9, 2002.

24. Marilyn Elias, "What Makes People Happy, Psychologists Now Know," *USA Today*, December 9, 2002.

CHAPTER 4—THE FEMININE PHYSIQUE

1. Magazine Audience Estimates, spring 2003, Mediamark Research, Inc.

2. Peter Allen, "The G Spot," *Daily Mail* (London), January 15, 2003.

3. *Working Mother* magazine, June 2001, quoted in "A New Perspective on Appearance," *Yankelovich Monitor Magazine*, August 2001.

4. Cynthia Crossen, "Americans Are Gaining but 'Ideal' Weight Keeps Shrinking," *The Wall Street Journal*, July 16, 2003.

5. "Weight-Loss Market Grows as Over One in Six Americans Diet," *Research Alert*, November 1, 2002.

6. Figures reported by American Dietetic Association.

7. "Weight-Loss Market Grows as Over One in Six Americans Diet," *Research Alert*, November 1, 2002.

8. Kristyn Kusek, "5 Minutes to a Better Body," *Redbook*, February 2003.

9. Jill Foster and Rebecca Smith, "Quick Fixes for Party Foxes," *The Mirror* (London), December 3, 2003; "A Wide Range of Alternative Regimes, None of Them Recommended," *The Times* (London), August 13, 2003; "Sweetie, Who's Slimming You This Season?" Kate Betts, *The New York Times*, September 15, 2002; "Detox? What Rubbish," Peta Bee, *The Times* (London), August 3, 2001; "Fad Diets Are a Con Which Can Do More Harm Than Good," Chris Millar, *The Evening Standard* (London), June 20, 2002.

10. Survey of the American Woman, *Ladies' Home Journal*, 1997, 1998, 1999.

11. Linda Villarosa, "Dangerous Eating," *Essence*, January 1994.

12. *Marketing to Women*, EPM Communications, "Women in Advertisements Are Getting Younger, Thinner and More Racially Diverse," June 1, 2002.

13. "Watch Out, Listen Up," 2002 Feminist Primetime Report, National Organization of Women.

14. Jean Kilbourne, "Deadly Persuasion" (The Free Press, 1999), excerpted in *AdWeek*, June 5, 2000.

15. *The O'Reilly Factor*, Fox News Network, October 1, 2002.

16. Anna Wintour and Grace Coddington, "Remembering Liz Tilberis," *Vogue*, June 1999.

17. Kate Betts, "The Tyranny of Skinny; Fashion's Insider Secrets," *The New York Times*, March 31, 2002.

18. Neil Sears, "Is This Size 8 Model Too Fat for Milan's Catwalk?" *Daily Mail* (London), March 6, 1998.

19. Kate Betts, "The Tyranny of Skinny," *The New York Times*, March 31, 2002.

20. Leora Tanenbaum, *Cat Fight* (Seven Stories Press, 2002), p. 121.

21. Courtney Kane, "The Media Business: Advertising," *The New York Times*, August 15, 2002.

22. Donna Freydkin, "Doctored Cover Photos Add Up to Controversy," *USA Today*, June 17, 2003.

23. Baz Bamigboye and Tania Shakinovsky, "Kate's Digital Diet," *Daily Mail* (London), January 10, 2003.

24. Figures reported by National Clearinghouse of Plastic Surgery Statistics, American Society of Plastic Surgeons, 2001.

25. "A New Perspective on Appearance," *Yankelovich Monitor Magazine*, August 2001.

26. Ibid.

27. Guy Trebay, "Bring on the Clowns: Goofy Today, in Stores Tomorrow," *The New York Times*, January 7, 2003.

28. "Pot Scarcity Peeves Patients," *New York Post*, October 25, 2002.

29. Michael Gross, "'Jerry! It's Shimon,'" New York *Daily News*, September 29, 2002.

30. Peter Carlson, "What Matters to Us; Wenner Weekly Makes a Study of Stars," *The Washington Post*, September 24, 2002.

31. Karen Duffy, "Deconstructing Duffy," *The New York Times*, October 13, 2002.

32. Ann Oldenburg, "Parker's One Hot Mama," *USA Today*, May 6, 2003.

CHAPTER 5—THE FEMALE FEAR FACTOR

1. *Good Morning America*, March 30, 2000.

2. Lydia Denworth, "The Poison That Hid in Our Home," *Redbook*, November 2002.

3. Mick Hume, "Warning: Worry Can Damage Your Health," *The Times* (London), November 30, 2002.

4. David Shaw, "Living Scared," *Los Angeles Times*, September 11, 1994.

5. Ibid.

6. Marilyn Elias, "Thinking It Over, and Over, and Over," *USA Today*, February 6, 2003.

7. Women's Magazines: A Liberal Pipeline to Soccer Moms, November 21, 1996, Media Research Center, mediaresearchcenter.org.

8. David Shaw, "Living Scared," *Los Angeles Times*, September 11, 1994.

9. "Getting Nailed," *20/20*, May 18, 2001.

10. Jane Spencer and Cynthia Crossen, "Why Do Americans Feel That Danger Lurks Everywhere?" *The Wall Street Journal*, Thursday, April 24, 2002.

11. Eleanor Singer and Phyllis Endreny, "Reporting on Risk: How the Mass Media Portray Accidents, Diseases, Disasters and Other Hazards," *Risk: Health, Safety and Environment*, vol. 5, summer 1994.

12. David Shaw, "Living Scared," *Los Angeles Times*, September 11, 1994.

13. "Plastics and Your Food: Do Chemicals in Plastic Taint Our Food?" *20/20*, April 19, 1999.

14. Dr. Kimberly M. Thompson, "Kids at Risk," *Risk in Perspective*, Harvard Center of Risk Analysis, vol. 8, issue 4, April 2000.

15. "A Closer Look," *World News Tonight*, February 16, 1998.

16. Douglas S. Barasch, "How Safe Are Kids' Vaccines?" *Good Housekeeping*, September 2000.

17. Women's Magazines: A Liberal Pipeline to Soccer Moms, November 21, 1996, Media Research Center, mediaresearchcenter.org.

18. Lisa Collier Cool, "Is There Celery in That Tuna?" *Good Housekeeping*, February 2000.

19. Andrew Tyndall, "Climbing Down from Olympus," *Media Studies Journal*, fall 1998. Change in news coverage is also analyzed in "Changing Definition of the News," Committee of Concerned Journalists report issued March 6, 1998.

20. Daryl Chen, "Pregnant? Know Someone Who Is? You Must Read This Urgent Health Warning," *Glamour*, April 2002.

21. Hallie Levine, "5 Down-There Diseases You Don't Know About—But Should," *Glamour*, May 2002.

22. Eva Rubin, M.D., as told to Susan Ince, "The Hidden Threat to Your Breast Health," *Glamour*, June 2002.

23. Peg Rosen, "How to Shrug off Shoulder Pain," *Good Housekeeping*, May 2002.

24. *Oprah Winfrey Show*, February 6, 2002.

25. Alex Kuczynski, "Menopause Forever," *The New York Times*, June 23, 2002.

26. Sheila M. Rothman, *Women's Proper Place* (Basic Books, 1978), p. 23.

27. *48 Hours*, July 26, 2002.

28. Christina Hoff Sommers, *Who Stole Feminism?* (Simon & Schuster, 1994), pp. 11–12.

29. Jim Stingl, "Violence Task Force Jumps on Bandwagon," *Milwaukee Journal Sentinel*, January 17, 1997.

30. Elizabeth Jensen, D. M. Osborne, Abigail Pogrebin, Ted Rose, "Consumer Alert," *Brill's Content*, October 1998.

31. Todd Gitlin, *Media Unlimited* (Henry Holt & Company, 2001), p. 121.

32. "The Politics of Personal Destruction," *Ex Femina quarterly newsletter*, Independent Women's Forum, October 14, 1999.

33. "Hype with John Stossel," ABC, December 22, 2000

34. Marcia Angell, M.D., *Science on Trial* (W. W. Norton & Co., 1996). In this book Dr. Angell discusses in depth the breast implant case and the interrelationship of medicine, the law, and media.

35. Lydia Denworth, "The Poison That Hid in Our Home," *Redbook*, November 2002.

36. Kenneth Smith, "Toxic Lawyers Threaten Health," *The Washington Times*, November 18, 1999.

37. Julie Haursman, "The Hidden Danger in Your Backyard," *Family Circle*, February 11, 2003. Debra Gordon, "Is Your Child's School Toxic?" *Parents*, March 2003.

38. Michelle Malkin, "Environmental Tricksters," *Philadelphia Enquirer*, February 11, 2002.

39. Sarah Foster, "Eco-Group Violated Tax Laws, Free Enterprise Organization Files Complaint with IRS," February 17, 2002, WorldNetDaily.com.

Chapter 6—The Victim Virus

1. Abby Goodnough, "In the Park a Usually Tough Crowd Bares Hearts for Diana," *The New York Times*, September 15, 1997.

2. Francine du Plessix Gray, "Department of Second Thoughts," *The New Yorker*, September 15, 1997.

3. Mark Harris, "It Had Become Almost Impossible to Retrieve One's Own Sorrow from the Carnival Atmosphere," *Entertainment Weekly*, September 19, 1997.

4. Walter Goodman, "Critic's Notebook: As Much Mourning as the Market Will Bear," *The New York Times*, September 2, 1997.

5. Interview with Judy Milestone, June, 2002.

6. S. J. Taylor, "The Making of the *Mail*," *Daily Mail* (London), October 15, 2002.

7. Tina Brown, "Magazine Editor Urges Tough, Lively Papers," *Presstime* magazine, June 1, 1991, adapted from a speech given by Tina Brown at the ANPA convention, May 7, 1991.

8. "Changing Definition of News," Committee of Concerned Journalists, report issued March 6, 1998.

9. David Shaw, "Media Matters," *Los Angeles Times*, January 19, 2003.

10. "Public News Habits Little Changed by September 11," Pew Research Center for the People and the Press, June 9, 2002.

11. Linda Stasi, "How to Wed a Million-air Head," *New York Post*, January 12, 2003.

12. "New Media Improved Image Proves Short-Lived," Pew Research Center for the People and the Press, August 4, 2002.

13. Mark Gillespie, "Public Remains Skeptical of News Media," *Gallup Poll News Service*, May 30, 2003.

14. Interview with Dr. Valerie Crane, November 2002.

15. Joke Hermes, *Reading Women's Magazines: An Analysis of Everyday Media Use* (Polity Press, Cambridge, U.K., 1995), pp. 41–46.

16. Elizabeth Kolbert, "The Thomas Nomination, Most in National Survey Say Judge Is More Believable," *The New York Times*, October 15, 1991.

17. Dr. Turhan Canli study published by the American Psychological Association cited in CNN.com Health, July 23, 2002.

18. Interview with Cathy Chamberlain, February 2003.

19. "Crime in the United States 2001," *Uniform Crime Reports*, Federal Bureau of Investigations.

20. Ibid.

21. Ibid.

22. Murray Weiss, "City Has Thugs on the Run," *New York Post*, June 15, 2003.

23. Liz Welch, "Could You Be a Predator's Next Target?" *Cosmopolitan*, November 2002.

24. Eve Ensler, "Imagine a World without Violence," *Marie Claire*, March 2003.

25. David Carr, "Media: Two Magazines Going for Grit, Not for Glamour," *The New York Times*, December 9, 2002.

26. "Fancy Footwork," *20/20*, July 14, 2001.

27. *Good Morning America*, January 28, 2002.

28. Dick Morris, "Hillary Plays the Victim Card The Talk Piece Restored the Sad Image that Tugs at the Voters' Hearts," *New York Post*, August 10, 1999.

29. Margery Eagan, "Hillary Polls Prove We Love a Loser," *Boston Herald*, August 30, 1998. Ellen Warren, "Why Does Humiliation Become Her?" *Chicago Tribune*, November 22, 1998.

30. Karen Tumulty and Nancy Gibbs, "The Better Half," *Time* magazine, December 28, 1998.

31. Hillary Rodham Clinton, *Living History* (Simon & Schuster, 2003), p. 466.

32. Ann Douglas, *The Feminization of American Culture* (The Noonday Press, 1977, 1978), p. 73

33. Ann Douglas, "The Extraordinary Hillary Clinton," *Vogue*, December 1998.

34. Ibid.
35. "Sex, Lies and TV News," *Media Monitor*, September/October 1998, Center for Media and Public Affairs.
36. "Angry and Hurt, but No Quitter," *People*, August 31, 1998.
37. Karen Tumulty and Nancy Gibbs, "The Better Half," *Time* magazine, December 28, 1998.
38. Maggie Gallagher, "What's a Good Wife?" *New York Post*, August 31, 1998.

CHAPTER 7—MEDIA QUEENS AT WORK AND PLAY

1. Erika Kinetz, "The Cool Table," *The New York Times*, August 4, 2002.
2. J. D. Reed, Anne-Marie O'Neill, K. C. Baker, Michelle Caruso, Lyndon Stambler, Brian Karem, Margery Sellinger, "Katie's New Life," *People*, November 27, 2000.
3. Jim Rutenberg, "Anchor's Pay Package May Change Standards," *The New York Times*, December 20, 2001.
4. Joanna Powell, "Katie's New Life," *Good Housekeeping*, November 2000.
5. Gene Warner, "Couric's Whirlwind Talk Is Uplifting," *Buffalo News*, October 14, 2002.
6. "Rudy Plans Race for Albany," *New York Post*, July 18, 2003.
7. James Grant, "The Prime Times of Diane Sawyer," *Life* magazine, August 1989.
8. Harry F. Waters with George Hackett, "CBS's New Morning Star," *Newsweek*, March 14, 1983.
9. Howard Kurtz, "Diane Sawyer's Maalox Moment," *The Washington Post*, February 4, 1999.
10. Exchange on *Good Morning America*, October 2, 2002.
11. Liz Smith, "The Mouse That Soared," *Newsday*, July 3, 2002.
12. Liz Smith, "A New Cycle in His Life," *Newsday*, July 7, 2003.
13. Liz Smith, "A Great American Mind," *Newsday*, February 16, 2003.
14. Tina Brown's description of President Clinton quoted in Judy Bachrach, *Tina and Harry Come to America* (The Free Press, 2001), p. 271.
15. "100 Influential Business Leaders," *Crain's New York Business*, June 17, 2002.
16. Kimberly Schuld, *Guide to Feminist Organizations* (Capital Research Center, 2002).
17. Gini Sikes, "Why Are Women Who Escape Genital Mutilation Being Jailed in America?" *Marie Claire*, May 1998.
18. Ibid.
19. Winnie Hu, "Woman Fleeing Mutilation Savors Freedom," *The New York Times*, August 20, 1999.
20. "Why It Was Important for *Marie Claire*'s Glenda Bailey to Have Her Day in Court," *Media Industry Newsletter*, May 10, 1999.
21. Michelle Malkin, "Hillary and the Clitoridectomy Hoax," Townhall.com, September 18, 2002. Malkin also discussed the case in her book *Invasion: How America Still Welcomes Terrorists. Criminals and Other Foreign Menaces to Our Shores* (Regnery Press, 2002).
22. "Media Bias Basics," Media Research Center, mediaresearchcenter.org.
23. George Lardner Jr., "Chappaquiddick: A Tale Time Has Not Resolved," *The Washington Post*, November 12, 1979.
24. Erika Kinetz, "The Cool Table," *The New York Times*, August 4, 2002.

25. Andrea M. Grossman, "PARSA to Open Beauty School in Kabul," *Women's Wear Daily*, August 23, 2002.

26. Helen Schulman, "Hall of Fame: Vanity Fair Nominates Kabul Beauty School," *Vanity Fair*, August 2003.

27. Lindsay Faber, "No Degrees of Separation," *Columbia Journalism Review*, March/April 2001.

28. "The Dish on Dinner," *New York* magazine, May 5, 2003.

29. Christopher Byron, *Martha Inc.* (John Wiley & Sons, 2002), p. 319.

30. "The Power Book," *Ladies' Home Journal*, November 2001.

31. "News Media's Improved Image Proves Short-Lived," Pew Research Center for the People and the Press, August 4, 2002.

CHAPTER 8—GETTING THE "GET" (AND OTHER ADVENTURES)

1. CBS affiliates meeting, May 27, 1993.

2. Connie Chung, "The Business of Getting 'The Get': Nailing an Exclusive Interview in Prime Time," discussion paper, the Joan Shorenstein Center on Press, Politics and Public Policy, Harvard University, April 1998.

3. Interview with Amy Rosenblum, October 2002.

4. Elizabeth Jensen, "Battle over Victims a Sign of Pressure in TV Industry," *Los Angeles Times*, August 8, 2002.

5. Peter Johnson, " 'GMA' Gets the Miner; Couric Gets the Shaft," *USA Today*, July 30, 2002.

6. Lisa de Moraes, "Katie Bars the Door on *Today*'s Executive Producer," *The Washington Post*, October 11, 2002.

7. *Today*, December 16, 2002.

8. David Bauder, " 'Today' Tears Worth It?" New York *Daily News*, December 25, 2002.

9. Ibid.

10. *20/20*, February 13, 2003.

11. Interview with Neal Gabler in *Bold Type* on www.randomhouse.com.

12. Interview with Fidel Castro, *20/20*, October 11, 2002.

13. Connie Chung, "The Business of Getting 'The Get': Nailing an Exclusive Interview in Prime Time, discussion paper, the Joan Shorenstein Center on Press, Politics and Public Policy, Harvard University, April 1998.

14. Ibid.

15. Alessandra Stanley, "In Hometown of Slain Girl, a Veiled Fear Lurks," *The New York Times*, July 19, 2002.

16. Jim Rutenberg, "To Inteview Former P.O.W. CBS Offers Stardom," *The New York Times*, June 16, 2003.

17. A. J. Benza and Michael Lewittes, "Couric's Nanny Isn't Kiddin'," New York *Daily News*, June 12, 1995.

18. Barbara Matusow, "Big Name Hunting," *Washingtonian*, March 1999.

19. "The Unabomber's Media Pen Pals," TheSmokingGun.com.

20. Maureen Dowd, "Getting the 'Get' of the Century," *The New York Times*, June 14, 1998.

21. Exchange on *The View*, September 13, 2002 (on mediaresearchcenter.org).

22. Lisa de Moraes, "Whitney's Weird Chat Gives ABC Fat Ratings," *The Washington Post*, December 6, 2002.

23. David Shaw, "Lights, Camera, Reaction," *Los Angeles Times*, February 13, 2001.

24. James Barron, "Boldface Names," *The New York Times*, February 19, 2002.

25. Jennifer Benjamin, "Cosmo Confessions," *Cosmopolitan*, September 2002.

26. Liza Featherstone, "Sex, Lies and Women's Magazines," *Columbia Journalism Review*, March/April 2002.

27. Ibid.

28. Peter Carlson, "A Breath of Fresh Stupidity," *The Washington Post*, April 8, 2003.

29. Lynya Floyd, "5 Things That Freak Him Out in Bed," *Cosmopolitan*, April 2003.

30. Liesa Goins, "Flirting Moves No Man Can Resist," *Cosmopolitan*, April 2003.

31. Deanna Kizis, "Achin' for Ashton," *Cosmopolitan*, April 2003.

32. Esther Crain, "50 Ways to Make Great Sack Sessions Sex-traordinary," *Cosmpolitan*, April 2003.

33. "Hooking Up, Hanging Out, and Hoping for Mr. Right—College Women on Dating and Mating Today," Independent Women's Forum, July 26, 2001, based on research conducted by the Institute for American Values, Courtship Research Team, headed by Norval Glenn, professor of sociology at the University of Texas. Study published July 26, 2001, by the Independent Women's Forum.

34. Ibid.

CHAPTER 9—"IF ONLY WOMEN VOTED"

1. Bernard Goldberg, *Bias* (Regnery, 2002), p. 24.

2. Interview with Cal Thomas, *AfterHours*, Fox News Channel, January 18, 2003.

3. Michael Kelly, "Left Everlasting (Cont'd)," *The Washington Post*, December 18, 2002.

4. Katie Couric interview of Ann Richards, C-Span, April 3, 1999.

5. Interview of Oliver North, *Today*, March 13, 1995.

6. *Today*, July 16, 2001.

7. *Today*, October 30, 2001.

8. *Today*, May 11, 2001.

9. Susan Schindehette, "A Mother Strikes Back," *People*, May 8, 2000.

10. Michael Kelly, "Left Everlasting (Cont'd)," *The Washington Post*, December 18, 2002.

11. Bernard Goldberg, *Bias* (Regnery, 2002), p. 25.

12. Interview with Av Westin, October 2002.

13. Interview with Susan Winston, August 2002.

14. Interview with Kate O'Beirne, August 2002.

15. David Shaw, "Media Matters: Journalists Losing Touch with Man on the Street," *Los Angeles Times*, December 8, 2002.

16. Interview with David Corvo, August 4, 2002.

17. *Dateline NBC*, June 11, 2002.

18. Interview with Dr. Samir Husni, May 2003.

19. "2002's Hottest Sex News," *Cosmopolitan*, December 2002.

20. "Portfolio: Moment of Silence," *The New York Times*, April 13, 2003.

21. *Marketing to Women*, EPM Communications Inc., 2003, citing the Gallup Organization, "Religion and Gender: A Congregation Divided," 2002.

22. 2000 General Social Survey, National Opinion Research Center, University of Chicago, cited in *American Women: Who They Are & How They Live* (New Strategist, 2002).

23. Michael Giltz, "American Dreams: Oh, TV of Little Faith," *New York Post*, April 13, 2003.

24. David Bauder, "ABC Bleeps 'Jesus' out of Broadcast," Associated Press, June 6, 2002.

25. Interview with Jill Montaigne, March 2002.

26. Interview with Mary Knowles, August 2002.

27. Interview with Kellyanne Conway, July 2002.

28. Exchange between Jane Fonda and Star Jones on *The View*, March 14, 2002.

29. Interview with Nancy Pfotenhauer, November 2002.

30. Mark Potok, "Texas Hutchison a Battler and Survivor," *USA Today*, June 11, 1993.

31. Robin Givhan, "The Eyelashes Have It," *The Washington Post*, November 18, 2000.

32. Larkin Warren, "Journey of Hope," *Good Housekeeping*, September 2000; "A Hero Speaks," *Glamour*, February 2000; Gail Collins, "Perfect Balance," *McCall's*, January 2000; "Susan Sarandon Speaks Her Mind," *Rosie*, February 2002; Lisa Cohen Lee and Kimberly Goad, "Mothers and Shakers," *Redbook*, October 2000.

33. Larkin Warren, "Journey of Hope," *Good Housekeeping*, September 2000.

34. Lisa Cohen and Kimberly Goad, "Mothers and Shakers," *Redbook*, October 2000.

35. Lloyd Grove, "The Reliable Source," *The Washington Post*, March 18, 2003.

36. Lloyd Grove, "The Reliable Source," *The Washington Post*, March 25, 2003.

37. Jonathan Van Meter, "SuperJane," *Vogue*, March 2001; Jane Fonda, "Help Jane Fonda Save These Girls' Lives," *Marie Claire*, June 2002; Joanna Powell, "Jane Fonda: Starting Over Again," *Good Housekeeping*, November 2000.

38. Joanna Powell, "Katie's New Life," *Good Housekeeping*, November 2000; Joanna Powell, "Jane Fonda: Starting Over Again," *Good Housekeeping*, November 2000; Patt Morrison, "Changing the Rules," *Good Housekeeping*, November 2000.

39. Jonathan Van Meter, "SuperJane," *Vogue*, March 2001.

40. Ibid.

41. Editorial, "Add Your Voice to the Million Moms vs. Guns," *Glamour*, June 2000; Stephanie Dolgoff, "Glamour Woman of the Year," *Glamour*, 2000; Tracy Eberhart, "Moms Take Aim at Guns," *Parenting*, February 2000; "A Mom Who Stops Bullets," *Parents*, May 2000; Mary Alice Kellogg, "25 Moms We Love!" *Working Mother*, December 2000; Jan Goodwin, "Every Day 10 Children Are Killed by Guns in the U.S," *Marie Claire*, January 2001; Lisa Cohen Lee and Kimberly Goad, "Mothers and Shakers," *Redbook*, October 2000.

42. "Mothers and Shakers," *Redbook*, October 2000.

43. Susan Kirkwood, "Women's Magazines in Election 2000," Media Watch, Final Report, mediawatch.com.

44. *Glamour*'s anti-Bush, pro-Gore features included: Margot Magowan, "Don't Get

Bushwacked," February 2000; Editorial, "The Abortion Election," May 2000; David France, "George W. Bush. Who Is the Real Man in the Picture?" June 2000; Editorial, "Add Your Voice to a Million Moms vs. Guns," June 2000; Julianne Moore as told to Anastasia Higginbotham, "Abortion Rights—You Could Lose Yours," July 2000; Susan Cullman, "A Pro-Choice Republican on How She's Planning to Crowbar Her Party into the Woman-centric Twenty-first Century," August 2000; Editorial, "Election 2000, Time for a Supreme Decision," September 2000; Editorial, "Why a Vote for Gore Is a Vote for You," November 2000.

45. David France, "Gore Exclusive: Karenna to the Rescue," *Glamour,* February 2000.

46. Karenna Gore Schiff, "Where Are America's Family Values?" *Glamour,* November 2002.

47. Jonathan E. Kaplan, "Karenna Gore Schiff: A Different Poltical Tack—for Now," *The Hill,* April 22, 2003.

48. "Gore Daughter Scores $200K Miramax Book/TV Deal," *New York Post,* April 16, 2003.

49. Editorial, "Election 2000: Time for a Supreme Decision," *Glamour,* September 2000.

50. Ibid.

51. Ibid.

52. Ibid.

53. Susan Kirkwood, "Women's Magazines in Election 2000," Media Watch, Final Report, mediawatch.com.

54. "Why a Vote for Gore Is a Vote for You," *Glamour,* November 2000.

55. "Who Readers Would Vote For?" *Glamour,* July 2000.

56. Harvey Weinstein, "State of the Nation," *Marie Claire,* November 2000.

57. Christie Brinkley, "On My Mind: Why You Need to Vote," *Cosmopolitan,* November 2000.

58. Karenna Gore Schiff, "Karenna Gore Schiff's Guide to Not Getting Bush-whacked," *Glamour,* August 2001.

59. Sally Horchow and Liz Goldhirsh, "Cosmo's Guide for the Bush Twins," *Cosmopolitan,* April 2001.

60. Alexandra Lynch, "Vote for Your Rights," *Marie Claire,* November 2002.

61. Christine Stolba and Diana Furchtgott-Roth, "Women's Figures: An Illustrated Guide to the Economic Progress of Women in America," Independent Women's Forum; "Bridging the Gap: More Women Outearning the Typical Man," Employment Policy Foundation, March 26, 2003, analyzing data from the Bureau of Labor Statistics March Current Population Survey; "Single Women Earn More Than Men," *Marketing to Women,* EPM Communicative, Inc., May 2002.

62. Interview with Nancy Pfotenhauer, November 2002.

63. Richard Morin and Claudia Deane, "Women's Forum Challenges Feminsts, Gains Influence," *The Washington Post,* May 1, 2001.

64. Mary Remuzzi, "Are Your Rights in Jeopardy?" *Marie Claire,* October 2001.

65. Lisa Bennett-Haigney, "National NOW Times," January 1997, quoting Patricia Ireland; Kathryn Jean Lopez, "NOW—So Very THEN," Women's Quarterly, Independent Women's Forum, winter 2001.

66. Dana Milbank, "Ashcroft Appointment Assailed," *The Washington Post,* September 5, 2002.

67. Joanna Powell, "A Passion for Kids," *Good Housekeeping*, October 2001; Lizette Alvarez, "The Widow Goes to Washington," *Good Housekeeping*, April 2001; Leah Eckerg Feldman, "I Want to Live for My Grandbabies," *Good Housekeeping*, April 2002; Ellen Goodman and Pat O'Brien, "Girl Friends Are Forever," *Good Housekeeping*, May 2000; Joanne Kaufman, "Lessons from a Straight Shooter," *Good Housekeeping*, March 2003.

68. "2002 *Glamour* Women of the Year," *Glamour*, December 2002.

69. Editorial, "Bringing Up Baby," *The Wall Street Journal*, September 6, 2002.

70. Interview with Dr. Laura Schlessinger, February 2003.

71. Tammy Bruce in her book, *The New Thought Police* (Prima Publishing, 2001), details the campaign against Dr. Laura Schlessinger, pp. 59–72.

CHAPTER 10—NOT A BIT LIKE YOU

1. Carol M. Mueller, ed., *The Politics of the Gender Gap: The Social Construction of Political Influence* (Sage Publications, 1988), pp. 82–101.

2. Tom Diemer, "Voter Loyalties Turn Politics into Battle of the Sexes," *The Plain Dealer* (Cleveland), November 14, 1996.

3. Richard Morin and Claudia Deane, "Sex in Elections: It's Not What You Think," *The Washington Post*, April 9, 2000.

4. Ibid.

5. Anna Greenberg, "Deconstructing the Gender Gap," John F. Kennedy School of Government, Harvard University, 1998.

6. Sidebar "Anatomy of a Female Voter," in "The Votes Are In: What Women Really Want," *Ladies' Home Journal*, August 2000.

7. Anna Greenberg, "Deconstructing the Gender Gap," John F. Kennedy School of Government, Harvard University, 1998.

8. Ibid.

9. "The Gender Gap: Real or Hype?" Independent Women's Forum Conference, October 24, 2000.

10. "The Cost of Living," *Dateline NBC*, August 18, 2000.

11. Interview with Kathy Bonk, April 2003.

12. "The Voice of Real Americans," The Polling Company, survey reported January 2002.

13. The Winston Group Survey, October 2001.

14. Karen Tumulty and Viveca Novak, "Goodbye, Soccer Moms. Hello, Security Mom," *Time* magazine, June 2, 2003.

15. DYG Scan, "A Closer Look at Gender-ations," March 12, 2002, dyg.com.

16. Interview with Madelyn Hochstein, April 2003.

17. 2000 General Social Survey, National Opinion Research Center, University of Chicago, cited in *American Women: Who They Are & How They Live* (New Strategist, 2002).

18. Yankelovich Partners poll, November 1995. Surveying 4,787 nationally registered voters.

19. 2000 General Social Survey, National Opinion Research Center, University of Chicago, cited in *American Women: Who They Are & How They Live* (New Strategist, 2002).

20. Ibid.

21. Julianne Moore as told to Anastasia Higginbotham, "Abortion Rights—You Could Lose Yours," *Glamour*, July 2000.

22. Lucy Liu, "Losing the Right to Choose," *Glamour*, April 2001.

23. 2000 General Social Survey, National Opinion Research Center, University of Chicago, cited in *American Women: Who They Are & How They Live* (New Strategist, 2002).

24. William McGowan, *Coloring the News* (Encounter Books, 2001) p. 123.

25. David Shaw, "Abortion Bias Seeps into News," *Los Angeles Times*, July 1, 1990.

26. David Shaw, "Abortion Foes Stereotyped Some in the Media Believe," *Los Angeles Times*, July 2, 1990.

27. William McGowan, *Coloring the News* (Encounter Books, 2001), p. 124.

28. "Partial-Birth Abortion," *60 Minutes*, June 2, 1996.

29. Ruth Pradawer, "The Facts on Partial-Birth Abortion," *The Record* (Bergen), September 15, 1996.

30. David Brown, "Late Term Abortion; Who Gets Them and Why," *The Washington Post*, September 17, 1996.

31. Gina Gonzalez as told to Barry Yeoman, "I Had an Abortion When I Was Six Months Pregnant," *Glamour*, October 2001.

32. 2000 General Social Survey, National Opinion Research Center, University of Chicago, cited in *American Women: Who They Are & How They Live* (New Strategist, 2002).

33. "Stop! Your Feelings About Abortion Are About to Change," *Marie Claire*, November 2001.

34. Elizabeth Hayt, "Surprise Mom, I'm Against Abortion," *The New York Times*, March 30, 2003.

35. Ibid.

36. Top issues facing the nation in all polls remain the economy, security, and education. See "Problems and Priorities" on PollingReport.com, which includes CBS News Poll, FOX News/Opinion Dynamics Poll, The Harris Poll, NBC News/*Wall Street Journal* Poll, *Newsweek* Poll, CBS News/*New York Times* Poll, and the CNN/*USA Today*/Gallup Poll.

CHAPTER 11—NEVER UNDERESTIMATE THE POWER

1. Editorial, "Hillary Clinton Hits All the Right Points," *St. Paul Pioneer Press*, September 7, 1995.

2. Ying Chang, "$50,000 Piece of Hope; Asian Donor Under Fire for Gifts to the Prez," New York *Daily News*, February 9, 1997.

3. "Women's Magazines: A Liberal Pipeline to Soccer Moms," Media Research Center, 1997, mediaresearchcenter.org.

4. Interview with Madelyn Hochstein, April 2003.

5. "Women's Titles Hit Hard on the Newsstand," *Advertising Age*, September 8, 2003.

6. Mary Lou Quinlan, *Just Ask a Woman* (John Wiley & Sons, 2003), p. 45.

7. Jane Spencer, "Are You Stressed Out Yet?" *The Wall Street Journal*, March 11, 2003.

8. Elaine Sciolino, "Woman in the News: Compulsion to Achieve!—Condoleezza Rice," *The New York Times*, December 18, 2000.

9. O Calendar: *O, The Oprah Magazine*, April 2003.

10. Dr. Martha Beck, "Balance," *O, The Oprah Magazine*, April 2003.

11. Ibid.

12. Stephen Goode and Michael Fumento, "Love's Role as Dispeller of Modern Myths," *Insight on the News, The Washington Times*, September 29, 1997.

13. "Health Insight: Taking Charge of Health Information," Harvard Center for Risk Analysis.

14. "Appealing or Appalling: Images of Women in Advertising" (survey). www.frankabout women.com.

15. Cindi Leive, "Are We Loving Our Bodies Yet?" *Glamour*, May 2003.

16. Ibid.

17. James Chapman, "Do You Suffer from Celebrity Worship Syndrome?" *Daily Mail* (London), April 14, 2003.

18. John Carlin, "Celebrity Power," *The Independent*, March 1, 1998.

19. Tad Friend, "This Is Going to Be Big: How Publicity Really Works in Hollywood," *The New Yorker*, September 23, 2002.

20. Jancee Dunn, "This Is Faith," *Lifetime Magazine*, May/June 2003.

21. Caroline Doyle Karasyov, "Michelle Gets Personal," *Harper's Bazaar*, October 2002.

22. Liza Porteus, "Anti-War Celebrities May Face Backlash," Foxnews.com, April 17, 2003.

23. "Digest of Education Statistics 2002," National Center for Education Statistics, June 2003.

24. Ibid.

25. Ibid.

26. Stephanie Armour, "More Women Cruise to the Top," *USA Today*, June 25, 2003.

27. Center for Women's Business Research, statistics as of 2002, http://www.nfwbo.org.

28. Bureau of the Census, Current Population Survey, cited in *American Women: Who They Are & How They Live* (New Strategist, 2002).

29. Ibid.

30. Census Bureau statistic cited in "Paths to Power, Women Today," Bill Torpy, *Atlanta Journal and Constitution*, April 8, 2003.

31. *National Vital Statistics Reports*, vol. 51, no. 3, December 19, 2000.

32. 2000 General Social Survey, National Opinion Research Center, University of Chicago, cited in *American Women: Who They Are & How They Live* (New Strategist, 2002).

33. National Cancer Society, "Surveillance, Epidemiology and End Results," 1975–2000.

34. Center for Women's Business Research, statistics as of 2002, http://www.nfwbo.org/. "Women-Owned Businesses in 2002; Trends in the U.S. and 50 States," Center for Women's Business Research, 2001.

35. Cathi Hanauer, ed., *The Bitch in the House* (William Morrow & Co., 2002), Introduction, p. xix.

ACKNOWLEDGMENTS

As an editor, I always said it was a lot easier to tell others what to write than to do it yourself. I found in working on this book that I was absolutely right! Still, I have several to thank who assisted in making the process interesting and—at least some of the time—enjoyable.

First of all, my agent, the shrewd and sensible Richard Pine, whom I like and admire as much as I did his dad, Arthur Pine, who was my friend for many years.

I want to thank as well, Elizabeth Beier, my editor at St. Martin's, and Sally Richardson, St. Martin's esteemed publisher, another longtime friend.

Others to thank: my researchers, Ann Sherman, Natasha Randall, and Michelle Suarez. I am also grateful for the Media Research Center's carefully organized library of television tapes.

Most of all I want to express my appreciation to Chriss Winston, my smart, witty colleague and friend, who was an enormous help, day in and day out, every step of the way.

My other great helpmate was my husband, Jeffrey, who, besides reading and rereading, commenting and editing, told me—as he always has—that I could handle the challenge. It was his confidence and support that really helped to make it so.

INDEX

329